STRACOMER PRESS

GW00599376

Bordertown Blues

The Story of a Forgotten Part of Ireland

Marc Geagan

Published by Stracomer Press, Bundoran. Co. Donegal

www.stracomerpress.com

First published 2015

Copyright © Marc Geagan 2015

10 9 8 7 6 5 4 3 2 1

ISBN: 978-0-9568847-1-8

Front Cover: British soldiers and police officers on the Border at Belleek in 1924 (courtesy of British Pathé News)

ACKNOWLEDGEMENTS

I would like to thank the following people for their help when I was writing this book. Sean Carty, Michael McMahon, Reverend Noel Regan, Tony Talbot, Joe O'Loughlin, Anthony Begley, Thomas Dillon, Peter Ogle, Darach MacDonald (thank you for your deft editing skills), Marc McMenamin, Rory and all the staff at Bundoran Library, Michael McHugh (for all the support), Hugh Óg and Martina Fergus, Charlie Fergus, Brian Drummond, Basil Dalton. Father Joe McVeigh. Dr. Eugene Deeney. Sean McEniff and Jonathan Ball. I would also like to thank my wife Michele and children David, Zoe and Aoife for giving me time and support to write this book.

I would also like to acknowledge the massive contribution of retired members of the Gardaí, the RUC, British and Irish soldiers and former paramilitaries who very graciously provided me with information that allows this book to be as balanced as possible.

Finally, I would like to dedicate this book to all those people in this area who lost their lives in the vortex and British and Irish history. Lest we forget.

Bordertown Blues

Borderland: 'a vague intermediate state or region'. (Merriam-Webster dictionary)

On a warm sunny evening in August 1994, the sleepy Border village of Belleek had come alive. Young revellers were getting ready to go to the nightclubs in the nearby seaside resort of Bundoran. Many locals were enjoying music in the local bars. The IRA had just announced a ceasefire and there was a general feeling of relief and euphoria sweeping across Ulster, north and south.

With just one hour to go before the ceasefire was due to begin, a local IRA active service unit, known for their autonomous actions, had decided to have one last 'parting shot'. A sniper with a high-powered rifle lay in wait just over the Border on the grounds of an ancient fortification known as the Battery. He was waiting for the patrolling RUC officers to appear in his crosshairs. The RUC officer in charge that night decided to patrol the area by the rear of the shops. They avoided the main street, a decision that no doubt saved their lives. When they returned to the station, the noise of the massive iron gate opening signalled to the sniper that the police officers were now beyond his scope. Undeterred, he fired over a dozen shots with some striking the station fence. The sound of high velocity rounds reverberated off the buildings in the main street. Although not a regular occurrence, locals knew instinctively to get their heads down and avoid any stray bullets. One of the bullets struck the bedroom of a local doctor. Then, as quick as it began, the firing stopped. The IRA unit melted into the night.

This event marked the last time that the Provisional IRA mounted an attack on security forces in Belleek. There would be intermittent incidents over the next 20 years, staged by dissident republicans but essentially the Irish Border, with its substantial military presence would never be the same.

Despite the genteel feel of this quaint Border village, Belleek has been a highly contested area for many centuries. The Vikings came and plundered in the 9th century. The Normans built a castle in the 13th century, which was quickly destroyed by locals. This part of Ireland would remain resolutely Gaelic for the next several centuries. Shortly, before the plantation, local chieftains, the Maguires, O'Donnells and the O'Neills, waged war with the British Empire for nine years before their sclf-imposed exile. Patrick Sarsfield fought here in 1689. The United Irishmen Rebellion of

1798 saw the area engulfed in conflict. Secret societies, like the Ribbonmen and the Fenians kept the republican flame flickering throughout the 19th century. In 1922, the struggle for national unity erupted with the only pitched battle between Irish and British troops. The Battle of Belleek almost proved to be a deal-breaker between Michael Collins and Winston Churchill in their negotiations over Irish independence. In World War 2, both the IRA and the British Army planned to use Belleek as a staging area for the invasion of the North and South respectively. At the outbreak of the Troubles, the British Army considered invading Ballyshannon from Belleek if the Irish Army invaded Northern Ireland. In 1987, a young British soldier was shot and killed from the same position in the south as the 1994 sniper. The Battery, as it is known, was built on the site of the original Norman castle. Control the high ground and you control Belleek. Rebuilt during the 1798 Rebellion, the British Army occupied it until 1924, almost 3 years after the Treaty was signed though still technically in the South.

This contested piece of ground presents a microcosm of the Irish Border. An anomaly that fosters ambiguity and a dark dystopian space that presents a tranquil bucolic facade. The partition of Ireland created a deeply complex set of scenarios in the towns and villages dotted along its frontier.

At various times, partition has hindered cooperation and commerce between both jurisdictions. This has presented major challenges for communities in its proximity who find themselves constrained by a lack of infrastructure, high unemployment and emigration. The immediate impact of the Border was a dramatic decrease in trade. Cross-Border business is estimated to have reduced by up to forty per cent following the imposition of customs tariffs.[1] Financial interactions between both jurisdictions continued to decline as Border towns found themselves cut off from their hinterlands and market access.[2] The situation was exacerbated by the transport policies of both governments. In Northern Ireland, the transport authorities favoured the development of its road network over rail. This rendered some of the cross-Border rail lines effectively redundant. The three Ulster Border counties of Donegal, Cavan and Monaghan, are the only counties with no railway connection in the Republic of Ireland. Many towns and villages along the Fermanagh, Leitrim and Donegal Borders were adversely affected by the railway closures and the destruction of roads deemed 'unapproved routes'. With no major industries to sustain employment, the area looked to tourism to provide income. However, when the Troubles erupted, the Border counties became the most militarised part of Western Europe and tourists stayed away.

Kiltyclogher

The quaint village of Kiltyclogher was originally known as Sarahville in memory of the local landlord's daughter. Charles Henry Tottenham founded the village around 1828 near the place where his daughter Sarah was killed in a hunting accident. The market village was laid out with wide streets. Tottenham built the first four houses on the corners where the roads converged. The village subsequently developed from there. The Market House bears the inscription C.H.T. Sarahville 1831. However, the people of the area persisted in calling it Coillte Clochair – the Stony Woodlands that became Kiltyclogher. During the Land War, Tottenham had an extremely adversarial relationship with their tenants. When writer Margaret Dixon McDougall visited the area in 1882 she noted, "This man has a very evil name among the tenants."[3]

Colonel Tottenham was unrepentant in his approach to land management. He announced in the House of Commons that, 'the best manuring land could receive would be to salt it well with rent'.[4] The impact of his policies was recorded in the Freeman's Journal in 1882, 'I found, wherever I turned yesterday the empty homes of evicted tenants rising up before me. I found that thirty or forty families have been dispossessed of the farms and the houses where they and their ancestors struggled to gain a livelihood, some for twenty years, some during half a century, and many others for a time contemporaneous with the meeting of the Irish Volunteers. I found that these evicted families number over one hundred individuals – equal to the occupants of many an Irish workhouse. For miles, I found these desolated homes and these idle farms which are already showing signs of returning wildness studding the face of the country.' After the Land Acts transferred land ownership to tenants, the Tottenhams link with Kiltyclogher began to fade.

Seán Mac Diarmada was born near Kiltyclogher in 1883. He grew up in a small thatched cottage in the townland of Laughty Barr, also known locally as Scregg. He became active in nationalist politics in the early 1900s. He was sworn into the Irish Republican Brotherhood (IRB), and rose to prominence in both Sinn Féin and the Gaelic League. Shortly after the establishment of the Sinn Féin party, he became director of elections in the North Leitrim area, travelling throughout the country making speeches and rallying volunteers to the Nationalist cause.

Mac Diarmada was one of the seven signatories of the 1916 Proclamation, which declared Irish independence from Britain and stated a commitment to 'religious and civil liberty, equal rights and equal opportunities to all its citizens'. On Easter Monday 1916, members of the Irish Volunteers, the Irish Citizen Army and

Cumann na mBan took over key buildings in Dublin and declared Irish independence. The Easter Rising had begun. After a week of heavy fighting against vastly superior numbers of British troops, the Volunteers were forced to surrender. The leaders of the 1916 Rising were brought before a court martial and sentenced to death. Seán Mac Diarmada was shot dead in Kilmainham Jail in Dublin in May 1916.

Seán Mac Diarmada's statue in Kiltyclogher

One of Kiltyclogher's most famous sons, musician Ben Lennon describes the Kiltyclogher of his 1930s childhood as a 'great market town' with 'three tailors, two shoemakers, a blacksmith, carpenter, stonemason, cooper, wheelwright, milkman and butcher'.[5] Most houses in the area had some land attached where they kept animals and grew vegetables. This became a necessity during The Emergency (1939-45). Like many other places in rural Ireland, the people developed a distinct sense of self-sufficiency.

The IRA's Border Campaign (1956-1962) caused disruption in the area when the British security forces blew up the roads leading into Northern Ireland. In December 1956, local man James Seely's house was badly damaged by an explosion when the road near Kiltyclogher was destroyed by dynamite.[6]

Yet Kiltyclogher remained a prosperous market town and a hub of local commercial and social activity until the Troubles began in the 1970s. It was one of the few urban areas in the Republic that suffered directly. Both the Blue Haven Dance Hall and the Technical College were blown up. All roads from Fermanagh were either blocked or blown up and Kiltyclogher found itself cut off from its natural environs around Cashel and West Fermanagh.[7]

The writer Colm Tóibín walked along the Border in 1986, a year after the Anglo-Irish Agreement. His book, 'Bad Blood', reports on the impact of the Border on ordinary lives and the historical legacy of life in an unforgiving environment, 'The road between Rossinver and Kiltyclogher, the heart of rural Ireland, was a convincing testament to the failure of Éamon de Valera's vision, which now seemed like a joke from some bitter satirical sketch. He wasn't a drinking man, but it is likely that even he would have taken a dim view of the plight of the publicans of Kiltyclogher, right on the Border with County Fermanagh. There were six pubs in the town and four were closed completely for lack of trade, one was open only at the weekends and the other, where I drank to de Valera's poor old ghost, was the only hostelry in the town open all day. And even here trade was bad on weekdays, the owner told me.'[8]

The reopening of the roads in the mid-90s brought an opportunity for Kiltyclogher to reconnect once more with its neighbours but the area's transport infrastructure remained underdeveloped. Public transport was limited and unemployment remained high (male unemployment was 16.7% in Kiltyclogher in 2006). Despite the poor quality of the land, agriculture remains one of the areas dominant employment sectors. Between 2006 and 2011, the population of Kiltyclogher declined by over 8%.[9]

Rossinver

'I've strolled along Rossinver braes where lakeside breezes blow,
And I've gazed in awe and wonder at the great world below.'

From 'The Fields around Kinlough': Author Unknown

The tiny hamlet of Rossinver lies just over four miles to the northwest of Kiltyclogher, near the shores of Lough Melvin. Since the 1990s, the area has become synonymous with the Organic Centre. It was established in 1995 with the aim of providing education and training about organic food production and sustainable living. Its continued success has raised the profile of Rossinver and attracted many like-minded people to the area. Across the road from the Organic Centre lie the ruins of Rossinver Abbey, which was founded by St Mogue.

St Mogue founded many churches throughout Ireland. He was born on Port Island on Templeport Lake in County Cavan. His father was said to have descended from Conn of the Hundred Battles. In his youth, Mogue was apparently given as a hostage to Ard-Rí Ainmire but later returned to his family because of his pious nature. Later he went to study at St Finnian's monastery of Clonard where he became friends with St Molaise. He travelled to England and Wales.

On his return to Ireland, he cured Brandubh, the king of Leinster, and in return was granted land in Ferns, Wexford, where he established a monastery. St Mogue died in 632 and buried at Ferns.

Mogue had four main confidants and loyal friends to whom he conveyed in inheritance the ownership (coarbship) of his churches and lands.[10] Towards the end of his life he travelled to Rossinver accompanied by Fergus, his foster-child and companion. He appointed Fergus (and his descendants) to assume responsibility for the place. The Fergus clan thus became were the coarbs of Rossinver Abbey and their descendants continue to live in the area.

Rossinver Braes

Adieu! My native home must I leave you here behind
To go and seek my fortune in a far and distant clime?
To leave the land that gave me birth it grieves my heart full sore
Adieu! My aged parents shall I ever see you more

According to tradition, a local man thought of turning the local graveyard of St Mogue's church in Rossinver into a commercial enterprise. There was a belief that burial in this graveyard meant an assurance of heaven and people brought their dead from distant districts to be interred there. The man mounted a gun in the gap of the south wall, assisted by a servant and a bloodhound. No one was allowed to be buried there unless they paid him a fee. However, when a man from a distant district arrived to bury his brother, he refused to pay, and he shot the man who claimed to own the graveyard. The breach in the south wall is still known as the Corpse Gap.

Rossinver Abbey

Many years ago, there was an annual festival called the 'Fair of Mogue' that took place on the Hill of Mogue near Rossinver village.

Thousands gathered to honour the saint but over time, it degenerated into a drunken affair in which public order incidents became common. The festival tradition eventually died out.

Lough Melvin: The Lake of Legends
According to legend, Lough Melvin was formed from a single well. The well was covered by a lid in the belief that if it were exposed to the elements it would overflow. One day, a local woman went to the well for water and as she was about to replace the lid, she heard her young child crying. She ran home to comfort the child and in her haste forgot to replace the lid. The water gushed forth and in the deluge that followed the woman was drowned and the surrounding area was flooded, forming Lough Melvin.

The Annals of the Four Masters provide a different account, 'Melghe Molbhthach, son of Cobhthach Cael Breagh, after having been seventeen years in the sovereignty of Ireland, fell in the battle of Claire, by Modhcorb. When his grave was being dug, Loch Melghe burst forth over the land in Cairbre, so that it was named from him.'
[11]

Inishkeen from the Irish, Inis Caoin meaning 'Beautiful Island', is sometimes referred to as 'Wood Island' or 'Maguire's Island'. The local chieftains, the MacClancys used it as a naval base. In 1421, it was attacked by the O'Rourkes. Five MacClancy brothers were killed and twenty boats were destroyed. The MacClancys later reclaimed the island and made the Gallaghers guards of the lake (a tradition that arguably continues to this day). During Penal times, friars took refuge on the island, which was then connected to the shore by a ridge of stones called the friar's pass. Captain Croft of Finner Camp bought the island in the 19th century. He planted the island with some impressive trees. The next owner was a Dr Maguire who imported exotic plants and shrubs. Republicans occupied the house on the island during the Civil War. Charlie Fergus bought it in the 1970s. Inistemple or 'Church Island' contains the remnants of a church thought to have been built in the 14th century and associated with the MacClancys. There is a cemetery on the island that was used until the beginning of the 20th century.

Inishkeen Island

Rossinver's modern fate mirrors that of Kiltyclogher. Both areas in North Leitrim found themselves isolated by road closures throughout the 1970s and 1980s. Yet when William F. Wakeman travelled through the area in 1870, he too found the Leitrim-Fermanagh Border difficult to navigate, 'About three miles inland from Garrison in a wild district unapproachable to all but the pedestrian was formerly another foundation of St Aidan or Mogue.' By the early 1990s, things had not improved. Young people were leaving the area in droves due to lack of potential employment. When a journalist from the Irish Times visited, she found an area that was struggling to sustain itself. She spoke to a local woman who was serving an elderly man in the family bar in Rossinver. This woman told the journalist that on a good night she could expect at most half a dozen customers. Her children had all left the area to seek employment. The population was aging and shrinking. Before the road closures, many people from nearby areas in Fermanagh came to pubs like theirs to drink, play music and socialise. People from Fermanagh stopped coming because it was simply 'too far'. When one young man from Garrison was asked how often he had travelled the few miles to Rossinver to visit his relatives during the Troubles, he replied, 'I was over there a couple of times, but it was basically too far because of the roads blown up... It was probably harder for my own family in the area to be cut off because my grandmother was from Rossinver across the Border. So it was tougher on them, you know, that that contact then was stopped with that community, you know. And it was only recently back when the ceasefires [happened] that all those roads were re-opened.'[12]

Road closures on the Leitrim/Fermanagh Border during the Troubles

The Legend of the Gillaroo

The gillaroo or 'salmo stomachius' is a species of trout that is unique to Lough Melvin. Its name is derived from the Irish Giolla Ruadh meaning 'red fellow' due to the fish's distinctive colour. It has a bright buttery golden colour on its flanks with bight crimson and vermillion spots. The gillaroo is characterised by deep red spots and a 'gizzard', which is used to aid the digestion of hard food objects such as, water snails.

According to local tradition, one evening St Mogue sat down to dinner only to find that the chief item on the menu was chicken. As he was fasting at the time, meat was proscribed and there were no fish immediately available. His solution was to raise his hand and turn the chicken into a fish, thus creating a unique species of fish that had a 'gizzard' similar to that of a chicken. The chicken was turned into a trout and placed in the lake. Another legend states that St Brigid was offered a chicken to eat on a Friday as she walked through the Garrison area in County Fermanagh. Meat was not allowed on Fridays for Christians. She was so incensed that she threw the bird into the river, upon which it changed into a fish with a gizzard.

Garrison

In the early 1970s, the British army closed all the roads connecting counties Leitrim and Fermanagh to prevent cross Border attacks by the IRA. As a direct result, local cross-border trade ceased and many social networks were severed. This led to the stagnation of local economies and a depopulation of the Border villages. Even more young people started to migrate out of the area due to the lack of local employment and intermittent paramilitary activity. The villages could no longer provide a sustainable living for its younger generation. Consequently, the population profile of the area began to age and services declined. Despite the adversity, this area maintained a strong tradition of good cross-community relations and today many groups and networks continue to work together in an effort to improve living standards.

Near Fermanagh's Border with Leitrim is the site of an old barracks and ironworks built by Sir John Dunbar in 1621 and 1622 respectively. They were destroyed during the 1641 Rebellion. After the Battle of Aughrim in 1691, some of King William's troops garrisoned there on their return journey. The village retained the name 'Garrison' and during the mid-1700s, it had a distillery and a milling industry. Most of the churches in the village were built in the 1800s. The building of the bridge over the Rogagh River in 1866 consolidated the village.

The village was the scene of mass protests during the Land War. Strongly supported by both Protestant and Catholic tenants, a group of around 3,000 protesters gathered outside the village in November 1883. The authorities had banned the meeting. As the protesters made their way towards Garrison, their numbers swelled to 7,000. The meeting attracted a lot of media coverage and helped bring the Land War to international attention.[13]

The effects of partition on the village were similar to those experienced by other towns and villages along the Border. Decline in trade and services, emigration and high unemployment were the recurring themes of division. The sense of isolation gave rise to a culture of self-sufficiency in the area and local people from both Catholic and Protestant communities worked together to maintain an infrastructure that supported tourism. By the 1950s and 1960s, Garrison became an internationally recognised angling location. It owed much of its success to its proximity to Lough Melvin, one of Ireland's premier fishing lakes. Hollywood star Charlie Chaplin, a keen angler, often fished Lough Melvin and stayed in McGovern's Hotel in Garrison. Hotels and shops catered for the needs of the visiting anglers and tourists. However, shortly after the Troubles began, the IRA blew up one hotel and the other was burned down. Many of the tourists who came to fish were English and, when they stopped coming, the hotels were not rebuilt.

Garrison hotel destroyed by a bomb during the Troubles

When Colm Tóibín visited Garrison in 1986, a local man told him that 'there had been thirty-one houses in this townland twenty years before... now there were only seven. People were getting out.' When Tóibín asked a local Catholic farmer why there were not as many police or British army on the roads, the farmer told him that 'they didn't come in by land anymore... the area was too dangerous. They flew in by helicopter.' He told Tóibín that 'there were strict divisions between Catholics and Protestants in this are... if Catholic land went up for sale, no Protestant would be let bid for it and vice versa.'

The lack of development in the border area between Fermanagh and Leitrim led to infrastructural issues. A 1994 report identified the area as the second most deprived ward in Fermanagh and the 23rd most deprived ward in Northern Ireland (out of 566 wards), in terms of degree of deprivation.[14] In the surrounding rural areas on both sides of the Border, many of the homes where old age pensioners lived alone lacked central heating, access to public sewage and bathing facilities. Unemployment was high and the youth were leaving.

> Adieu to Lovely Garrison,
> Where I was bred and born.
> Though far away I love you still,
> As the sunshine of the morn.

Despite the adverse circumstances, the people of Garrison rallied in 1991 and formed the Garrison and District Development Association. Their first chairperson was the then Church of Ireland rector, though his congregation did not endorse his involvement.[15]

The association's persistence led to the establishment of several new local facilities such as a cultural centre to include all traditions, a day-care centre and the Bilberry restaurant. Strong cross-community ties ensured that all events were supported by both traditions. Community relations in the area remained strong throughout the Troubles despite the fact that many UDR families were forced to leave their homes in the early 1970s.[16]

Blocked Border road at Garrison during the 1980s

Garrison experienced some growth between 1991 and 2001 as its population increased by twelve per cent.[17] The development of the local economy remained undermined by the poor quality of the surrounding road network but Garrison's greatest asset has always been its community spirit, which has regularly outperformed much bigger communities.[18]

Belleek
The name Belleek comes from the Irish Béal Leice, meaning 'mouth of the flagstones'. According to legend, Fionn mac Cumhaill's men sharpened their swords on the big limestone rock at Belleek Falls. The strategic location of Belleek as a fording place on the Erne has ensured that it remained a hotly contested area for thousands of years. The Gaels, Vikings, Normans and Planters have all left heavy footprints on the area around the village.

The Normans were quick to try to consolidate control of the area. In 1211, Gilbert de Costelloe built a fort at Caol Uisce, near the present day Belleek Fort, only to be destroyed by fire the following year. It was rebuilt forty years later but destroyed by the O'Donnells who were very adept at resisting Norman encroachment.

In the 16th century, Sir Richard Bingham, the English governor of Connacht also recognised the significance of controlling Belleek, 'There is no better means to conquer Ulster than by first taking Tyrconnell and placing garrisons at Ballyshannon and Belleek.'[19] During the Nine Years War (1594-1603), the Gaelic chieftains O'Neill and O'Donnell repelled repeated efforts by Queen Elizabeth's army to take control of the area. However, after the Flight of the Earls in 1607, the lands were forfeit to the crown and Sir Edward Blennerhassett became the local landowner. His family built Hassetts Fort. It later became Castle Caldwell after the Blennerhassetts fled to Ballyshannon during the 1641 rebellion and then sold their estate to James Caldwell. During the Williamite War, Patrick Sarsfield's forces attempted to seize the strategically vital towns of Ballyshannon and Belleek to prevent supplies reaching the besieged town of Enniskillen. The defeat of King James by King William at the Battle of the Boyne essentially consolidated English control of the region.

In 1776 a visitor to Belleek village was taken in by the natural beauty of the area, 'Crossing the bridge, stopped to see the salmon leaping up the rocky barrier. The water seemed to be quite alive with them. Came to Belleek, a little village with one of the most beautiful cascades anywhere to be seen.'[20] His comments about the local people were not so flattering, 'The vulgar here are remarkably addicted to thieving, though living is so extremely moderate.'[21]

A contemporary search of the word 'Belleek' on Google will reveal thousands of pages relating to the pottery. The village is synonymous with the high quality earthenware products it produces. John Caldwell Bloomfield established the pottery at Belleek in 1857. His architect Robert Williams Armstrong later became the manager of the factory. Caldwell Bloomfield discovered china clay and feldspar on his estate and with the financial backing of David Mc Birney, a wealthy department store owner from Dublin, he developed Belleek Pottery. For over a century and a half, it has provided a stable source of employment in the area. Caldwell Bloomfield was instrumental in the development of the local railway network. This brought prosperity to the town. The growing international reputation of the pottery has made Belleek synonymous with fine craftsmanship and it continues to attract thousands of tourists to the town. Belleek Pottery continues to play a central role in the economic life of the village. In 2009, for example, more than 160,000 people visited the factory.

By 1900, Belleek was a busy market town with a thriving tourist industry. The trains between Enniskillen and Bundoran ran through the village three times a day. The Belleek Co-Operative enabled local farmers to sell their produce and the building of sluice gates to regulate the water levels enabled farmers to reclaim land by the lakeside. The Lady of the Lake boat also ferried passengers from Enniskillen to Castlecaldwell in a connection with the Bundoran-bound train.

Belleek on a busy market day

After partition, tensions between North and South led to a major incident on the Border in the 'Belleek Triangle' of west Fermanagh. Free State forces (in alliance with Republicans) were expelled from the area by an overwhelming British military force. After the event, a local buffer zone was created stretching from Belleek to Pettigo. Partition and the establishment of customs posts led to a sharp decline in cross-border trade and towns and villages on both sides of the Border suffered as a consequence. Manufacturing that relied on the waters of the Erne for production and transport had always played a significant role in the development of Belleek. Many local industries were adversely impacted by the border closures during the by early 1930s and this caused some to leave the area.

However, the influx of American soldiers during the Second World War brought some colour to the quiet Border village. Phil Callaghan was an American soldier who was based in Belleek during this time. Historian Joe O'Loughlin recorded his recollection of that time.

'Life in Belleek itself was quiet but not without some excitement. The highlight of each month was fair day on the 17th. On that day, the farmers from miles around Belleek would drive their cattle into town to sell and buy. On that day also, the wide Main Street of Belleek became a quagmire of cow manure and the air odoriferous with the animalistic scents of sweat and Irish whiskey. Bartering for beef took the form of unintelligible – for the outsider that is – shouting between two Irish farmers facing one another. To the casual observer, it might resemble a violent argument, which it was not. Time and again during the process, one would slam his fist down into the hand of his counterpart with a vigor that would shake them both to the tips of their Wellington boots. When the final thunderclap of hand-slapping had died away and the deal was set, the two would adjourn to the pub and seal the agreement with a nip from the wee bottle.'

The closure of the railway in the 1950s affected the town's economic development. The IRA Border campaign was mostly concentrated in the south of the county and throughout the 1950s and 1960s; life in Belleek was relatively peaceful. The first fatality in Belleek during the Troubles occurred in 1972 and the last in 1992. During this 20-year period, violence was sporadic but there was a substantial security presence along the Border. The British Army, the Royal Ulster Constabulary (RUC), the Garda Síochána and the Irish Army all monitored the steady flow of cars crossing the Border. Economic trends were dictated by the currency exchange rate between the punt and the pound and local entrepreneurs on both sides of the Border became extremely adept at exploiting the circumstances.

Cross-community relations have always been good in the area and this quiet corner of Fermanagh managed to escape the inter-ethnic violence that enveloped other parts of the Border. Between 1981 and 2001, Belleek's population increased by eight per cent but this figure was still below its pre-Troubles level. At the dawn of the 21st century, Belleek's proximity to the Border continued to hamper its economic growth. The Overall Unemployment Rate was 10.5%, that was higher than both the County Fermanagh average (8.2%), and the Northern Irish average of (6.6%). The high proportion of 'self-employed' persons represents the mainly agricultural base of the area but it alludes to a local culture of entrepreneurship fostered by decades of political and economic exclusion.[22]

Kinlough

On the north western tip of Lough Melvin lays the charming village of Kinlough. It evolved from the Oakfield Estate, home of the Johnstons. The Johnstons originally came from the Scottish Borders. They arrived in Leitrim via Fermanagh in the late 17th century. The estate and the Kinlough Johnstons are no more but their echoes reverberate against the high walls still visible on the leafy main street and in the place names dotted around the village.

Prior to the arrival of the Johnstons, the MacClancy clan ruled the surrounding Dartry area. Their lands were confiscated after the 1641 Rebellion. By the beginning of the eighteenth century, the lands around Kinlough were owned by John Rynd, who was High

Sheriff for Leitrim in 1722. His daughter married Robert Johnston and they moved to Kinlough around 1740, when they built Oakfield House on the estate. Thus began a dynasty that would last for over 200 years and see Kinlough village grow up around the estate.

Oakfield House was remodelled in the 1820s and renamed Kinlough House. In the mid-19th century, Kinlough House was occupied by William Johnston and valued at £45. Samuel Lewis describes Kinlough and the estate in his 1837 book, A Topographical Dictionary of Ireland, 'This village contains about 30 houses. It has a chief constabulary police station, and has fairs on the sixth of each month. Petty sessions are held every third Monday and there is a dispensary. Here are the parish church, a R. C. chapel, and a school. At the north-eastern extremity of Lough Melvyn is Kinlough House, the beautiful villa of R. Johnston, Esq., in a very fine demesne. Near the village is a chalybeate spa which was formerly much frequented.'

Oakfield House

Political upheaval brought about the demise of Oakfield estate. The establishment of the Irish Land League and the subsequent Land War triggered the decline of landlord rule. The various Land Acts from 1870 to 1909 transferred Irish land from the landlords to the tenant occupiers. In 1906, James Johnston was the owner of the mansion house at Kinlough, then valued at £43. In 1943, the Irish Tourist Association Survey recorded that the house had been damaged by fire some twenty years previously but that the gardens were still open to the public.[23] Over time, Oakfield has become dilapidated. The timber was cut down and the roof was taken off the building. The last member of the Kinlough Johnstons died in the late 1950s.

The first recorded meeting of Kinlough Rural District Council took place in 1901. Analysis of the surnames present at the meeting reveals the shifting dynamic in Irish politics. The Johnston and Dickson names are no longer present in the area but the McGowan, Rooney, McGloin and Connolly names still proliferate. After 1916, that process was accelerated by national events. In 1918, Pat Gilvarry of Kinlough became adjutant of the South Donegal No. 1 Battalion of the IRA with volunteers from Bundoran, Ballyshannon, Kinlough, Belleek and Pettigo. The IRA began targeting RIC stations in the area. In 1920, members of the infamous Black and Tans raided the home of IRA Volunteer James Connolly at Unshinagh. His father was shot dead by the British soldiers. As the War of Independence, ended, local IRA volunteers took over the Kinlough RIC barracks. As the Civil War raged throughout Ireland, Captain James Connolly was killed in a gun battle with Free State Forces at Finner Camp.

The Johnstons

At the end of the Civil War, post boxes in the area were painted green to erase the regal red. In the midst of the global economic recession, Kinlough Creamery was destroyed by fire in 1931. It was rebuilt the following year only to be robbed and gutted by fire eight months later.[24] The Emergency brought hardship and opportunities for locals. Food shortages prompted many people from the area to indulge in some cross-border smuggling. Lough Melvin (which was completely frozen over in February 1940) was the ideal discreet location for exchanging illicit goods.

A secret agreement between the British and Irish governments at this time meant that RAF planes could fly over part of neutral

Ireland's airspace. There were several plane crashes in the Dartry Mountains and surrounding area. In 1941, a funeral cortege bearing the Union Jack draped over the bodies of British airmen solemnly made its way through Kinlough village. Locals lined the street to pay their respects and placed a wreath of daffodils on each coffin.

British Sunderland flying along the Donegal Corridor during WW2.

The 1950s and 60s saw large numbers of locals emigrating to London to find work. They centred on places like Harlesden and Cricklewood. The pace of change was slow for the village and in particular, the rural area surrounding it. It was not until the 1960s that some parts of the parish finally had electricity. During the 1970s, many families returned from London to raise their families in Kinlough. Small factories like Abbotts and Donegal Rubber provided employment. Some local men even took seasonal employment on the oilrigs of the North Sea at this time, using their considerable earnings to build new houses that began to replace the traditional archetype. Community centres were opened and the people of the village were very proactive in promoting sports and music in the area. The village was never directly affected by the Troubles but, like most Border villages in the Republic, it was cut off from Northern Ireland. As one local man observed, 'I had never been to Garrison (a distance of three miles from his house as the crow flies) until they opened the roads in the nineties.'

The village's population figures over the past two centuries mirror that of County Leitrim. The county population had been in decline since 1841, although the trend was reversed briefly during the 1970s and again between 1996 and 2006 during the Celtic Tiger era. Between 1996 and 2002, the village population grew by 17.1%. From 2002 to 2006, Kinlough became one of the most rapidly expanding villages in the County Leitrim. The hurried expansion combined with the near collapse of the Irish economy resulted in a number of unfinished estates with high vacancy levels within the village.[25]

Bundoran

This seaside town of Bundoran has both suffered and prospered because of partition. During the 1939-45 Emergency, the town experienced a mini-boom when many people crossed the Border to escape the realities of war and enjoy some leisure time in the 'Brighton of Ireland'. When the railway closed in the 1950s, the numbers of tourist visiting Bundoran decreased dramatically. When the Troubles began, Catholics from Northern Ireland flocked to Bundoran in droves, particularly during the summer marching season of July and August to escape the sectarian violence in Northern Ireland. Despite the convivial appearance of the seaside resort, however, Bundoran became synonymous with militant republicanism during the Troubles, not unlike other border towns such as Buncrana and Dundalk.

The modern town of Bundoran developed from two separate villages, the Protestant Ascendancy resort of Bundoran in the West End and the Catholic village of Single Street in the East End. The Viscount of Enniskillen built the first residence, Bundoran Lodge in 1777, and during the early 19th century, Bundoran became increasingly fashionable as a holiday destination for the Ascendancy. At the other end of the coastal plain, in the townland of Finner, the small village of Single Street was also developing. Throughout the 19th century, its population grew steadily. Both villages began to expand into the Drumacrin townland. When the railway arrived in 1866, the two villages amalgamated to become the modern town of Bundoran. The town grew up with the railway and its arrival brought unprecedented prosperity. During the early years of the 20th century, Bundoran experienced the most spectacular population growth in Ulster.

Bay View Terrace, Bundoran

By the end of the First World War, however, the railway company was in trouble. Partition exacerbated its problems as both governments had opposing transport policies concerning the railway network. In Northern Ireland, the transport authorities preferred the development of the road network to rail. Yet because of the rationing of petrol during the Second World War, the railway once again became popular. The trains made it possible for most people to smuggle goods across the Border to and from Northern Ireland. Rationing meant that flour and butter were not readily available. People from Northern Ireland regularly smuggled sugar back across the Border where it was in short supply.

The pressure of a post-war economy took its toll. By the early 1950s, the railway company was in difficulty and by the end of the decade, it had ceased to exist. The Northern Irish Government closed its lines in 1957 leaving small sections of railway scattered throughout the south. A 1956 Seanad Éireann report stated that the railway closure would be a devastating blow for Bundoran, which was largely dependent on its tourism industry. An inquiry at the time revealed that up to 40,000 Sunday day-trippers went to Bundoran during July and August.

Bundoran became an increasingly popular holiday destination for the Catholic community of Northern Ireland during the Troubles due to its immediacy to the Border. However, foreign visitors, particularly those from Britain, stopped coming to Bundoran for just that reason. As the Battle of the Bogside erupted in Derry, the Taoiseach Jack Lynch ordered the Irish Army to set up field hospitals and refugee camps in Donegal in 1969. Finner Camp, just outside Bundoran, was used to house some of the large numbers of refugees who began streaming over the Border. In 1972, the British Army cracked down on 'no-go' areas such as the Bogside in Derry with 'Operation Motorman'. This forced the IRA to move some of its resources to border areas. A British government document, Prominent Members of Provisional IRA Active Service Units Operating in a Cross-Border Role, stated there were five active service units (ASUs) on the Border, including one based in Bundoran. One of the names mentioned in the document was Dáithí Ó Conaill. A senior figure and strategist in the IRA, Ó Conaill was in hiding in the Bundoran area at the time. He left Sinn Féin in 1986 with Ruairí Ó Brádaigh, local republican Joe O'Neill and others to form Republican Sinn Féin.

Nine prisoner candidates were nominated by the National H-Block committee to run for the Dáil after Charles Haughey called a general election in June 1981. Two of the candidates, Kieran Doherty and Martin Hurson, had strong connections with Bundoran. Tensions were high in the town when the then Taoiseach Charles Haughey arrived to canvass support for the upcoming general election. H-Block supporters jeered the Taoiseach as he appeared in Bundoran to speak on a mobile platform. Haughey was struck by an egg when he spoke at Ballyshannon and the Gardaí and H-Block supporters came to blows. Throughout the 1980s, the presence of members of the New York Police Department pipe band at the IRA Hunger Strike commemoration in Bundoran continued to cause controversy. Then in the mid-1980s, Bundoran was dubbed the 'dirtiest town in Ireland'.

By the mid-1990s, however, the property boom had begun to take hold in Bundoran. The extensive investment in holiday homes was fired by the Irish Government's tax-incentive schemes and many people from Northern Ireland bought properties in the town. In 1995, an article in the Irish Times suggested that in order for Bundoran to develop, it was simply a 'question of good planning control and a concerted effort to deal with the image problem'. Surfing provided the solution to the town's image crisis. In 1997, Bundoran hosted the European Surfing Championships. It was Europe's largest-ever surfing championship at the time with more than 360 competitors from seventeen different countries. The championships marked Bundoran's first official recognition as a world-class area for surfing.

Between 2002 and 2006, Bundoran's population grew by seven per cent to almost 2,000. The construction boom that began in the 1990s continued unrestricted, leading to increased expansion in the town. In 2008, the banking crisis led to the downfall of the construction industry and, like many other towns all over Ireland, some developments in the town remained unfinished.

Ballyshannon: The Oldest Town in Ireland

'At present the town appears to be utterly neglected by those who should care for it' - (Comment made by a travel writer in 1858). [26]

In 2014, violent storms damaged the clock face on one of Ballyshannon's most iconic buildings, forcing it to be removed. That same year, in the same building, the jewellery shop on the ground floor closed its doors for the last time after more than 150 years of trading. Another local family business had already closed down in the town. When asked about that closure, the owner told the Donegal Democrat, 'There has been plenty of talk about the end of the recession, but I see no sign of it here.'[27] Although the closure was possibly prompted by global economics, the unfortunate event was a microcosm of the declining fortunes of Ireland's 'oldest town'. For of all the Border towns in the area, Ballyshannon appears to be the one most adversely affected by partition.

Ballyshannon retains the character of a 19th century market town but its history stretches back to the first settlement of humans in Ireland. Evidence of settlement dating back to the Neolithic Period (4000-2500 BC) has been discovered within the town and throughout the surrounding area. According to tradition, Inis Saimer Island in the Erne Estuary was the place where the first inhabitants of Ireland disembarked around 2700 BC. They are thought to have arrived from the Mediterranean region. These pre-historic people were named by the 17th historian Geoffrey Keating (Seathrún Ceitinn c.1569-1644) as Parthalón and his people. Different annalists cite Parthalón's origins as Greece, Macedonia or Sicily. For centuries, the river Erne and the surrounding topography acted as a barrier for the first settlers and their descendants. A little further up the river from Inis Saimer was the strategic crossing point or ford. Its location ensured that it became a hotly contested area throughout history.

Many centuries later, when war broke out between the Ulaidh (Ulster) and the Connachta (Connacht), the Ulaidh killed Conall Gulban's foster-father. Conall Gulban (died c. 464) established the kingdom of Tír Conaill (much of what is now County Donegal) in the fifth century. His descendants became known as the Cenél Conaill. A distressed young Conall swore revenge. He marched towards the ford on the Erne River at Ballyshannon aided by his brothers and some three thousand Connacht men. Conall's troops were triumphant. He decapitated Senach (son of King Cana of Ulster) in the ford and it subsequently became known as Áth Seanaigh (Senach's ford). Although the Drowes was traditionally recognised as the boundary between Ulster and Connacht, for the next few centuries this line was occasionally revised to the Erne as the various tribes battled for control of the ford.

By the 830s, large Viking fleets began to arrive in Donegal Bay and sail up the Erne. They attacked Devenish Island monastery on Lough Erne in 837. The attacks continued well into the next century. An order of the Cistercians was established on Abbey Island by the estuary during the 12th century. The Normans arrived in Ballyshannon area in the early 13th century but were repelled by the O'Donnells. In 1423, the O'Donnells built their castle overlooking the ford of Áth Seanaigh on the Erne. The castle was ideally located to defend against any incursions by invading armies. The Erne was a valuable resource for the O'Donnells, so much so that they exported its abundant salmon and they became known as 'the kings of the fishe'.[28] The fish were exported internationally in exchange for wine and other goods.

In 1603, James I granted Henry Folliott Ballyshannon Castle and some of the adjacent lands. In 1613, Ballyshannon received Royal Charter and became a British garrison town. The barracks built in 1700 brought business to the town. Improvements to the harbour in the 1830s led to the town's evolution as an important port and began a period of sustained economic growth. As the foremost merchant town in the region, its main industries included brewing, distilling, tanning, saw-milling and tobacco processing. Many of the historic buildings that characterise the town were built during this period, which also corresponded with a phase of high design standards in Europe. These buildings include period houses such as Portnason (c.1820), Inis Saimer House (c.1885), the Royal Bank of Ireland with clock and bell tower (1878), Mulligans Warehouse (c.1860), the Tudoresque Workhouse (1842), the Convent (1880) and the many churches throughout the town.

Ballyshannon on Harvest Fair Day.

The advent of the railway marked the decline of Ballyshannon's importance as a port. This was compounded by the build-up of the sand bar at the mouth of the Erne, which acted as a barrier to nautical navigation and the lack of political will to address the problem (an issue that would resurface early in the 21st century). By the late 19th century, many of the town's industries were in decline. Although the deterioration of the port's significance adversely affected the town's economy, partition in the early 20th century exacerbated an already delicate situation.

As a market town, Ballyshannon served a wide area that included West Fermanagh and North Leitrim. Agricultural goods such as flax, pork and grain were sold in its markets. In its heyday, the town had three banks, two newspapers, two railways, a brewery and a distillery. It was an important centre for fairs, hosted on the second day of the month. Its electoral divisions stretched from Bundoran to Churchill (Fermanagh) and Glenade (Leitrim). Post-partition, Ballyshannon found itself cut off from its natural hinterland and trade and commerce quickly declined.

On 2 May 1925, three men from Ballyshannon James Campbell, Michael Maguire and Cecil Stephens representing the Ballyshannon Harbour Commission travelled to the Killyhevlin Hotel in Enniskillen to meet the members of the Boundary Commission. They made their case for the restoration of the natural hinterlands. Whilst there was some initial optimism that places like Belleek, Castlecaldwell and Garrison would be incorporated into the Irish Free State, the de facto Border remained and Ballyshannon would be adversely affected by the loss of approximately 7,000 people from its official district. By 1925, it was estimated that the Border resulted in the loss of markets with a reduction of one third in trade. Markets in

Ballyshannon were getting smaller. Shopkeepers did less business and the town suffered a drop in employment resulting in more emigration to England and America. The imposition of customs tariffs followed by the Land Annuities war with Britain further aggravated the town's economic woes.

On the 8th of November the news it was sent,
That the tariff was raised to forty percent
From the town of the Erne there was a great drive
And into Belleek they all did arrive
When Gavigan heard it I'm thinking said he,
I'll put out my cattle and they will be free
Going up Belleek street he hit on a plan
And he put them out to his mother-in-law's land
At Belleek station a meeting took place
Pat O'Brien and his son were discussing the case
Says Pat to the son 'Our big bullocks won't thrive
We must have them here at a quarter to five
The land it is clear of all bullocks just now
Instead we will see the horse and the plough
We will never hear the bullock's big roar
The dog will be keeping the wolf from the door.'

The Emergency brought more austerity as rationing was introduced. The black market economy developed as various products were smuggled back and forth across the Border. However, the Erne Hydro Electric Scheme brought a short-lived prosperity providing employment. The controversial project is still seen by some as having a negative impact on the Ballyshannon area. The Troubles ensured that tourists stayed away from 'the oldest inhabited town in Ireland'. In 1969, the UVF attempted to blow up the power station. The political instability and the proximity to the Border affected the entire Erne area. Like many towns in Donegal that had a strong manufacturing tradition, Ballyshannon was affected by increased global competition and this led to industrial closures. In 1996, more than 120 jobs were lost with the closure of Donegal Rubber. Between 1981 and 2002, Ballyshannon's population fell by 11%. In 2002, the national unemployment rate was around nine per cent but Ballyshannon's unemployment rate was 14%. Donegal Parian China closed in 2005 with the loss of fifty-four jobs and an average of 60,000 visitors per annum.[29] By 2010, the position had not improved and this area of south Donegal had the fastest-growing unemployment rate in any part in the Border counties.[30]

Pettigo: *'Who fears to speak of '98?'*
The area around the old market town of Pettigo contains many reminders of its historic past. Until the early Christian period in Ireland, this frontier was home to faithfully pagan people. Cam

townland was a centre of the ancient religion of the Celts and its name is derived from a pagan burial-place. The vestiges of the Stone Age architectural legacy can be found in Tamlaght townland.[31] In Celtic times, it was known as the 'Place of the Blacksmith'. In the Middle Ages, St Patrick's Purgatory on Lough Derg rose to international prominence. From the 13th century until the late 16th century, the area remained firmly in the hands of one family, Mac Craith (or Mag Craith) of the Termon. This surname has some variations, the most common being McGrath. Following the Plantation of Ulster, Pettigo became a popular market town. The arrival of the railway increased the amount of goods flowing into the town. It also brought increased numbers of pilgrims to the area. However, partition cut the town off from its locality and it reverted to its boundary status. Its frontier location made it a 'smugglers' paradise'.

During the Second World War, Pettigo experienced a curious phenomenon. During the blackout, half the village remained in the dark, whilst the part of the village in the Republic remained fully lit and open for business. Many British soldiers crossed the Border to wine and dine in the local hostelries. The village suffered from the closure of the railway in the 1950s and from the closing of numerous cross-Border roads during the Troubles in Northern Ireland.

The area around Pettigo is known as the Termon, meaning church lands or sanctuary from the Latin *terminus*. For more than a thousand years, this area had been established as a neutral territory. Even though it found itself wedged in between three Gaelic fiefdoms, Tír Conaill, Tír Eóghan and the Fir Manaigh, each of them engaged in internecine battles and land grabs, the termon's boundaries guaranteed refuge for fugitives.[32] Though it was regarded as a nonaligned territory, it was more and more looked on as part of Fir Manaigh during the Maguire dynasty.[33]

The Plantation
Through Torlogh's rebellion in 1641, the McGraths forfeited their ancestral lands to the Crown. The Plantation then saw the Termon lands come under the control of a Scottish settler family, the Leslies. They were less than impressed with what they found, 'The land, I assure you, is the worst and most unprofitable in the Province of Ulster and will afford fourteen hundred acres useful to the tenant, though the bog and mountains be of larger extent. My interest in Termon McGra is nothing but a lease from the See of Clogher, for which I have already paid more than it is worth.' Bishop John Leslie, author of that passage, passed on the land to his son. During the early 1700s, more Scottish settlers arrived in this remote area. Their

settlement concentrated around Pettigo, which developed into the town, as we know it today.

Then here's their memory, let it be
To us a guiding light
To cheer our fight for liberty
And teach us to unite!
Though good and ill be Ireland's still,
Though sad as their your fate,
Yet true men, be you, men,
Like those of 'Ninety-eight.

John Kells Ingram (1823-1907)

The town has many famous sons and daughters who played a significant role in shaping political and cultural events in Ireland both north and south of the Border.

Miler McGrath is best described as a Border Borgia. Miler was born about the year 1522. He joined the Franciscans and he was appointed by the Pope as bishop of Down and Connor in 1565. Events in 1567, triggered by the death of his foster-brother and protector Shane O'Neill, prompted him to submit to the Crown's authority. Ever the political pragmatist, he renounced his religion, but only after he was imprisoned and tortured in England. In 1570, he became the first Protestant bishop of Clogher by appointment of Queen Elizabeth I. Miler McGrath was described by one historian as 'a very complex character, a consummate bluffer who for half a century led a life of the most brazen duplicity... He had all the sagacity and astuteness of a successful, if unscrupulous politician.'[34]

Much of Miler's success can be attributed to his Machiavellian duplicity. He ingratiated himself with the court of Elizabeth I. His diplomatic skills and deceitful actions, such as feeding false information to both Dublin and London, caused one English official to remark that 'he runs with the hare and hunts with the hound'. He became very rich and extremely powerful. He died aged 100, despite being a notorious bon-vivant. He was archbishop for 52 years. Even in death, he remained an ambiguous figure. His epitaph ran:

Patrick, the glory of our isle and gown,
first sat a bishop in the See of Down.
I wish that I succeeding him in place
as bishop had an equal share of grace.
I served thee, England, fifty years in jars,
and pleased thy Princes in the midst of wars; is,

here, where I'm placed, I'm not; and thus the case
I'm not in both, yet am in both the places."

Reverend Philip Skelton was at the polar opposite of Miler on the spiritual scale. He was rector of the parish from 1750 to 1759. A pugilistic, non-conforming philanthropist, he was described as a man of 'gigantic size... adept at cudgels and the use of his fists, and was not backward in the use of either when he considered occasion required.' [35] He survived two famines in the area, whilst securing food for the starving masses of all beliefs. Twice, he sold his much beloved library to feed the poor. During the famines, he sustained himself on an austere diet stating, 'Will I feed myself while my poor are starving?' In what appears to be a recurring theme for the area, he maintained a close relationship with his Catholic counterparts.

Proinsias Dubh Mc Hugh was one of the last highwaymen of Ireland. He gained notoriety in the late 18th century. His headquarters was in the wild Scraghy hills near Pettigo. He was eventually caught and hanged in Enniskillen in May 1780 along with his companions. He is buried in Carne Graveyard, near Pettigo. He is eulogised in local songs as a gallant humanitarian who 'robbed the rich and paid the poor':

> My name it is bold Frank McHugh
> As game a cock as ever crew.
> In Meencloghore I was bred and born,
> Free from all disgrace and scorn.

In an act of true Christian harmony, the Catholic priest Reverend Neal Ryan lent his congregation to his Church of Ireland friend Reverend James Benson Tuttle on the day of a church inspection by his bishop. The story was retold in Maurice Walsh's novel *Green Rushes,* which became the screenplay for the film *The Quiet Man,* starring John Wayne and Maureen O'Hara.

Another priest, Fr Lorcan O'Ciarain (1863-1945), delivered sermons that were famous their brevity and political overtones.[36] He lived in Magheramena Castle and he was a close friend of both Eamonn de Valera and Michael Collins. During the War of Independence, his home was taken over by the Black and Tans who destroyed his collection of books. An ardent Irish nationalist, he was present at the first meetings the organisation that would later become Sinn Féin. It is believed that it was he actually, who coined the phrase that became the party's title.

Andrew Barton Patterson, one of the best-loved figures of Australian literature and the author of the song *Waltzing Matilda,* also has roots in Pettigo. Another Barton, 'French Tom', was born in Pettigo in 1695 and attended school in Ballyshannon. After emigrating to France, he founded the now world-famous Barton and Guestier wine company. Robert Childers Barton, (1881-1975) cousin of Erskine Childers and related to the Barton family of Waterfoot, was a British Army officer stationed in Dublin during the Easter Rising of 1916. He resigned his commission after the execution of the leaders of the revolt. He then joined the Republican movement and was elected to Parliament as the Sinn Féin member for West Wicklow In 1918.[37] Basil McIvor (1928-2004) was born in Tullyhommon, Pettigo. Regarded by many as a liberal Unionist, he was one of the champions of Integrated Education in Northern Ireland. He believed that a non-inclusive education system based along religious lines would only foster sectarianism. He was a member of the Ulster Unionist group that negotiated the Sunningdale Agreement in 1973. In 1981, he became chairperson of Northern Ireland's first integrated school, Lagan College.

During the early 1970s, the British Army attempted to seal the Border by destroying what they deemed were 'unapproved roads'. This had an adverse effect on border villages such as Pettigo. The legacy of the road closures continued to affect border towns into the 21st century. In 2001, an article in the Irish Times noted that the people in Pettigo felt that they had 'the worst of both worlds, north and south'. There was no public transport service in the area; the banks had closed their branches; and there was no doctor's surgery. As services were withdrawn, investment declined, unemployment rose and emigration became commonplace.[38]

'Draw a Line': The Origins of the Border

'Ulster is different… This was so before Partition; indeed to some extent, it was true before Plantation.'
- Historian Liam de Paor, [1]

From 1870 until 1918, Home Rule remained the main goal of constitutional nationalists in Ireland. The founder of the Home Rule movement, Donegal-born Protestant Isaac Butt, proposed an arrangement whereby Ireland England and Scotland would each have their own parliaments with a shared 'national council' at Westminster. His successor, Charles Stewart Parnell, pursued a similar policy. British Prime Minister William Gladstone backed the idea but failed to have it passed in 1886. A second attempt in 1893 was also defeated. Parliament passed the Third Home Rule act in 1914 but it was bitterly opposed by the Unionist community. The outbreak of the First World War postponed its implementation and so it never came into effect. Ironically, the only part of Ireland granted Home Rule after partition was Northern Ireland.

Lord Randolph Churchill (1849-1895) was quick to realise that getting Unionists on side would help undermine the Gladstone government, commenting, 'The Orange card was the one to play.' However, his rallying cry of 'Ulster will fight and Ulster will be right' was in stark contrast to comments he made earlier, in which he said 'Ulsteria is not so much an argument as a disease'.[2] This Orange card forged a political alliance between Conservatives and Ulster Unionists which was to last almost a century until the fallout from the Anglo-Irish Agreement in 1985. In 1948, as Ireland was exiting the Commonwealth, Lord Randolph Churchill's son and war-time Prime Minister Sir Winston Churchill hoped, in later years, 'that someday there will be a united Ireland', insisting that this could come about only with the consent of the Unionists of Northern Ireland.

Unionist opposition to Irish nationalism was nothing new. One British Home Secretary remarked that if Daniel O'Connell's repeal campaign against the 1801 Act of Union resulted in violence, 'We must call on the Protestant yeomanry in the North and put arms in their hands.' [3] During the Fenian violence of the 1860s, some Ulster landlords armed their tenants and announced that 'the North will take care of itself, and let the government send troops to the South and West'.[4]

Ulster unionism had become better organised in its opposition to Home Rule after Edward Carson took over the reins. The union was in crisis and unionist fears were emphasised by Rudyard Kipling, whose ancestors came from Ballinamallard, County Fermanagh, in his poem, Ulster 1912.

> The blood our fathers spilt,
> Our love, our toils, our pains,
> Are counted us for guilt,
> Before an Empire's eyes
> The traitor claims his price.
> What need of further lies?
> We are the sacrifice.

In 1911, Unionist leader Edward Carson declared that unionists should take over 'those places we are able to control' and they would become part of the 'Protestant Province of Ulster'.[5] The revived Ulster Volunteers pressured the Liberal government to propose an amendment that would exclude the Protestant-dominated counties of Antrim, Down, Armagh and Derry. In a general election two years previously, Fermanagh and Tyrone had voted for Home Rule by 51.5% to 48.5%. However, Carson insisted that he would never agree to give up either county.[6]

As the campaign for Home Rule continued to gather impetus, the Ulster Unionists drafted the Ulster Covenant of 1912 in which they declared their intent to use 'all means which may be found necessary' to stop Home Rule. They also formed the Ulster Volunteers in 1913. The Irish Volunteers were formed in 1914 as a result. Both groups grew steadily in numbers and drilled openly in public areas. Ireland looked as if it was heading for civil war. On March 4th 1914, more than 600 Ulster Volunteers drawn from Ballyshannon to Ardara began drilling on Rossnowlagh beach in the pouring rain. They were a minority group in South Donegal but they were nonetheless determined to uphold their Solemn League and Covenant. The battalion was divided into eight companies led by James Sproule Myles of Ballyshannon.

Under intense pressure to avoid bloodshed, Liberal MP Thomas Agar-Robartes (1844-1930) recommended a revision to the contentious Third Home Rule Bill to omit the counties of Antrim, Armagh, Derry and Down with their Protestant majorities.[7] As the Omagh-born writer, Benedict Kiely noted in his 1945 book, Counties of Contention, 'the mind of the young Liberal politician saw a sensible and obvious solution... draw a line.'[8] Even so, the Third Home Rule Bill highlighted the latent difficulties in trying to partition Ireland.

Carson initially proposed a nine-county exclusion in December 1912 but after a religious headcount, the Unionists opted to go with six counties rather than nine on the basis that a rise in the Catholic population would change the political balance against them and that demographic shift could eventually lead to Irish reunification. Over the next few years, discussion about the prospect of a six-county state continued. The government opted to implement the 'county option' to avoid civil war. However, the pragmatic northern Unionists continued to campaign effectively for control over the largest area they could hold safely.[9] Unionist politician Charles Craig concluded, 'We quite frankly admit that we cannot hold the nine counties.'[10] In 1920, he observed, 'if we had a nine-county parliament with 64 members, the unionist majority would be about three or four: but in a six-county parliament, with 52 members, the unionist majority would be about ten.'[11]

In 1914, as the Unionists prepared to defend 'Ulster', members of the Irish Volunteers, congregated at the market yard in Ballyshannon. Both militias drilled openly and at the same time, large numbers of British soldiers marched through the streets of Bundoran, and Ballyshannon on recruitment drives for the 'war to end all wars'. The area represented a microcosm of the cataclysmic events that would unfold over the next decade and continue to dominate social and economic life throughout the 20th century.

Irish Volunteers drilling at the Market Yard, Ballyshannon

Before the 1918 election, the pro-Home Rule Irish Parliamentary Party was the only show in town for nationalists. The Land War of the 1880s had marked a significant shift in the political landscape of

South Donegal. Thousands of people in the area took to the streets to demand a redistribution of land ownership to tenants from their landlords. In a series of subsequent Irish Land Acts, the Westminster Government granted the people their rights. However, nationalists were no longer content with the 'three Fs' (fair rent, freedom of sale and fixity of tenure) and their crosshairs became sharply focused on the devolution of political power from Westminster. Unionists vowed to oppose any such move. In 1913, more than 260 Protestants signed the Ulster Covenant in the Great Northern Hotel in Bundoran. Over 300 signed the same pledge in Ballyshannon. Guns were smuggled, bought, borrowed or stolen as both nationalists and unionists armed themselves for a showdown. Then the actions of the Bosnian Serb nationalist assassin Gavrilo Princip changed all of that.

With the outbreak of war after Princip killed the Austro-Hungarian Archduke Ferdinand, Irish Parliamentary Party leader John Redmond called on the Irish Volunteers to enlist in the Crown forces. Major Joe Sweeney from Dungloe, who later fought alongside Patrick Pearse during the Easter Week rising in Dublin, stated that there was an initial enthusiasm among Irish Volunteers in Donegal to fight 'for the freedom of small nations'. Donegal had around 10,000 volunteers. The majority took up the call to arms and enlisted. The British Secretary of State for War, Lord Kitchener, had already convinced the Ulster Volunteers to join up. Approximately 8,000 Donegal men joined the British army to fight in the First World War. Over 1,200 would never come home and 55 of those were from Ballyshannon, 44 from Donegal Town, 13 from Ballintra and 12 from Bundoran. The Glenties-born writer Patrick MacGill fought in the trenches and recorded the true horror of war. His poem, A Lament, is featured on the First World War Ulster Memorial in Thiepval, France.

I wish the sea were not so wide
That parts me from my love;
I wish the things men do below
Were known to God above.
I wish that I were back again
In the glens of Donegal,
They'll call me coward if I return
But a hero if I fall.

Then during Easter week 1916, Irish republicans launched an armed rebellion to end British rule in Ireland and establish an independent Irish Republic. The Rising was organised by the Military Council of the Irish Republican Brotherhood and it began on Easter Monday. The fighting lasted for six days and Patrick Pearse, fighting alongside James Connolly's Irish Citizen Army and

Cumann na mBan, led the Volunteers. They seized strategic locations in Dublin and in a Proclamation declared the Irish Republic, independent of the United Kingdom.

General Sir John Maxwell arrived in Dublin on Friday, 28 April 1916 after receiving orders from Minister for War Lord Kitchener to suppress the Rising and pacify Ireland. The British Army, with vastly superior numbers of combatants and military resources suppressed the Rising, forcing the Irish Volunteers to agree to an unconditional surrender on 29 April. The subsequent decision to execute the leaders of the Rising was Maxwell's. He could never have anticipated the consequences of his actions. However, the poet W.B. Yeats knew intuitively that everything had changed:

I write it out in a verse--
MacDonagh and MacBride
And Connolly and Pearse
Now and in time to be,
Wherever green is worn,
Are changed, changed utterly:
A terrible beauty is born.
W.B. Yeats, Easter 1916

In the aftermath of the executions, the majority of Irish people were galvanised into a unified opposition to British rule in Ireland. The blood-sacrifice made by the Volunteers set in motion a series of events that continue to resonate to this day.

After 1916, many nationalists in Donegal withdrew support from the Ancient Order of Hibernians (AOH), closely linked with the Irish Parliamentary Party, and joined the Irish Volunteers. Support for Sinn Féin soared within the county. Sinn Féin flags began appearing on unionist properties around Donegal in late 1917. By the end of year, Sinn Féin had 34 clubs in Donegal. In 1918, Eamon de Valera visited the county. Both Unionists and the AOH attacked the Sinn Féin rallies. The AOH had warned Sinn Féin not to march in Ballybofey, as they did not allow the Orange Order to do so. However, Sinn Féin defiantly held their rallies in the town, as elsewhere in Donegal.

When Sinn Féin gained control of the Board of Guardians and the District Council at the Local Government Elections, one of their first acts was to purge from the records a 1916 resolution passed by the Donegal Board of Guardians condemning the Rising. The extract was torn from the minute book and burned.

Around the same time, a number of Bundoran volunteers were on trial in Ballyshannon for unlawful assembly. Hundreds of British

Army soldiers from Finner Camp were called in to assist armed police in guarding the prisoners while large groups of their local supporters surrounded the court. The Conscription Bill was announced in April 1918. The Irish people were united in their opposition to the Bill and drafted the National Pledge, 'Denying the right of the British Government to enforce compulsory service in this country, we pledge ourselves solemnly one to another to resist conscription by the most effective means at our disposal.'

One of the first anti-conscription meetings in County Donegal was at Milford. The next mass rally was at Frosses and around 6,000 people attended it. Another meeting in Letterkenny united the AOH, Sinn Féin and the Irish Labour movement. Thousands signed the pledge and Dr McGinley warned, 'There is only one way... We will resist this threat at the point of the rifle.' The people of the county gave their definitive response in the 1918 general election when three Sinn Féin and one Nationalist were elected to the first Dáil Éireann.

Sinn Féin won 73 out of the 103 Irish seats in that 1918 general election. Yet in Ulster, the Ulster Unionists gained 23 out of 37 seats. The political realities in Ireland forced the British to commit towards the establishment of Home Rule. In 1919, the British Cabinet's Committee for Ireland suggested the formation of two parliaments for Northern Ireland and Southern Ireland. It suggested that the northern area should comprise the nine counties of Ulster in a bid to preserve an estimated religious balance.[12] The Ulster Unionists opposed the nine counties option because of the risk of a future Nationalist majority when the Northern Parliament might vote itself out of existence. Their preference was that the arrangement should be restricted only to the six counties of Antrim, Down, Derry, Armagh, Tyrone and Fermanagh.[13] The British government decided that the only possible way to resolve the opposing aims of both Unionists and Nationalists was to group those six northern counties of Ireland together and give them an assembly of their own.[14]

The Liberals, in association with Irish nationalists, were the architects of the first three Home Rule Bills in 1886, 1893 and 1912. However, a Conservative-dominated government in association with Ulster Unionists drafted the fourth Home Rule Bill, which became the Government of Ireland Act of 1920.[15] The Better Government of Ireland Bill had proposed a six-county Northern Ireland that the majority of Unionists accepted.[16] It meant that the opening of the Northern Irish parliament 'closed the door' on Irish unity and the collapse of the Boundary Commission in 1925 'turned the key'. Indeed, in giving primacy to the Ulster Unionist cause, it provided the template for the later treaty settlement in stating that, 'Northern Ireland shall consist of the parliamentary counties of Antrim,

Armagh, Down, Fermanagh, Londonderry and Tyrone, and the parliamentary boroughs of Belfast and Londonderry, and Southern Ireland shall consist of so much of Ireland as is not comprised within the said parliamentary counties and boroughs.'

However, northern Nationalists adopted a policy of non-recognition of the new Belfast assembly. They saw the 1920 partition decision as a violation of their democratic rights and believed that they would soon be incorporated into the Free State. Nationalists sardonically referred to the new state as 'Carsonia' and believed that their case for inclusion in the Free State would inevitably lead to reunification.[17]

In Fermanagh, the Unionist population were acutely aware of the political threat posed by the Nationalist majority, especially with voting under the proportional representation (PR) system. When the Nationalists gained control of Enniskillen Urban Council, Lisnaskea Rural Council and the Fermanagh County Council, they demanded that the entire county should be included in an independent Ireland.[18] The Belfast parliament moved quickly to crush dissent and passed a bill dissolving local authorities that refused to recognise the new Northern Irish State and dispensing with PR voting. These laws were backed up with a show of force by the police as they moved in and took over the Enniskillen offices of Fermanagh County Council. Fermanagh and Tyrone County Councils were both dissolved.[19] When Unionist premier William Craig met Michael Collins of the Dublin government, he informed him that unionists would never 'abandon places like Enniskillen or Londonderry' because of their historical and sentimental significance.

The discontinuation of proportional representation resulted in Unionist political control over the new state. In Fermanagh, Catholics made up 56% of the population but their representation on local bodies fell from 52.5% to 36.75%. At the time, Craig was also busy preparing the Representation of the People Bill (No. 2). This resulted in gerrymandering to assert firm Unionist control in both counties.[20]

The census of 1911 had shown a Catholic majority of 7,644 in Fermanagh.[21] Yet since that census, there had been a considerable and mostly Protestant, immigration into Fermanagh and a corresponding emigration of Catholics from Fermanagh into the Free State.[22] Yet British Prime Minister David Lloyd George told the House of Commons, 'There is no doubt... that the people of the two counties (Fermanagh and Tyrone) prefer being with their southern neighbours to being in the northern parliament.'
Conversely, for unionists on the 'wrong' side of the Border, the hard-headed strategy adopted by Carson and Craig constituted both an

insensitive duplicity and a negation of Unionism. The fight against Home Rule for Ireland had resulted in Home Rule for Northern Ireland and southern Unionists, now including thousands from the Ulster counties of Cavan, Monaghan and Donegal, found themselves on the wrong side of the fence. They felt betrayed by their northern brethren. In 1912, many of these southern unionists had signed the Ulster Covenant that had abandoned the unionist minorities in Leinster, Munster and Connacht.[23] Eight years later Unionists in Donegal, Cavan and Monaghan were themselves abandoned by their fellow Covenanters. Sir James Stronge, the Unionist politician stated, 'the three counties have been thrown to the wolves with very little compunction'.[24]

The terms of Article 12 of the Anglo-Irish Treaty of 6 December 1921 enabled the Northern Irish parliament to separate itself from the Irish Free State.[25] In 1922, Conservative politician Austen Chamberlain described the partition of Ireland as 'a compromise, and like all compromises, (it) is illogical and indefensible'.[26]

'Turning the Key': The Boundary Commission

Fermanagh Border 1957

Under the Anglo-Irish treaty of 1921, a commission was set up to demarcate the Border between Northern Ireland and the Irish Free State. Arthur Griffith agreed to the establishment of a Boundary Commission in the hope that this would transfer at least Derry city and large parts of Fermanagh and Tyrone to the Irish Free State and thus render the fledgling Northern Irish state unviable. Article 12 of the Anglo-Irish Treaty outlined the process of partitioning Ireland, 'A Commission consisting of three persons... shall determine in accordance with the wishes of the inhabitants, so far as may be compatible with economic and geographic conditions, the boundaries between Northern Ireland and the rest of Ireland.'

Michael Collins also felt that the Boundary Commission would eventually lead to a united Ireland. It was his belief that the unification of the north with the rest of Ireland was 'an inevitable necessity' and the 1921 treaty was just a 'stepping stone' to that outcome. The Boundary Commission began work in 1924. Eoin MacNeill represented the Irish Free State, J. R. Fisher was the Northern Ireland representative and South African jurist Richard Feetham was appointed as chairperson. The Boundary Commission tour commenced in Armagh, and then travelled to Enniskillen, Omagh and Derry. Representative bodies from south Donegal and

Fermanagh met the Boundary Commission to make their respective cases.

Fisher was a Belfast barrister and former editor of the unionist *Northern Whig* newspaper. In 1922, Fisher had advised James Craig to seek the inclusion of Donegal in Northern Ireland, 'We *ought* to bear *our* share of the burden of congestion and misery, and Ulster can never be complete without Donegal. Donegal belongs to Derry, and Derry to Donegal. With North Monaghan *in* Ulster and South Armagh *out*, we should have a solid ethnographic frontier to the South, and a hostile 'Afghanistan' on our north-west frontier would be placed in safekeeping. A Southern frontier from the end of Lough Erne to Bessbrook or thereabouts would be ideal; it would take in a fair share of the people we want and leave out those we don't want.'[1]

Donegal, however, posed major logistical problems for partition. The fertile Lagan Valley and the farmland around Donegal Town were Protestant-dominated but much of the rest of the county was poor, Catholic and Irish speaking. The Ballyshannon Harbour Commissioners highlighted the detrimental effect that the Border had on the town. They urged the Commission to incorporate areas such as Belleek and Garrison into the Free State. Ballyshannon served as the market town for a large area that encompassed South Donegal, West Fermanagh and North Leitrim before the 1920 Border was established. Post-partition Ballyshannon had lost much of its natural hinterland. The representatives of the Ballyshannon Harbour Commissioners told the Boundary Commission delegation that 'the markets in Ballyshannon are now much smaller, the merchants and shopkeepers do less business, and generally the town has suffered by the boundary line. The people in the Northern area have ceased to do business at Ballyshannon, and have gone elsewhere.'

The County Donegal Protestant Registration Association also met with the Boundary Commission delegation and outlined its three proposals for the county: (1) the whole county should be transferred to Northern Ireland; failing that (2) the former 'East Donegal' and a small portion of North and South Donegal should be transferred; and finally (3) as the minimum, that the areas Londonderry No.2 Rural District, Strabane No. 2 Rural District, with the Manorcunningham area, Convoy area, Cliff area, and Pettigo area, should be so transferred on the grounds of population and geographic and economic conditions.[2]

In a submission to the Boundary Commission on behalf of Donegal Protestants Association the following claim was also made, 'The county of Donegal is one of the first four counties in Ireland most suitable for the development of the tourist traffic. Given the support of the Government, railways and hotel associations, together with security for capital, it would undoubtedly be possible to build up what would be a very important industry in what is now an impoverished country... It would certainly be in Donegal's interests to join Northern Ireland.'

In making the case for Pettigo they stated, 'This area has been very badly hit commercially owing to the customs duties. Derry and Belfast (the natural buying centres) formerly supplied the great bulk of the goods required and there is considerable trade in drapery goods direct with Manchester. To avoid the customs duties some of the merchants have purchased in Dublin, but that city does not cater for the class of goods required.' In reference to the Cliff area, the association pointed out that 'residents on North Bank of river (Cliff), in order to get to Belleek, (which by direct road is only a half-a-mile distant) by motor, have to go round by Ballyshannon a distance of nine or ten miles for the return journey.'

In local terms, under the Boundary Commission's recommendations, parts of north-west Fermanagh such as Garrison, Belleek and Castlecaldwell were to be transferred to the Free State and Pettigo and Templecarn were assigned to Northern Ireland. The sluice gates and gatekeeper's lodge at Belleek would also remain part of the North. If the recommendations had been implemented, County Donegal would have lost 42,627 acres to the North and the Irish Free State would have gained 40,614 acres from parts of Fermanagh and Tyrone adjoining Donegal.[3]

Nationalists had naively hoped that each Ulster County could opt for exclusion from Home Rule, while Unionists were now demanding a six-county block, which came 'with no plebiscitary determination of [a] boundary and without assurance that the demand for the exclusion of the whole nine counties of Ulster had been discarded.'[4] The parish priest of Garrison, Fr. Eugene Coyle was intuitively pessimistic about the potential findings of the Commission. He wrote to the Free State Minister for Finance Ernest Blythe several weeks before the leaked news report warning him 'that the Free State government will soon have to revise its repeated, and unnecessarily repeated talk about the fairness of England.'[5]

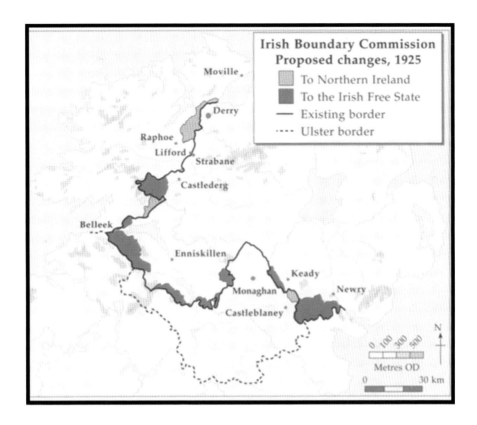

Commission chairperson Feetham refused to transfer Fermanagh
and Tyrone to the Free State, insisting that the terms of the treaty
prohibited him from reconstituting Northern Ireland anew. Derry
and Newry were retained due to the economic clause of the treaty. [6]
In Border counties such as Tyrone, Catholics formed the majority in
the poorer upland areas of the interior, while the Protestant-owned
land was concentrated near the Border. This made any resultant
land transfer difficult to settle. Pettigo found itself divided by the
Border. The small Protestant block on the Free State side could be
transferred without too much discord. In the predominantly Catholic
West Fermanagh, the Boundary Commission acted with more care.
At the edges of Lower Lough Erne, there was a concentration of
Protestant famers who had had invested in the lake's drainage. They
were anxious to retain control of the water levels to avoid flooding.[7]
In October 1925, Commissioner Fisher wrote to Carson, thus
breaking his pledge of secrecy, stating, 'I think there is no harm in
letting you know that I am well satisfied with the result which will
not shift a stone or tile of your enduring work for Ulster... It will
control the gates to its own waters at Belleek... and your handiwork
will survive.'[8]

The Commission recommended the transfer of seventy square miles of West Fermanagh, a strip of territory that ran from Garrison and Belcoo to the Free State. The wish to maintain control over watersheds, which left substantial Catholic majorities within the Six Counties. The boundary recommendations were that 286 square miles would go to the Free State and 77 miles would go to Northern Ireland. This would have shortened the Border from 280 to 229 miles. It might have strengthened Northern Ireland's position but was still longer than the Bundoran to Bessbrook line that had been advocated previously.[9]

In November 1925, these recommendations were leaked to the Morning Post. The leak caused a political crisis in Dublin and Eoin MacNeill resigned from the Boundary Commission in protest. The commission was abandoned and the report was suppressed. Winston Churchill predicted that 'someday it might be expected to emerge as an historical document'.[10] A new tripartite agreement was put into place confirming the existing Border. The debt write-off that released the Free State and Northern Ireland from certain financial commitments to Britain sweetened the bitter pill. In negotiating the new deal, Kevin O'Higgins remarked that the debt write-off would 'deaden in the twenty-six counties the echo of the outcry of the Catholics in North East Ulster'.[11] When the accusation was levelled at him that he had in fact 'sold northern nationalists' he claimed that this was 'no more than a half truth'.[12] In December, the Northern Ireland parliament presented Premier William Craig with a silver cup, which had the words 'Not an inch' inscribed on it.[13]

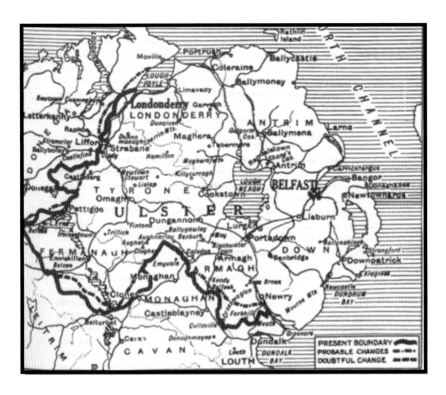

Map of Boundary Commission recommendations leaked to the Morning Post, 1925

On 3 December 1925, the governments of the Irish Free State, Northern Ireland and the United Kingdom signed the boundary agreement and registered it with the League of Nations. This gave the 1920 interim partition a permanent status.[14] Northern Nationalists already felt dejected after the failure of the Boundary Commission to deliver any considerable changes to the Border. They now felt abandoned by the Free State government and trapped in a Unionist state that would always regard them as second-class citizens. Over time, many marginalised nationalists turned from moderate forms of nationalism to the uncompromising resolve of Irish republicanism and this further toughened the unionist mind-set.[15] The combination of Unionist intransigence and Free State indifference sowed the seeds of future conflicts. De Valera became the main beneficiary of Northern Catholic disaffection. His 1937 constitution asserted the 'national territory' as comprising the entire island of Ireland, thus revoking the recognition of partition contained in the December 1925 agreement.[16]

The outcome was a legacy of distrust and a deep sense of betrayal on both sides. A poem published in the Donegal Democrat in 1925,

Partition of Ireland, illustrated and mourned the breakdown between the two traditions.

> The noblest patriots of our land,
> Some noble martyrs too'
> Who for our country tool their stand
> Still wore the orange and blue.
> The greatest writers of our land,
> From hill and dale and crag,
> Oft times marched in the orange band,
> And bore the orange flag.

Therefore, the Irish Border established a legacy of isolation and disillusionment for many members of both communities on both sides of the line. It created large minorities in both states that felt discarded by both Dublin and Belfast. The nationalist minority in Northern Ireland resented the Border. For them it was an obstacle to an independent 32-county Ireland and a morally unjustifiable continuance of British involvement in Ireland. They found themselves trapped inside a 'Protestant State' with a 'Protestant Parliament', while southern Unionists were marooned in a state where the Catholic Church enjoyed a 'special position' and determined political and social attitudes.

For Northern Ireland's Unionist majority, the Border strengthened their ties with Britain and guaranteed their independence from the Free State. Yet it also left them with a deep sense of vulnerability. In their view, the Border had to be defended and the mass mobilisation of the Special Constabulary, many of whom were former militia, ensured that Northern Ireland remained separate from the irredentist Free State. Consequently, the contested Border became one of the root causes of sectarian and political conflict on the island throughout the 20th century. In the run-up to the fiftieth anniversary of the 1916 Rising, Unionists in Northern Ireland became increasingly concerned that the celebrations might rekindle Nationalist aspirations to recapture the 'fourth green field'.[17] Then the worst phase of violence, referred to as the 'Troubles' claimed over 3,500 lives between 1969 and 1999.[18] As Northern Ireland descended into a spiral of violence, the Irish Border became the most heavily militarised area in Western Europe.

In 1873 Hugh de F. Montgomery, a senator of the Northern Ireland Parliament from 1922-24, wrote: 'It is impossible that a country can be truly free and prosperous unless its inhabitants live and work together as one people and cease to be divided into two tribes by barriers of race or creed. There are two influences at work to keep Irishmen so divided, the one Popish bigotry... and.... Protestant bigotry.'[19] One hundred years later, Ireland and Britain joined the

European Union. The Single Market project that lifted Border controls within the EC brought attention to the Irish Border. Hopes were raised that the conflict over the Irish Border would 'be dissolved in a wider European "constellation of regions".'[20] However, the transformation of the Border from a militarised zone only really began after the first IRA ceasefire in 1994. Almost immediately, local residents in Garrison and Rossinver re-opened the roads that had been closed for more than twenty years.

After the demilitarisation of the Border, trade between North and South increased. Growing numbers of tourists from the south ventured north, where many had never even dreamed of travelling. By January 1999, the British Army installation at Roscor was vacated and by November of the following year, it was demolished.[21] The Irish Border today is barely discernible. Sometimes the only indicators that you are in Northern Ireland is the prevalence of yellow number plates. The Peace Process has delivered some modest prosperity in some Border areas such as Derry but in south Donegal, west Fermanagh and north Leitrim, many of the villages dotted along the boundary are still reeling from the effects of partition.

Donegal: The Forgotten County

Almost sixty per cent of voters in Donegal returned an unambiguous 'No' in the November 2012 referendum on children. The previous June, the county rejected the European fiscal treaty and previously it said No to both Lisbon treaties in 2008 and 2009. As the county was being hit hard by emigration following the economic collapse, unemployment continued to rise and household incomes dropped sharply. There were rumblings that a large percentage of the county's population would refuse to pay the Household Charge. What was the reason for this disconnect? There was a pervasive feeling among Donegal people that they live in the 'forgotten county' and that its peripheral location has defined its lack of economic development.

In 2002, County Donegal's unemployment rate was fifteen per cent, compared with nine per cent at the national level.[1] Even during the peak of the so-called Celtic Tiger boom, Donegal continued to have a much higher unemployment rate compared to the national average. In Ballyshannon, the world-renowned Rogans angling business and then Donegal Parian China closed their doors. The ESB reduced its workforce from a peak of 200 to about forty staff. Donegal lost more jobs during the boom years than were created within the county. The county has had the highest deprivation rates in the country since 1991 and the highest rate of unemployment since 2002.[2] By 2010, the situation had not improved and south Donegal had the fastest-growing unemployment rate of any area in the Border counties.[3] According to the 2011 census, youth unemployment in the county was at forty-nine per cent. The rate of overall unemployment at 26.2% compared with nineteen per cent for the State. A report published by the Area Development Management/Combat Poverty Agency (ADM/CPA) revealed that Donegal was the 'most deprived Border county' in terms of social deprivation.[4] In 2012, it was revealed that Donegal did not even exist on the maps of the Irish Government's crisis response headquarters. Senator Joe McHugh made the claim that the omission by National Emergency Co-ordinating Centre was 'a continuation of the inglorious attitude towards the forgotten county'.[5]

Yet Donegal has always existed on the periphery. According to tradition, Donegal was established as a geographical entity when Conall Gulban carved out the kingdom of Tír Conaill (from the Drowes to the Swilly) in the fifth century. His brother Eógan ruled Inishowen and later by extension Tyrone (Tír Eóghan).[6] Another brother, Cairbre (after whom Duncarbry is named) ruled the area from the Drowes to the Owenmore River at Ballysadare. From the late sixth century onwards, the descendants of Cairbre and Conall

50

sought to expand their territories. The stage was set for the area around south Donegal and north Leitrim to become a highly contested area. For over a thousand years, this area would remain a Borderland with the frontline periodically shifting north and south.

Cenél Conaill was facing a threat from its northern neighbours also. Cenél nEóghain defeated them at the battle of Clóiteach (Clady on the River Finn) and forced them to move south of the Barnesmore Gap. The giant cashel Grianán of Aileach may have been built around this time to celebrate this victory. This cashel, with walls four metres thick, was built in the ninth century. Its construction coincided with the expansion of the Cenél nEóghain dynasty. It was around this time that these rulers of 'the North' began to be described as the kings of Aileach. However, Cenél Conaill, their 'unloved cousins' to the south continued to act as a bulwark against their hegemony.[7]

In 807 AD, the Norse men made their presence felt with an attack on Inis Muiredaig in Donegal Bay. By the 830s, large Viking fleets began to arrive in Donegal Bay and sail up the Erne. The Cenél Conaill repelled a Viking incursion in a battle at Es Ruaid (Ballyshannon) in 837. The Vikings attacked Devenish Island monastery on Lough Erne that same year. The attacks continued into the next century. In the ninth and tenth centuries, the Vikings appear to have established temporary settlements in the area at Dún na nGall (Donegal town) and Cáel Uisce (Belleek). Donegal (Dún na nGall: meaning 'fort of the foreigners' may have been named after these Nordic invaders.

In the tenth century, the Ó Canannáin dynasty (Cannon) ruled their area between the Ballintra River and the Barnesmore Gap. Mag nÉne (Magh Éne), the plain between the Drowes and the Erne, was home to the Muintir Maíl Doraid (Dorrian). Their rulers were inaugurated at the famous flagstone Lecc Uí Maíl Doraid on the southern banks of the Erne. The area around Ballyshannon (Es Ruaid) was reserved for the dynasty that held the kingship of Cenél Conaill. Ruaidhrí Ó Canannáin ruled Tír Conaill from 941 to 950. He became 'the most powerful Irish king' of his time.

Throughout the eleventh and twelfth centuries, the Muintir Chanannáin and Muintir Maíl Doraid families battled for control of Tír Chonaill. From 1085 to 1181 the Uí Channannáin ruled Tír Chonaill with the result that Tír Áeda (south Donegal) was renamed Trí Saorthuatha Mhuinntire Chanannáin ('the three free territories of the Cannon clan'). The Uí Maíl Doraid, expanded their territory into northern Connacht. By the end of the thirteenth century, the hegemony enjoyed by the south Donegal families was ending and the Ó Domhnaill (O'Donnell) clan stepped onto the stage, where they would remain for the next few centuries.

The O'Donnell lords, who claimed the Cenél Conaill as ancestors, extended the traditional boundaries of Donegal. These areas remained under their control until 1603. Their rule was consolidated by a strong dynasty despite some succession disputes. Their success in resisting Norman invasion was in part due to their strong military organisation and use of mercenary fighters who had come from Scotland (gallóglaigh). This was subsidised by taxing subordinate lords and chiefs.

The Norman threat to O'Donnell power arrived in the form of Maurice Fitzgerald, described by Henry III as being 'harsh in executing the King's mandates'. He built Sligo Castle in 1245 after Connacht was brought under Norman rule and he planned to expand his rule northwards into Donegal. This resulted in the battle of Creadran Cille, north of Sligo in 1257 and defeat for the Normans. The conflict with Fitzgerald extended the southern Border of Tír Conaill as far as the Drowes. At the time, the area (Magh Éne) was under the control of the chieftain O'Flanagan of Tuatha Ratha (West Fermanagh).[8]

During the mid-14th century internal rivalries within the O'Donnell clan undermined the stability of Tír Conaill. A bitter territorial dispute emerged between the O'Donnells and the O'Connors of north Connacht that continued to dominate the political landscape of south Donegal throughout the 15th century. Brian O'Connor began to build a castle at Bundrowes in 1420 to prevent the O'Donnells from extending the southern boundary of Tír Conaill. This resulted in a continuous struggle by both families to establish control over south Donegal.

After Henry VIII was declared King of Ireland in 1541, English plans became sharply focused on the strategic town of Ballyshannon. Captain Thomas Lee, an English soldier of fortune proposed setting up a garrison there suggesting that 'once settled in that place, (we) will procure great quietness in (the) province of Connacht, and stop the only passage which they (the O'Donnells) have to go to and fro to assist any traitor that may rebel there'.[9]

In July 1597, Sir Conyers Clifford, the governor of Connacht, attempted to capture O'Donnell's Castle at Ballyshannon with a large army. Even though there was a small garrison stationed there, they managed to hold out until O'Donnell arrived with reinforcements. The English soldiers were routed and forced to retreat southwards towards Sligo. O'Donnell's forces intercepted the troops in the boggy terrain of Magheracar, just south of the present day town of Bundoran. The result was carnage and slaughter with an estimated six hundred English casualties. The name Magheracar translates as the 'Plain of the Slaughter'.

The O'Neills and O'Donnells joined forces to oppose the English invasion during the Nine Years War. Despite some early successes, the war ended in defeat for the Irish chieftains. On 14 September 1607, Hugh O'Neill and Rory O'Donnell, along with members of their families and retinue boarded a ship at Rathmullan and set sail for Spain, never to return. With the removal of the last rebel chieftains of Ireland, the English began to implement their next colonial project, the Plantation of Ulster.

The architect of the Plantation of Ulster, Sir Arthur Chichester, once described Donegal people as being 'inclined to blood and trouble'. In 1608, a commission was set up to gather information about the newly confiscated lands. In south Donegal, there was no government-sponsored attempt to remove the native Irish from the area and the region was sparsely planted with settlers making up just fifteen per cent of the population. The land in south Donegal (Barony of Tirhugh) was granted to Trinity College Dublin, former army officers (servitors) and the Church of Ireland.

Tír Conaill was historically divided into four 'cantreds'. These ancient divisions were later used to form the baronies after Donegal became a county in 1585. The barony of Tirhugh (from the Drowes to the Eske and Bearnas Mór) was more or less based on the ancient territory of Tír Áeda.

In 1603, James I granted Ballyshannon Castle to Henry Folliott along with some of the neighbouring lands. In 1610, Folliott agreed to maintain the castles at Ballyshannon and Bundrowes in a 'defensible state' in the event of a native uprising in the area. The Folliotts also leased the south Donegal townlands of Bundrowes, Drumacrin, Ardfarna and Rathmore from Trinity College Dublin. Henry Folliott, who had held the lands from the time of the Plantation (as a reward for distinguishing himself at the battle of Kinsale), died in 1622. He passed the lands onto his son Thomas Folliott. When Thomas Folliott died in 1696, the estate was passed onto his son Henry. Henry Folliott died in 1716 without an heir. In 1718, much of the estate was sold to his legal advisor William Speaker Connolly.

After William Connolly died in 1729, he left his estate to his nephew William (M.P. for Ballyshannon) who died in 1754. Thomas Connolly then inherited the estates. When he died without a genetic heir, he passed the land to a Colonel Pakenham, who took the name Connolly. His son, Thomas Connolly, inherited the estate. This

Thomas Connolly appears as the main property owner in Magh Éne in Griffith's evaluation in the middle of the 19th century.

Like many areas in the west of Ireland, the Great Famine ravaged Donegal. In 1845, the blight was reported in the Donegal town area. By 1846, Bundoran had lost some of its crop to the disease. Dr Sheil recorded that at the time, there was 'great distress' among the poorest members of society. In 1846, the local priest Fr. Francis Kelaghan appealed to the Lieutenant General to help some of the underprivileged people of Bundoran, claiming that their food stocks were rapidly running out and they faced starvation. In 1847, reports of fever and dysentery outbreaks in south Donegal began to appear. Despite the government's initial indifference, relief committees were set up to deal with the humanitarian disaster. Local landlords Colonel Connolly and Dr. Sheil were among the most generous contributors to the local Relief Committee.

While Donegal had extensive maritime assets, its fisheries remained underdeveloped due to high levels of emigration after the Famine.[10] In the early 1880s large-scale evictions forced many people from Donegal to emigrate during the Land War.[11] By the time the Congested Districts Board was established, Donegal farms had the lowest valuation in Ulster. Poor infrastructure hampered access to markets. The development of the railway lagged behind the rest of the country. Periodic calamities compounded the problem and contributed to general levels of impoverishment. The population had a low level of literacy and limited employment opportunities. There was an over-dependence on hiring and child labour as a source of income.[12]

By 1891, Ballyshannon, then the largest town in Donegal, had lost its booming maritime trade in iron and wine. Gone too was its extensive salt industry. At one time it thrived as a banking and industrial centre. It had strong brewing and distilling industries. Other industries thrived such as tobacco and snuff manufacture, weaving and dyeing.[13]

Partition was disastrous for Donegal. Its impact on the county is still being felt. Not only was it geographically isolated from the new Irish Free State but also it was cut off from its natural hinterlands in the new Northern Ireland state. Both governments neglected to adopt a strategic approach in developing the local area and that resulted in economic stagnation. Then the railway network was dismantled, further diminishing cross-Border trade.

The issue of chronic unemployment continued in south Donegal and was raised by Deputy Brennan in Dáil Éireann in November 1955. He asked the Minister for Industry and Commerce if there were any proposals before his Department to alleviate the unemployment. The Minister replied that there were no proposals at that time.[14]

Thirty years of political violence in Northern Ireland hampered any socio-economic development or investment in the area. Cross-Border trade was seriously affected by the closure of many roads. Despite all, Donegal became a holiday haven for both Catholics and Protestants from Northern Ireland during the Troubles, albeit with some degree of segregation. Catholics generally went to towns like Bundoran and Buncrana, while Protestants mostly went to Rossnowlagh and Dunfanaghy.

During the 1990s, Donegal's rural economic structure began to change. The traditional dependence on agriculture and fishing began to diminish. This had a substantial bearing on the capacity of the county to entice international investment.[15] Therefore, by the mid-1990s, Donegal was still lagging behind the rest of the country. The Department of Finance conducted research on socio-economic trends from 1993 to 1996. It revealed that Donegal ranked twenty-sixth among the twenty-six counties of the Republic in terms of employment growth, twenty-sixth in the reduction of unemployment decrease, twenty-fourth in new car registrations, and twentieth in growth of tourism revenues.[16]

Inured to Toil: North Leitrim

In 1588, Captain Francisco de Cuellar, a survivor of the shipwrecked Spanish Armada, sought refuge in north Leitrim. He recorded the events in a diary, which provides a fascinating insight into life in sixteenth century Dartry. He described the locals as being 'inured to toil', a description that has as much resonance now as it did back then.

Broadly speaking, Leitrim's diverse landscape allows it to be geographically divided into north and south Leitrim with Lough Allen as the dividing line. Rocky outcrops, loughs and peat bogs permeate South Leitrim's landscape of drumlin farmland. North Leitrim by contrast is dominated by the Dartry mountain range that separates the extensive glens featuring loughs and drumlins. The drumlins blocked the drainage systems and forced water back to form a multitude of small lakes that characterise the north Leitrim landscape. To this day, the alignment of the tightly packed drumlins governs the patterns of roads, farms and fields. This has limited the agricultural development of the north of the county where small dairy and cattle farms form the primary land use. Despite technological advances in agriculture, the wet drumlin region remains a difficult area to farm. The wet soils that react poorly to drainage, combined with precipitous slopes, limit animal movement and hinder mechanisation. Conversely, the water retentive soil of Leitrim is ideal for growing certain types of trees. Sitka spruce thrives in the wet mineral drumlin soils and can grow faster there than anywhere else in Europe.

Leitrim still has the smallest and most rurally based population (more than ninety per cent) in the republic. The effects of rural decline and emigration have taken their toll. Studies have shown that North Leitrim men in particular have suffered from higher than average suicide levels. Poor health and low educational achievement are contributing factors. The reduction of public services to rural areas resulted in an increased sense of isolation and exclusion. The decline in customs and traditions such as the céilí, fair days and holy days, has meant that there are now fewer opportunities outside the public house for people to socialise with their neighbours and people from other villages and towns. This has had a big impact, particularly on single men who do not have a wide range of opportunities for socialising.[1] The quality of life for some in North Leitrim is seen as contributing to factor to the above-average rate of mental health problems.

Leitrim's first inhabitants found a landscape where the high grounds were covered with dense pine forests. The lowlands were blanketed by deciduous woodlands of hazel and elm. The Mesolithic hunter-gathers, who roamed the area around 9,000 years ago, moved between seasonal hunting grounds. Traces of their existence are rare in Leitrim but archaeological finds on the shores of Lough Allen may date to this period.

The Neolithic period (around 4000 BC) marked the introduction of farming and brought about a dramatic transformation of the landscape. Large swathes of land were cleared of trees and then farmed until the nutrients were depleted. Over time, this led to an extensive decline of native forests. Despite the fact that Leitrim's soil is unsuited to large-scale agriculture; the large number of megalithic tombs suggests that the area experienced large-scale settlement during the Neolithic era. Some of the best examples of these tombs can be found near the coast at Tullaghan.

With the arrival of the Bronze Age around 2,500 BC, metal tools enabled farmers to fell larger trees and work with heavier soils. This enabled settlements to expand into lowland areas. Territories were consolidated and kingdoms established sometime between the end of the Bronze Age and the beginning of the Iron Age. Much of the history of this time remains a matter of supposition because, as one notable local historian wrote, 'more blood was spilled than ink'.[2] The proliferation of spearheads and swords provides an insight into the violence and turmoil that characterised this period. The Iron Age hill forts and linear earthworks are an indication of the defensive nature of these local communities.

The topography of the Borderlands between Connacht and Ulster ensured they would become separate geographical districts. This was later consolidated by the construction of the defensive partition that became known as the 'Black Pig's Dyke'. In north Leitrim, the Black Pig's Dyke is still visible in the townland of Lattone, near Kiltyclogher. Despite the mythical tales, archaeologists agree that its principal role was as a defence against cattle raiding. It also had ritual significance, demarcating ancestral boundaries. It was not continuous but a series of ramparts built between lakes, bogs and drumlins.

Black Pig's Dyke at Magheracar

Improved agricultural productivity led to an increase in population during the early Christian period. During the fifth and sixth centuries, a number of small religious settlements were established such as Rossinver Abbey on the shores of Lough Melvin. During the period between the fourth and twelfth centuries, the development of the church coincided with the rise of political dynasties. Two of the most powerful of these were the Uí Néill in Ulster and Ua Conchobair in Connacht.

There was some Norman settlement in Leitrim beginning in the thirteenth century but, for the most part, the kingdom of Breffni remained largely under the control of the O'Rourkes up until the Elizabethan conquest. In 1603, the O'Rourke stronghold Leitrim Castle fell and the confiscated lands were given to English and Scottish settlers. The kingdom of Breffni was no more. After the demise of Brehon power in North Connacht, Sir John Perrott began the process of forming what was to become County Leitrim (from the Irish 'Liath Druim' - meaning grey ridge).[3] The county was comprised of lands originally belonging to Gaelic clans such as the O'Rourkes, O'Connors and the MacClancys. In 1620, large parts of the county were appropriated and given to planters such as Sir Frederick Hamilton, who founded the market town of Manorhamilton.

Sir Frederick Hamilton was a Scottish planter who built Manorhamilton Castle between 1634 and 1638. His estate comprised 6,300 acres of arable land and 10,650 acres of bog. This land had previously been under the control of the O'Rourke clan. When rebellion broke out in 1641, the native Irish tried unsuccessfully to destroy Manorhamilton. Hamilton responded with a 'scorched earth' policy of retribution. His forces burned Sligo town, including the Abbey, in 1642 and three hundred women and children were killed by rampaging soldiers. Hamilton is described in Dr. O'Rourke's 'History of Sligo' as the 'Tamerlane of the West'.

Described by historian Lorcán Ó Rúnaí as 'a hard, bitter, cold fanatic', he was also responsible for the burning of the abbey at Dromahair and his violent actions and war crimes have drawn comparison with those of Cromwell. According to local tradition, Hamilton's actions were so brutal that his name was used by mothers to hush their children for generations afterwards. He appears to have relished his work, however, and is reputed to have said 'you can never get rid of the rooks until you burn the nest'. He destroyed O'Rourke's stronghold at Glencar in 1641. His castle was attacked during the 1641 rebellion and Hamilton fled. He died in 1647. His castle was finally destroyed in 1652. His youngest son Gustavus was made Governor of Enniskillen in 1686 and fought on the side of William of Orange at the Battle of the Boyne in 1690.

Historian C.P. Meehan's diligent research revealed an excerpt from a diary that highlights his attitude towards the native Irish:

'March 17 (1642) being their Patron's Day, our colonel sending for one of his prisoners, the rogues (Irish) being drawn up in a body before us, we called to them to come and rescue the prisoner who was there to be hanged in honour of St Patrick, which prisoner being hanged, and proving to be but an old sack of straw, long stockings being sewed to it, as it was thrown over the gallows, our hangman sitting thereon, calling to them, if they had charity in them, to send the poor prisoner a priest. They, imagining that sack to be a man, fell all on their knees in our view, praying for the prisoner's soul.'

One of Hamilton's men, a Sergeant Scott, kept a diary of events that occurred in north Leitrim during the 1641 Rebellion. The first began with the burning of the iron works in Garrison by the MacLaughlins and MacMurrays of County Leitrim. The diary indicates that more than one hundred and fifty victims, mostly English, were robbed and fled to Manorhamilton for relief. Hamilton was in Derry at the time and returned home after hearing about the growing unrest in his area. At Donegal, he found Sir Ralph Gore and Basil Brooke 'robbed of their cattell, shortly expecting themselves to be destroyed'. Upon his return, the reprisals began almost immediately. On 4 December 1641, he had eight men hanged for the 'burning of Ballyshannon'. The gallows were kept busy over the following months as scores of 'rogues' were hanged. The diary provides an insight into the brutal campaign that Hamilton launched on the area:

9 April – 'a party of foote was this night sent to Glenden, (Glenade) from five or six miles off, where we kil'd and burned in their houses neere twenty rogues, bringing home a number of cowes and goates, and burning a many of Irish houses'.

13 May – 'this night we marcht into the county of Fermanagh, where we kil'd the wife of Donnogha Mac Flagherty Mac Gwire, with about forty more, whom we surprised in houses before day, and brought with us nine score cowes, about two hundred sheep and goates, and forty-seven horses and mares, thirty swine, and five prisoners which we hanged'.

20 May - 'This morning our castle is attempted to be taken by four or five hundred rogues from the Dartey (Dartry) or Rosenver (Rossinver), but our centriess timely giving us the alarmes, they are rescued, and the rogues retyred to the mountains'.

Leitrim developed a reputation as a place where 'land sold by the gallon rather than by the acre'. Roughly, one quarter of the county was inhabited and the architects of the plantation regarded more than half of Leitrim's land as waste. The civil survey of 1654-56 further described the County as 'generally very coarse and mountainous'.[4] The planters were obliged to construct a manor house or strong house surrounded by a bawn and wall off a number of acres as demesne lands. Outside of towns such as Manorhamilton, the new settlers cultivated the landscape by reclaiming Leitrim's extensive forests and establishing regular patterns of enclosed fields. Previously, the native inhabitants did not employ a neat, orderly system of landscape management. Their small, irregular-shaped fields dotted the area and the new system radically altered the landscape. Eventually the protective bawns transformed into walled gardens as the ruling landlord class, secure in their status, expressed their lavish tastes architecturally. The once defensive structures grew into big houses and elaborate gardens. Soon the location of picturesque lakeside houses, such as Lareen and Mount Prospect, was prompted more by aesthetics than security.

As the population increased during the eighteenth and nineteenth centuries, the native inhabitants began to cultivate marginal lands in the mountains. In this climate, however, they were restricted to planting potatoes. This was to have dire consequences. By the early 1800s, the native population was increasingly dependent on the potato. The crop grew well in the acidic soil of the west of Ireland on land that was previously uncultivated. The problem of single crop dependence was compounded by the fact that the vast proportion of the population in Leitrim lived on small plots of land, generally five acres or less. When Famine struck in 1845, Leitrim was devastated.

In 1841, the population of Leitrim was 155,297. By 1851, it had dropped to 111,915. Almost 20,000 people from the county died during the Famine, while many others emigrated. The following account, written twelve years after the Famine, provides an insight into the destitution of North Leitrim:

'Few counties suffered more severely than Leitrim during the famine. A vast number of the poorest class of the population were taken away by death and emigration; but some of them still linger in the mountain districts and contrive to drag on a wretched existence from year to year, always in distress and often on the verge of starvation. In rambling over the mountains to the north of Manorhamilton, about a mile from a place called Castletown, I came upon two or three hovels belonging to persons of this class, which was certainly as bad as any that I had previously seen in any part of Ireland… There were six children in the cabin, three of whom belonged to a strolling beggar woman who had sought and obtained hospitality on the previous evening.' [5]

A letter written by Dr O Higgins, the Bishop of Ardagh dated 19[t] May 1847 provides another disturbing account:

'Persons of twenty years appear to be bending in old age and in many instances become shameless and idiotic from want of every kind. In some instances, particularly in Leitrim, whole families are discovered to be dead in their cabins by the stench that proceeds from their putrid bodies. The dead are frequently buried in bogs, cabbage plots and even in the houses where they die. The most part of the land of Leitrim will be untilled this year and the Catholics will I fear before long have nearly all disappeared from death or emigration.' [6]

The Land Question
The establishment of the Congested Districts Board (CBD) paved the way for more changes in the Leitrim landscape as the clustered farm scttlements were replaced by owner-occupied strip holdings, which are still evident today. During the late nineteenth century, the conveyance of the land to owner tenancy enlarged farm sizes to between eight to twelve hectares. This has, for the most part endured in Leitrim because of the significance of owning land. In accordance with tradition, the eldest son inherited the farm. This forced other family members to emigrate and the rural population continued to decline. Between 1946 and 1996 Leitrim's population dropped from 44,591 to 25,032. There was a brief lull in population decline during the 1970s, but during the recessionary 1980s emigration resumed. Schools, shops and post offices were forced to close, propelling the rural infrastructure into a tailspin and fuelling further emigration. Between 1986 and 1996, the population of County Leitrim declined by a further seven per cent.

Leitrim's fortunes did not improve with Ireland's entry to the EEC in 1973. Its rural landscape had largely avoided large-scale industrialisation and many of Leitrim's part-time farmers found it difficult to obtain grants under the Common Agricultural Policy (CAP), forcing them to seek other employment opportunities. However, North Leitrim residents did begin to thrive during the 1970s. Factories in nearby Ballyshannon, Donegal and Sligo provided employment for them. Many emigrants returned from England to build new homes. Community centres in Tullaghan and Kinlough were opened and there was a revival in community sports and music. When emigration began again in the 1980s, it led to a further disintegration of the community infrastructures. Rural schools closed. Shops and post offices ceased to operate. During the early boom years of the twenty-first century, the pace of the decline slowed and some people decided to relocate within the county. Youth unemployment decreased and many opted to stay in Leitrim. The building boom provided much needed employment for the young people replacing the traditional industries. By 2002, the county had one of the highest levels of planning applications per capita in Ireland. Leitrim experienced a twenty-three per cent increase in population between 2002 and 2011. North Leitrim has a disproportionately large number of artists in residence. During the early 1990s, many artists were attracted to the area because of its isolation and its low house prices.

Between 1996 and 2006, Kinlough became one of the most rapidly expanding villages in Leitrim. However, the developments also resulted in a number of incomplete estates with high levels of vacancy within the village when the economic collapse happened.[7] The banking crisis of 2008 decimated employment opportunities within the construction sector and led to a new phenomenon, the ghost estate. In towns and villages throughout north Leitrim there are many examples of uninhabited dwellings in various phases of construction

Rather Inclined to be Scholars

Fermanagh is the smallest and most rural population in Northern Ireland. Yet for such a modest place, it has made a substantial contribution to the arts on these islands. Early monastic settlements like Devenish and Inishmacsaint served as seats of learning and reflection. Later, the Maguire courts were famous for the number of poets, bards, historians and musicians they retained. The Annals of Ulster and later The Book of Invasions were compiled in the county. The plaintive sounds of Turlough O'Carolan's airs filled the corridors of the Planters' Castles on the shores of Lough Ern during the eighteenth century. Two giants of drama and literature, Oscar Wilde and Samuel Beckett were schooled on the banks of the Erne at Royal Portora. Throughout its colourful history, this devotion to arts and peaceful disposition has remained a recurring theme. When the Attorney General of Ireland, Sir John Davies, came to Fermanagh in 1607, he commented, 'Generally the natives of this country are reputed the worst swordsmen in the north, being rather inclined to be scholars...'

One of Fermanagh's best-known landmarks, the stunning Marble Arch Caves can boast a history spanning 650 million years. However, events occurred during the last Great Ice Age, some 13,000 years ago that have dictated the narrative of the Fermanagh story. The glacial deposits that formed part of the drumlin belt, combined with the impenetrability of Lough Erne, marked the area as a Borderland from the time the first settlers arrived. Evidence of the last Ice Age is clearly visible in lakes and drumlin hills. The large sheets of retreating ice carved out the glacial valley of Lower Lough Erne. Many islands on the lake are actually 'drowned drumlins'. Enormous boulders, put in place by the retreating ice are still present on the shores of the lake, either too big to remove or left in place because of age-old superstitions.[1] According to one tradition, Lough Erne derived its name from Erna, Queen Maeve's favourite waiting-maid who drowned in the lake. [2]

The first people to settle in Fermanagh arrived about 8,000 years ago. They landed at Ballyshannon and made their way over the falls to settle in the district around Kesh. Others entered Fermanagh via Kiltyclogher and settled around Enniskillen.[3] The landscape they found was densely forested and navigation through the area was mostly by boat. Hazel, elm and ash woodlands saturated the area. The early settlers lived a hunter-gatherer lifestyle and built small wooden dwellings along the edges of the lakes and rivers. Evidence of their existence was found on Cushrush Island on Lower Lough MacNean.

Around 4000 BC, Neolithic famers arrived in the area from Britain. They introduced crops and livestock. To build farms they began clearing upland forest, mostly because it was easier to clear than lowland forest. These areas eventually evolved into peat bogs because of erosion from overgrazing. They left behind monuments to their dead, such the Dual Court Tomb at Aghanaglack near Boho.

Burial practices changed over time and Drumskinny Stone Circle near Kesh was constructed during the Bronze Age (2000 BC to 500 BC). When humankind added tin to copper to produce bronze, a new era in the human evolution had begun. This new material could be cast into any required shape and was much more durable and more effective for weapons and implements than stone.

At the end of the Bronze Age, the Celts arrived from central Europe, bringing with them a new, more refined material that would transform society; Fermanagh had entered the Iron Age. The Celts also introduced a new language (the basis of modern Irish) and new polytheistic religious practices.

In the first century AD, Ireland was divided into five provinces and Ulster at that time included Leitrim. Over the following centuries, major battles were fought between Connacht and Ulster placing the area between Lough Erne and Lough Melvin on the frontier.

When the Roman cartographer Ptolemy mapped Ireland in the first century, he referred to the inhabitants of the area as Erdini. Irish legend remembers the Ernai or the 'red armed Erainn' in the plain of Lough Erne, but makes them disappear when the lake burst over the land and over them. According to tradition, the next wave of settlers, the Fir Manach, Men of Manach arrived in the area from Leinster during the second century. They settled in the Lisnaskea area and developed their kingdom from there.

Boa Island is named after Badhbh, the Celtic goddess of war. Caldragh Cemetery is located in the townland of Dreenan (from 'draighneán' meaning 'blackthorn place'), towards the southern shore of Boa Island. The graveyard is home of the mysterious Janus figure and the Lusty Man. The carving of the large two-headed figure suggests a Celtic late pre-Christian or early Christian origin. The head was of great importance in Celtic culture. Celtic warriors decapitated their enemies after battle because they believed that their head contained their spirit after death. Severed heads were carried away in triumph after battle. In 1744, Isaac Butler wrote about Boa Island remarking that the people 'live in silent retreat... and are blest with all ye common necessaries of life'.[4] These island people were only connected to the mainland after partition for the purposes of military expediency. Boa Island Bridge was built during the 1920s to ensure that security forces in Northern Ireland did not have to traverse the Border via Pettigo to reach Belleek.

Caldragh Cemetery, Boa Island

Christianity arrived on Lough Erne in the fifth century and for a time Christian and pagan beliefs continued side by side until many of the pagan practices were fully appropriated by the new belief system. Saint Molaise established a monastery on Devenish Island during the sixth century. His peer, Saint Ninnidh established a monastery on another island, Inishmacsaint. Ninnidh is believed to have descended from Niall of the Nine Hostages and he was bishop of the area between Devenish and Bundoran.[5] Both saints were contemporaries of Saint Mogue of Rosclogher and all three were educated at Saint Finnian's school in Clonard. The other island on Lower Lough Erne of particular religious interest is White Island with the seven stone figures. Thought to date to the ninth or tenth century, these mostly represent various religious figures and a female fertility symbol, the sheela-na-gig.

The Annals of Ulster were written on Belle Isle on Upper Lough Erne. They record over 1,000 years of Ulster's history beginning in the mid-sixth century. The scribe Ruaidhrí Ó Luinín compiled them in the late fifteenth century for his patron Cathal Óg Mac Maghnusa. They were an important source for the Annals of the

65

Four Masters, which were compiled almost a century later along the banks of the Drowes River. One of the main architects of the Annals of the Four Masters was Brother Mícheál Ó Cléirigh, who also helped to compile the Leabhar Gabhála (The Book of Invasions) in 1631 at the Franciscan convent of Lisgoole on the shores of Lough Erne. It tells the story of the arrival of settlers such as Parthalon, the Fir Bolg and the Tuatha Dé Danann.

The Vikings appeared in the area in AD 836 when they 'destroyed all the churches on Lough Erne'. A temporary raiding camp was established in Belleek and The Annals of Ulster recorded that in 923 'a naval force of the foreigners went on Lough Erne, and they ravaged the islands of the lake and the surrounding peoples, to and fro'. They left Lough Erne the following summer.

The Normans then arrived in west Fermanagh in the early thirteenth century. They built a fort at Belleek, thought to be near the present location of Belleek Fort. Local opponents destroyed the castle. It was rebuilt in 1252, only to be destroyed again by the O'Donnells. The Normans never gained any more influence in West Fermanagh after that.

In the early fourteenth century, the Maguires stepped onto the Fermanagh stage and would continue to play a leading role for several centuries. The O'Donnell's of Tír Chonaill facilitated their rise to prominence.[6] Throughout their reign of Fermanagh, the Maguires were renowned for their love of arts and culture and (for the most part) their peaceful disposition. Sandwiched between the brooding O'Donnells and O'Neills, the Maguires maintained peace by tact and diplomacy. Of the sixteen Maguire chieftains, only one died a violent death. Despite having generally good relations with the O'Donnells, war between the two dynasties occasionally broke out. In 1369, Philip Maguire, Lord of the seven Tuaths, avenged the death of Donnell Muldoon, Lord of Lurg, in a naval battle near Boa Island.

The kingdom of Lough Erne had within its control around seven of the older tuatha and each tuath, instead of being ruled by a petty king, was held by one or more 'vassal chiefs', who rendered tribute and service to Maguire, and often belonged to the same royal dynasty.[7] These dynasties precipitated lasting social divisions. For instance, the parishes of Lurg and Magheraboy are based on historical boundaries between Gaelic clans. Lurg, (North Fermanagh) was the territory of the O'Muldoons and Toora, (West Fermanagh) was the seat of the O'Flanagans, comprised in the barony of Magheraboy. O'Flanagan's Tuatha Ratha (the District of the Fortress) extended from 'Belmore to Belleek and Lough Melvin to Lough Erne'. [8]

The lowlands of Fermanagh were farmed by about fifty Irish clans before the Ulster Plantation. Then the arrival of about one thousand initial settlers pushed some of the native Irish onto the less fertile uplands.[9] In the barony of Magheraboy, the O'Flanagans were the ruling family in the late medieval period and they were related to the ruling family of the Uí Neill branch of Cairbre Droma Cliabh (Drumcliff) in northeast County Sligo and north-west County Leitrim.

Historian and genealogist John O'Donovan recorded his impressions of Fermanagh in 1834 and documented some of family histories of local people. The McGraths were custodians the monastic lands about Lough Derg for over three centuries. Their most well-known and contentious figure was Bishop Miler McGrath who became the first Protestant bishop of Clogher after his conversion from Roman Catholicism. The McGoldricks appear to have been the ruling family around Belleek before the area came under the control of the Maguires. The Muldoons were the princes of the barony of Lurg for centuries and renowned as able fighting men. All of these families paid tribute to Maguire. Once a year, the Maguire chief would travel to Belleek where he stayed for one month, time spent collecting annual tributes, hunting and feasting. The principal tribute to Maguire was paid at Rath More Miodhbholg (the Great Rath of the Central Hollow) overlooking the waterfall of Belleek. During the fifth century, two sons of the King of Ulaidh had established a kingdom based at the Great Rath of Miodhbholg Belleek. Mulleek is a derivation of that name. In 1585, Cúchonnacht Maguire surrendered the Fermanagh lordship to the Crown whereupon it was re-granted to him in 1586 on condition that the old Gaelic gavelkind system would be replaced with English forms of land tenure.

Rival branches of the Maguire family took opposing sides during the Nine Year's War (1594-1603). Hugh Maguire ruled Fermanagh from 1589-1600). From the Enniskillen branch, he was the fifteenth chief of the Maguires and a major leader in the war, heading south to relieve the Spanish forces who had come to the aid of the Gaelic clans of Ulster but landed at Kinsale. Hugh was killed in March 1600 in a skirmish with English soldiers close to the city of Cork. He was succeeded by his half-brother Cúchonnacht Óg, organiser of the Flight of the Earls in 1607. Meanwhile, the Maguires who sided with the English in the Nine Years War were rewarded with land in the Barony of Magherasteffany. The rest of Fermanagh was parcelled out to British and, to a lesser extent, Gaelic undertakers.

Fearful that Spain might use Ireland as a staging area for an invasion of England, Elizabeth I vowed to bring the rebellious North to heel. She was incensed by the support that some Ulster clan chieftains had shown to the Spanish Armada survivors. By 1590, the English authorities had begun to consolidate control by dividing Ulster into counties for administrative purposes. Under the 'Surrender and Re-grant' scheme, the Maguires and others recognised the English crown as sovereign and surrendered their lands, receiving in return a charter for lands and noble titles.

The Ulster lords recognised that their power was in jeopardy and rose up in rebellion. Hugh Maguire of Fermanagh was one of the first who rebelled. In 1593, he fought the English near the present town of Ballyshannon. Both Ballyshannon and Enniskillen were strategically vital towns and both sides fought to control the area. In January 1594, the English captured Enniskillen Castle, which they held for fifteen months. The Maguires recaptured the castle in the spring of 1595. The Maguires, O'Neills and O'Donnells joined forces to oppose the English invasion. Despite many initial successes, the war ended in defeat at Kinsale in 1602 for the Irish chieftains. Having burnt his own castle at Dungannon and hid out in the woods, O'Neill finally surrendered in 1603. An uneasy peace followed with steady English encroachment on Ulster. The Flight of the Earls took place on 14 September 1607 when Hugh O'Neill and Rory O'Donnell, along with a small party of their families and followers boarded a ship at Rathmullan and sailed for Spain, never to return. With the removal of the last rebel chieftains, the English began to unfold their master plan for Ireland, the Plantation of Ulster.

During the early 1600s, wealthy landowners from Scotland and England arrived and began to build castles around Lower Lough Erne. Sir John Hume built Tully Castle in 1613. Castle Archdale was built in 1615. The Blennerhassetts from Norfolk built the manors of Crevenish and Castlecaldwell on Lough Erne and established the new villages of Ederney, Kesh and Belleek. In 1610, Thomas Blennerhassett issued the following proposal to his fellow colonists:

'The County of Fermanagh, sometimes Mack Guere's (Maguire's) country, rejoice! Many Undertakers, all incorporated in minde as one, they there with their followers, seeke, and are desirous to settle themselves. Woe to the wolfe and the wood-kerne! The islands in Loughearne shall have habitations, a fortified corporation, market towns and many new erected manors, shall now so beautifie her desolation that her inaccessible woods, with spaces made tractable, shall no longer nourish devowrers, but by the sweet society of a loving neighbourhood, shall entertaine humanity even in the best fashion. Goe on, worthy gentlemen, fear not! The God of Heaven will assist and protect you, the rather for that simply of your selves, you do desire to perform so honourable an action. And they, the successors of high-renowned Lud, will there re-edifie a new Troy.'

Sir Edward Blennerhassett, Thomas's brother, was granted a 1,500-acre estate in Bannaghmore in the Lurg district in 1610. He began erecting a fortified residence at Castle Caldwell, which was originally known as Hasset's Fort.[10] In 1618, Captain Pynnar visited the estate and the neighbouring embryonic village, noting: '...upon this proportion there is a strong bawn of lime and stone, being 80 foot long and 60 foot broad and a stone house three storeys high, all furnished himself and family dwelling in it. He hath also built a village near unto the bawn, consisting of nine houses of good cagework.'

Castle Caldwell

After Sir Edward died, his son Francis took over the estate. He was killed by the rebels at Ballyshannon during the 1641 Rebellion. After the war, his wife and family returned to Hasset's Fort. The estate passed through various family members until it was sold to James Caldwell in 1670.[11] He renamed Hasset's Fort as Castle Caldwell. He was described as 'a man of lifty [sic] principles, lover of sciences... a skillful head-piece in law suits, a terror to his adversaries'. During the Williamite War, Caldwell raised a regiment of foot and helped prevent Patrick Sarsfield's forces from capturing Ballyshannon. The estate continued to pass from father to son. In the mid-eighteenth century, Sir James Caldwell began to upgrade the estate. He renovated the house and built two large walled gardens. He planted four orchards that contained over 2,000 trees. Exotic plants were also grown in the greenhouses of Castle Caldwell.[12] Sir James published pamphlets on improving the estate and tenant conditions.[13] He experimented with a variety of agricultural endeavours from tree planting and livestock breeding to from flax cultivation and linen manufacture.[14] He was renowned for his lavish entertainment and hospitality, which included entertaining the travel writer Arthur Young when he visited Castle Caldwell in August 1776. Young commented that the locals were hard working but 'remarkably given to thieving' and that 'they bring up their children to "hoking" potatoes'. He was taken in by the scenery and lamented having to leave: 'It was with regret I turned my back on this charming scene, the most beautiful at Castle Caldwell and the most pleasing I have anywhere seen.' Young sailed away from the castle to the sound of a band playing on a warm August day, and he is not the only travel writer to have fallen for Fermanagh's charms. More than two hundred years later in her book, A Place Apart, Dervla Murphy wrote, 'I have fallen in love with Fermanagh.'

James Caldwell's son John took over the estate. He had two daughters, one of whom married Major John Bloomfield in 1817. It was this family that launched the world famous Belleek Pottery. Despite the pottery's success, the family's debts mounted and Major John's son Benjamin was forced to auction off the estate. The condition of the castle and estate deteriorated. In 1913, the government bought the land, which is currently maintained by the Forest Service of Northern Ireland.

By the end of the sixteenth century, Lough Erne remained a very remote part of Ulster due to its inaccessibility. Many of the large forests still remained. Some of the displaced natives sought refuge in the forests, where they continued to threaten the new settler population. Accounts of skirmishes with 'wood-kernes' in woods on the north shore begin to appear in the mid-seventeenth century.[15]

The Border Reivers were raiders along the Anglo–Scottish Border from the late thirteenth century to the beginning of the seventeenth century. Many of the Scottish settlers in Fermanagh came from that Border region with England. The area had a reputation of being unstable and disloyal. During the late thirteenth and early fourteenth century, the Anglo-Scottish conflict had a heavy impact on the socio-economic life of the Borders. In tensions between England and Scotland, its frontline position meant that the warring factions often reduced it to wasteland.

The Armstrongs and Elliotts were the largest families in Liddesdale (the valley of the Liddel Water in southern Scotland) and the Grahams came from an area on the western Border known as the Debatable Land.[16] Between the thirteenth and early seventeenth centuries, life on the frontline of those continuous wars between

England and Scotland was extremely perilous. Passing armies often attacked the local population, stealing or burning the crops in their wake. Arable farming was no longer a viable occupation. For these Border Reivers, the only societal arrangement that could offer true protection was kinship. Their community was comprised of large closely-knit family groups.

For more than three hundred years, cattle raiding or 'reiving' was their way of life. The word 'reive' comes from an old English word meaning 'to rob', from which we get the word 'bereaved'. Farmers had to pay protection money, known as 'black mal' (from the old Norse 'mal' meaning 'agreement') in exchange for immunity from pillage. This introduced the word 'blackmail' into the English language.

The Border Reivers regularly changed sides in the continuous wars between England and Scotland. Their deeds have been romanticised in ballads, but much like the 'rapparees' of Ireland, many of their actions were bloody and brutal. Throughout their reign on the Marches, the Reivers continued to feud amongst themselves. Blood feuds once begun, could last for generations almost to the point where contemporary clans could not even remember why it had started. In modern Albania, a similar code of 'gjakmarra', or blood feud, is still practised and it is not uncommon to see small siege towers (kullë), similar to the Pele towers of the Reivers, filled with men from a particular clan. Blood feuds have also been a feature of Basque and Corsican history.

Despite the lawless nature of the area, some rules did apply. According to Border Law, if someone had their livestock stolen they were allowed to cross the Border, 'without let or hindrance' for up to six days after the crime to try to get back their possessions. This was known as the 'hot trod.' They were obligated to each carry 'a lance tipped with burning peat' and follow the trail with 'hue and cry, and hound and horn' to let people know that they were on a counter-raid. Sir Walter Scott described such a foray in his 1816 novel, The Black Dwarf:

There's nae great skill needed; just put a lighted peat on the end of a spear, or hayfork, or siclike, and blaw a horn, and cry the gathering-word, and then it's lawful to follow gear into England, and recover it by the strong hand, or to take gear frae some other Englishman, providing ye lift nae mair than's been lifted frae you. That's the auld Border law.'

After Queen Elizabeth I died in 1603, the Reivers went on a spree of plunder and pillage. Such was the ferocity of their attacks that the event became known as the 'Ill Week'. Her successor decided to deal with the lawless Border area for the last time. When the thrones of

Scotland and England were united in 1603, King James VI of Scotland became James I of England. He saw the Border areas as a threat and mounted a sustained and brutal campaign known as the 'Pacification of the Borders'. Many members of the principal clans – the Armstrongs, Elliotts and the Grahams – were executed or banished from the area along with their families and sent to Ireland and elsewhere into the New World of the Americas.

In the rebranded 'Middle Shires', the King's rule was brutally enforced by the gallows and banishment. Most of the men from the Borders went to the most isolated parts of the new settlements, places such as Fermanagh. The proliferation of family names of Armstrong, Elliott and Johnson on the County Fermanagh Muster Rolls bears testimony to this.[17] James I's bloody campaign of pacification took seven years. The severest punishments were inflicted upon the Grahams. Their lands were confiscated, families were expelled and homes burned. In 1606, a large number of Grahams were sent to Roscommon. Broke and homeless, they drifted north into Ulster. Many others from the Borders fled to Ulster to evade persecution. Despite their rebellious reputation, some Plantation undertakers were content to settle these Border families on their land.[18] One of these was Sir John Hume, who became the greatest landowner in seventeenth century Fermanagh. Ironically, Hume was responsible for the 'pacification' of the eastern portion of the Anglo-Scottish Border. He knew what he was dealing with in the ferocious clans. Nonetheless, he encouraged many Border Reivers to make Fermanagh their new home. The Armstrongs, Elliotts and Grahams were all among the earliest and most widespread tenant settlers in Fermanagh.

The people of the Borders had been relatively untouched by the Reformation, and so were largely unaware of Puritan or Presbyterian theology. They finally conformed to the state-sponsored church. This is why such a large number became members of the established Church of Ireland, the Anglican Communion in their new home. Yet the Borderers' lack of evangelical enthusiasm is apparent in the shortage of churches built before the end of the seventeenth century. Political expediency ensured their support for the Anglican Church and to this day, Fermanagh's religious landscape differs significantly from the rest of Northern Ireland. Over time, their numbers increased and they continued to sculpt the landscape of Fermanagh as hard-working farmers.

The new settlers proved to be ideal candidates for the Plantation experiment. They had the skills of low intensity warfare, manufacturing weapons and designing and building fortifications deeply embedded in their collective DNA. They were tough, resilient and had spent the previous three centuries in a near constant state of war. Their resolve down the centuries can be attributed initially to their time spent on the Anglo-Scottish Borders where survival depended very often on your ability to fight and defend. Throughout the troubles of the seventeenth century, these tenacious Border settlers adapted to life on a new Border. Even after the bloody events of the 1641 Rebellion, the 1659 'Census' shows that the same names reappear in great numbers. They held Enniskillen in the 1640s and their sons and grandsons held it again during the Williamite campaign, making possible the Glorious Revolution. For, if Enniskillen had fallen then, would Derry have held out?[19]

When a new wave of planters began to arrive later in the seventeenth century, relatively few came to the settle in County Fermanagh. After the decisive Battle of the Boyne, the descendants of the native Irish and the first planters would continue to live side by side in Fermanagh in an uneasy peace.

Between 1717 and 1775, many of the descendants of the Border Scots and Northern English who had settled in Ulster left Ireland and sailed for America. When they arrived in America, most of the coastal lands had already been bought or were too expensive. The new settlers pushed on into the Appalachian Mountains. The ambiguous attitude of the fiercely independent Border Reivers was passed down to their American descendants.[20] The men who lived on the Border between West Virginia and Kentucky were rugged outdoorsmen who logged timber, fished and hunted. They were living on the 'cutting edge of the frontier'. Many had huge families creating extensive clan networks. They were noted for their marksmanship and illegal whiskey distillation.

In the most isolated parts of Appalachia, government barely existed and courts were few. During the American Revolutionary War, many of these frontiersmen formed militias to fight for American independence. These 'Over-mountain Men' defeated the loyalist militia forces in the Battle of King's Mountain. In his book, The Winning of the West, Theodore Roosevelt wrote of King's Mountain, 'This brilliant victory marked the turning point of the American Revolution.' One of those 'Over-mountain men' who took part in the battle was Davy Crockett's father, John, whose family emigrated to America from Castlederg in County Tyrone.

Despite the tough reputation that the new settlers in America enjoyed, many Appalachian scholars have argued that violent activities among the Scotch-Irish has been more a consequence of broader, shifting societal and economic circumstances than any intrinsically violent cultural traits.[21] However, these tenacious settlers did not bring with them only their 'fighting spirit'; they also brought a generational knowledge of whiskey production. This 'moonshine', as it became known because it was made with corn, provided another stream of revenue for the new settlers. After the American War of Independence, in which the Ulster Scots had fought against 'taxation without representation', the new government introduced a tax on alcohol production to relieve the war debt. The frontiersmen of Pennsylvania rose up in what in became known as 'The Whiskey Rebellion'. The tax was lifted in 1802 but the seeds of mutual distrust had been sown. The tax was reintroduced to fund the American Civil War. Then the government declared a war on moonshine and the moonshiners banded together in defiance. In this, they reverted to the clan structure they had inherited from the time that previous generations spent on the Scottish Borders.

No fewer than five American presidents – Andrew Jackson, Andrew and Lyndon Johnson, Richard Nixon and Woodrow Wilson – were descendants of the Border Reivers. One of the most famous Border Reiver descendants with Fermanagh links is Neil Armstrong, the first man to walk on the moon in 1969. His granduncle was Robert Armstrong from Lisnaskea.[22] Bill Clinton claims to be a relative of Lucas Cassidy, who left County Fermanagh for America around 1750.

By 1688, meanwhile, the policies of the Catholic King James II continued to alienate influential leaders of Britain's political and religious establishment. They called on his Protestant son-in-law and nephew from the Netherlands, William III of Orange, to take the English throne. After William's forces arrived on 5 November 1688, James's army deserted him and he fled to France. Even though he had lost control of England, most of Ireland was under the control of Richard Talbot, 1st Earl of Tyrconnell who remained loyal to him. Therefore, James II resurfaced in Ireland in 1689 in an attempt to win back his throne.

With the memories of 1641 still fresh in their minds, many Protestants from South Ulster and North Connacht fled to Enniskillen for protection. Their fears were heightened by the distribution of copies of a letter warning that the Irish were preparing to massacre the Protestants. Enniskillen's strategic location gave it a strong natural position for defence. Gustavus Hamilton was nominated as governor of the town with responsibility for its defence. Companies of cavalry and foot soldiers were created and more volunteers joined the group.[23] Enniskillen shut its gates and held out against the forces of King James II. During this time, Enniskillen founded two regiments, the Inniskilling Dragoons and the Royal Inniskilling Fusiliers.

In March 1689, Tyrconnell dispatched Lord Galmoy (Piers Butler) to deal with the defiant Enniskilleners. Galmoy ordered them to surrender in the name of King James but the Enniskilleners declared their allegiance to William and hostilities began. Many of those stationed at Enniskillen were descended from the Border Scots, the tough frontiersmen renowned for their marksmanship and horse-riding skills. They attacked Galmoy's men at Newtownbutler, forcing the Jacobites to retreat back across the Erne to Belturbet.

In a victory for the Jacobites, Patrick Sarsfield's forces captured Sligo in May 1689. He planned to press ahead and capture the strategically vital town of Ballyshannon, thereby cutting off supplies to Enniskillen. Sarsfield thought that Ballyshannon was poorly defended and that he would be able to take it easily. However, the town was heavily defended by a garrison commanded by Captain Folliott. Sarsfield attempted to block the roads leading into the town but Folliott had already dispatched riders to Enniskillen and Castle Caldwell to ask for reinforcements. Gustavus Hamilton ordered an army of over a thousand men under the command of Colonel Thomas Lloyd (also known as 'Little Cromwell') to relieve Ballyshannon. At the same time, an army led by Sir James Caldwell advanced on the Jacobite forces. Sarsfield was forced to withdraw towards Sligo. In the chaos of the retreat, sixty of his men were left stranded on Inis Saimer and taken prisoner. Hamilton recorded the events. 'All their foot fled away towards Sligo, except a few who were taken in the Fish Island (Inis Saimer) near the town, with their Captain, one MacDonagh, a Counsellor-at-Law, commonly known by the name of "blind MacDonagh".'[24]

After the crushing defeat at the Battle of Newtownbutler, the Jacobite army pulled back from Ulster. The Enniskilleners defended their own town and helped in the defence of Derry. The subsequent Battle of the Boyne then gave the Williamites control of the eastern part of Ireland and Dublin. The war was effectively over and James returned to France. Defeat for the Jacobites at Aughrim eventually led to the siege of Limerick and the final capitulation of their cause.[25]

For Enniskillen, however, victory was the launching pad for a proud martial tradition, which really began as many Protestants fled to the island stronghold on the Erne in 1688. Plans were made to defend the town from the advancing forces of James II and a local militia group was formed as two regiments, The Inniskillingers Foot and The Inniskillingers Dragoons. They successfully repelled repeated attacks and went on the offensive at Sligo, Ballyshannon and Newtownbutler. They were incorporated into the army of William III and later fought at the Battle of the Boyne and the sieges of

Limerick and Athlone. After the war, these militia forces were combined into two regiments in the British army.

From the Seven Years War (1756-63) to the War in Afghanistan (2001–present), the Inniskillingers in various forms fought with distinction in many theatres of war all over the world. During the First World War, 'The Skins' took part in the great battles in France and Flanders as well as Gallipoli, Macedonia and Palestine. In 1942, they fought in Burma helping to halt the Japanese advance and in 1943; they took part in the operations in the Arakan peninsula. In 1968, The Royal Inniskilling Fusiliers, The Royal Ulster Rifles and The Royal Irish Fusiliers became The Royal Irish Rangers (27th Inniskilling, 83rd and 87th). The Royal Irish Rangers later merged with The Ulster Defence Regiment and on 1 July 1992 became the Royal Irish Regiment. Meanwhile, the Royal Dragoons have served in Bosnia, Iraq and Afghanistan since their amalgamation in 1992.

Of all the counties that later became Northern Ireland, Fermanagh suffered the most during the Famine. Half of its baronies suffered population losses of around thirty per cent between 1841 and 1851. The first deaths from starvation were recorded in December 1846. Cholera began to spread early in 1847. The Erne Packet newspaper reported, 'In Garvary Wood hundreds of corpses are buried, they were the victims of cholera and their relatives too weak to carry them to the graveyard.' The county's workhouses became overcrowded with local families from both religious traditions.[26] In 1841, the population of County Fermanagh was 156,481. By 1851, it was 116,047. The population decline continued and today Fermanagh has only about one third of the population it had in 1841.

The arrival of the railway in the mid-19th century brought increased prosperity and employment for many local residents. Train passengers from Dublin could disembark at Enniskillen and take the Lough Erne steamer, the Countess of Milan, all the way to Belleek. From there to the Atlantic Ocean, the water route was impeded by a series of waterfalls and cascades. Throughout the 1880s, drainage schemes were introduced and the level of the lake subsequently dropped. Belleek Falls were finally removed and sluice gates were built there to control the level of the lake. Meanwhile, the railway connected Fermanagh to the rest of Ireland and to ferry services from Britain. By the mid-20th century, many of those lines of communication were closed.

For a brief time in the late nineteenth century, it appeared that Protestants and Catholics in Fermanagh had found common cause in the Land League. Clergy from all religious denominations spoke from Land League platforms. Nevertheless, with Home Rule looming in the 1880s, the landlords who from then on used the Orange Order to bring their Protestant tenants back into the fold of Unionism played the religion card once again.

Protestants in Ulster were in the majority. They would not accept Home Rule and quickly mobilised as they had done many times before to reject it with the familiar cry of 'No Surrender'. Their campaign of opposition really began in Fermanagh. On 18 September 1912, Ulster Unionist leader Edward Carson arrived in Enniskillen. He was met at Castlecoole by a troop of horse specially trained by William Copeland Trimble, owner of the Impartial Reporter newspaper. Trimble himself then led the procession through Enniskillen. Carson stood and watched while 40,000 Orangemen and Unionists marched past him. This was unquestionably the largest parade in Fermanagh's history, and there is no doubt that it was a clear show of strength for the Unionist cause.[27]

The famous Fermanagh fighting spirit produced some unusual scenarios. In 1916, George Irvine (1877-1954), whose descendants gave Irvinestown its name, fought alongside Connolly and Pearse in the Dublin G.P.O. His great-great-granduncle Colonel William Irvine had presided over the Dungannon Convention of Volunteers that called for Irish independence in 1782. In 1916, George was the officer in charge (O/C) of 'B' Company of the 4th Battalion. Other leaders of the battalion included Eamonn Ceannt and Con Colbert who were both executed. George was tried for his role in the Rising and sentenced to death, but this was later commuted to a ten-year sentence. He had been born in Enniskillen into a loyal Ulster Protestant family. He attended Portora Royal School and then Trinity College, Dublin. He was a dedicated member of the Church of Ireland and a fervent supporter of the Gaelic League. He moved back to Dublin where he became an important member of the Irish Republican Brotherhood (IRB). During the War of Independence (1919-21), he was Vice-Commandant of the 1st Battalion of the Dublin Brigade IRA. He took the Republican side after the Treaty and was interned in Mountjoy Prison. On his release after the Civil War, he returned to teaching.

George Irvine was highly regarded by the men who fought alongside him. Gerald Doyle who was with him during the Rising said of him, 'Captain George Irvine, one of the gentlest of men in manner. It was really only those of us who had been with him under fire who could realise the fighting spirit hidden beneath his gentleness.'[28] Another volunteer who served with him during the War of Independence described him as 'the embodiment of nobility, of honesty and of honour... He brought tact, devotion, and enthusiasm into his work as Second Officer of the Battalion'.[29]

During the Second World War, Castle Archdale was a coastal command base for the RAF. Sunderland and Catalina flying boats scoured the Atlantic and they notched up ten U-boat kills during the Battle of the North Atlantic that kept the supply lines open between North America and Britain. On 26 May 1941, a Catalina crew based at Castle Archdale spotted the German battleship Bismarck. Its location was passed on and the mighty ship was tracked down and sunk.

The period after the war saw life return to normal for west Fermanagh. Fair days and dances faded away from the social scene but interest in sport as a social occasion remained strong. In his 1968 book, The Fermanagh Story, historian Fr Peadar Livingstone wrote, 'On the whole, in most respects, relations between Catholics and Protestants are cordial. Socially they do not mix in many fields. At the same time they are good neighbours and, for most of the time, manage to live together in peace.'

British Army checkpoint at Roscor during the 1980s

The Road to Nowhere

Near Abhornaleha Bridge, on the Donegal-Fermanagh Border, lies the beginning a road that goes nowhere. It was built during the Great Famine to provide starving local people with the means to buy food. The road runs near Lough Melvin for half a mile and just ends abruptly. These nonsensical projects became known as 'The Hungry Roads'. During the greatest social disaster in Irish history, the government deemed it a good idea to employ the starving masses to build roads. Piece by piece, men broke apart large stones with hammers then placed the fragments in baskets, which were carried by the women to the road site where they were dumped and put into place. There were many reports of malnourished workers, weakened by fever, dying on these pointless projects.

After partition, more roads in the area came to an abrupt end when they were cratered or blown up to prevent unmonitored incursions from the south. The intended security outcome was never achieved. Instead, Border towns suddenly found themselves cut off from their natural environs and the result was social and economic stagnation in the area for decades.

Cross-Border road closures have been a feature of partition. As the two new states stood back to back, Northern Ireland looked east and the Free State quietly looked away from its Border districts. 'Nothing flows west of the Bann' was an adage increasingly murmured in the Northern Ireland Border counties. When the Northern government developed the M1 motorway during the 1960s, it took a turn for the west towards Dungannon, not south towards Dublin, which was arguably a more sensible choice from a commercial perspective. An indication of the attitude of the Northern Ireland authorities towards the south can be gauged by the fact that very few road signs in Northern Ireland even acknowledged southern destinations in the early 1970s. No major investment was placed on the cross-Border transport projects and most Border roads were, and remain, of poor quality.

In 1922, members of the RUC Special Constabulary trenched more roads and destroyed many bridges in Border areas to prevent further raids by republican forces into the six counties. The road was cratered at Dooard, cutting of communication between the communities of Garrison and Rossinver. When the Border was finalised in 1925, the Northern Ireland government designated a series of approved roads which people were forced to use. The aim was to control the flow of cross-Border traffic. Farmers who had land on both sides of the Border, found themselves making tortuous journeys in order to get into the other jurisdiction. This story was replicated all along the Border.

In 1941, the British War Cabinet published a report relating to control of the Border. The report stated that 'the land frontier is about 180 miles long and has been drawn without any regard to strategic considerations or the question of the control of traffic'. It concluded that there was 'no possibility of putting a completely effective control on the Border by means of any physical obstacles or by closely spaced patrols'.[1]

In the 1950s, during the IRA's disastrous Border Campaign, many Border roads in the area were repeatedly cratered or spiked with steel girders driven into the ground. In January 1957, the British military accompanied by the RUC from Castlederg and Tullyhommon dynamited roads along the Donegal Border. In February, the military cratered all the unapproved roads leading into Northern Ireland near *Kiltyclogher,* County Leitrim. This time, however, the roads were blown up further back from the Border. On a previous operation in December, the military did considerable damage to the house of James Seely when they were dynamiting a road near Kiltyclogher.[2] Local people filling in the holes left by the explosions repeatedly thwarted the attempts by the Northern Irish authorities to crater roads during the 1956-62 campaign.[3]

During the early days of the more recent Troubles, the British army placed steel tripods on many of the cross-Border routes in an attempt to prevent incursions by the IRA. In all over a hundred roads were estimated to have been cratered during the Troubles.[4] A campaign quickly began to reopen roads that were blocked or blown up. As soon as a road was blocked, local people worked hard to reopen the route. The cat and mouse game with the British Army continued. When the steel spikes were removed, the army replaced them with concrete-filled oil drums and massive concrete blocks, known colloquially as 'dragon's teeth'. Local resistance, which included the use of explosives, heavy construction plant and oxy-acetylene torches, meant that the operation was abandoned and many of the blockages were removed.[5]

Dragon's Teeth on the Irish Border

A substantial number of unapproved Border crossings were blocked in 1970. During the remainder of the Troubles, the British army cratered more than forty roads on the Fermanagh Border. Plastic explosives were used to blow holes roughly ten feet deep and twenty feet wide. During one such incident, a British soldier had a lucky escape when a sniper's bullet hit his rifle as he was guarding a team of sappers near Roslea, County Fermanagh. At the time, Colonel Simmonds of the Royal Engineers stated, 'Nobody is going to use this road for some time without a major piece of engineering repair work.' Six days later, local people had already repaired nine roads. The closure of the Border roads gave rise to a curious reactionary group who became known as the 'Border Busters'.

One former Border Buster from the Kinawley area described the consequence of the road closures. 'Normal activities such as tending to cattle, going to Mass, attending a funeral in your own parish, going to work, or even going home, could mean a detour of up to twenty miles or more, and the inevitable extra delay that going through a permanent checkpoint entailed. It became a bit of a game of cat-and-mouse with us and the British army – they kept putting barriers along the Border and we kept opening it back up.'[6]

Border Busters

Another Border buster from Kiltyclogher in County Leitrim worked on the Dooard blockade near Garrison, on the Leitrim-Fermanagh Border. The bridges around Kiltyclogher were blown up around the village in the 1970s, ultimately costing two local men Peter Brennan and Eddie McCaffrey their lives. 'One fella drowned as he was trying to cross over a remaining ridge of the bridge and the other got lost going through the fields.'[7]

The road closures were very unpopular with the overwhelming majority of local residents along the Border. In November 1971, Frank McManus MP for Fermanagh and South Tyrone was among twenty-two men arrested at Clogher, County Tyrone, after a confrontation involving the filling in of cratered roads. In 1973, senior security officials in the Northern Ireland Office outlined the problem policing the Border represented for the security forces: 'the Border is over 300 miles long; in many places it passes through difficult terrain and is not clearly delineated on the ground; moreover different maps give varying information on its location. Apart from authorised Border crossings, there are 187 unapproved roads crossing the Border as well as many tracks and farm trails."[8]

Even some senior British civil servants were opposed to the Border road closures, stating that it would put further pressure on the already-strained Anglo-Irish relationship. A military study concluded that it would be unsuccessful in stopping the IRA smuggling weapons. In any case, in 1971, the army implemented the 'Ashburton Programme' and closed all 'unapproved roads'. This provoked a storm of disputes and a litany of altercations between Gardaí and British soldiers over the precise line of the Border.[9] 'Clashes with infuriated Garda officers and fire fights with IRA units became so frequent that army patrols were provided with reports on Border incidents as a pure formality.'[10]

During the 1980s, the British army continued to destroy many Border roads and bridges in an effort to seal the Border and corral all traffic into their fixed military checkpoints. This security policy had a very negative effect on towns in the area. Towns that were already adversely affected by partition, now found their problems exacerbated by the road closures. Entire communities were cut off from market centres, neighbouring farms and their places of worship. Throughout the 1980s, the Conservative Government in Britain intensified security measures along the Border resulting in the lowest ever level of North-South interfacing.

Colm Tóibín's description of the Border at Garrison provides an insight into the devastating impact that this security imposition had on the area: 'At the Border, I saw that huge immoveable chunk of concrete with rusty iron bars coming out of it had been placed on the bridge. The road was overhung with trees, and there was a definite sense that no one had been here for a long time.'

In the early 1990s, with the prospect of an IRA ceasefire looming, the focus once again returned to the road closures. The British Army had begun to fortify the Border at this time in a bid to counter some of the IRA's new tactics, such as the 'bunker buster' mortar attacks and the insidious 'proxy bomb'. The Leitrim-Fermanagh Border area had become a no-man's land and towns on both sides had suffered as a result. Before the road closures, Garrison was a stopover on the main road to Sligo. The road ran along the striking windswept waters of Lough Melvin and now bore all the hallmarks of total neglect. Before the road reached the Border, it became a lane with massive ponds clogged with weeds where the Army had cratered it. The bridge at Dooard on the Border was blocked by large concrete blocks with rusty metal girders ('Dragon's Teeth') protruding from them. Local residents often came together to remove the blockades but each time the British Army put in more obstacles.

This barrier forced many people to make the long drive to Belcoo and Blacklion to get cross the Border, turning a 100-metre journey into a 38-kilometre drive. A journalist from the New Internationalist magazine visited the area in 1994 and was shocked by the dereliction of the area, noting 'Tourists haven't come this way for a long time.' The British and Irish governments commissioned a study of the area in 1986 and concluded that the strategy for tourism was central to future development of the Lough Melvin catchment area and yet eight years later nothing had been done to develop the sector in the area.

The journalist from the New Internationalist interviewed the local owner of a television repair business who described the closure of Dooard Bridge as 'a complete disaster'. He added that it had isolated the community with the result that young people in the town would not be able to name any person two miles up the road. If someone from the other side of the Border wanted to have their television repaired, he would have to meet them at the bridge and walk across to collect it. Circumstances were the same for the local vet. The New Internationalist journalist also interviewed two sisters who lived in Kiltyclogher. Their parents lived in Garrison, three kilometres away but now they had to make a 77-kilometre round trip if they wanted to visit. One of the sisters called the closure 'an absolute disgrace... All the Borders are opening in Europe, but we can't even cross to visit our families.'

During the previous year, customs barriers had come down in the European Union and along the Border in Ireland. However, the frontier remained stronger and more militarised than at any time in its history. The watchtowers, fortified checkpoints and cratered roads remained. It was around this time that people from the Spanish Ministry of the Interior visited the Border to study the towers and learn ways of fortifying their own coastline against immigration from Africa. [11]

The fall-out of the Border closure was distinctly felt in Leitrim that now found itself in the disadvantaged position of being the only Border County with no direct access to Northern Ireland. Leitrim County Council raised the matter with then Minister for Foreign Affairs Brian Lenihan Senior. He told the representatives that he would raise the matter with the Anglo-Irish Secretariat. In 1994, after almost twenty-five years of road closures, Irish politicians finally began to call for the roads to be reopened. Cavan-Monaghan TD Brendan Smith raised the issue in Dáil Éireann: 'Border road closures have caused immeasurable hardship to communities, North and South, and led in some instances to the destruction of normal commercial and social life.'[12] That same year, Senator Reynolds stated, 'Two Border crossings should be opened immediately. One is the Rossinver-Dooagh to Garrison crossing and the other is the crossing from Kiltyclogher to Cashel Bridge.' In response, he was told that Deputy David Andrews, and the then Foreign Affairs Minister Dick Spring visited the Border crossings in County Leitrim to familiarise themselves with the situation.' Senator Reynolds argued that Kiltyclogher was one of the comparatively few villages in the Republic which had suffered terrorist attacks when its vocational school was bombed in the mid-1970s. Since then 'Kiltyclogher has suffered as a result of devastating socio-economic factors and the village and community are dying a slow and painful economic death.' He argued, "Business people are depending on a hinterland that has been eroded by emigration and migration. The community has suffered in silence for long enough and the opening of a Border crossing which would give the village a greater hinterland would be the first step in re-awakening economic prosperity in the area.'[13] Meanwhile, a Leitrim County Council delegation complained to the Border Regional Authority that 'once self-reliant towns and villages [which] had become little more than ghost towns.'[14]

The sustainable development of villages such as Garrison and Rossinver was hampered by the lack of adequate public transport services and poor road networks.[15] The growth of tourism in the area has been promoted as a viable option and the region has vast array of natural resources to promote the sector. Getting the target market to the area is contingent, however, upon the upgrading of the road network and increased cross-Border cooperation. The poor transport infrastructure continues to hinder cross-Border trade in the area. There is no strategic east–west route and road conditions remain poor with many are in need of repair. For some local businesses, haulage costs from the North West of the Republic are as much as twenty-five to thirty per cent higher than the national average. Access to services is poor and circumstances are additional compounded by the lack of rail links.

Bundoran man Aidan Carty helping to open the Garrison/Rossinver road in 1994

Orange and Green Unite (Briefly): The Land War

The sectarian violence that broke out in the north-east in 1795-6 helped spread Defenderism and instilled it with vicious and ruthless characteristics. In the 'Armagh outrages' of those years, several thousand Catholics from Armagh, Tyrone, Down and Fermanagh were driven from their homes by the recently formed Orange Order. These Catholics migrated to Connacht where, as one commentator put it, 'They related their sufferings and I fear have excited a spirit of revenge among their Catholic brethren.' These expulsions also led to the alliance between Defenders and the United Irishmen in 1796.

Glenaniff, neatly tucked away in the Dartry Mountains, is a quiet and peaceful valley. It was thought to have been first settled after the Battle of the Diamond in Armagh when thousands of Catholics were driven out of Ulster. The Rooney family name is ubiquitous throughout the area. Historian Lorcan Ó Ruainí speculated that these Rooneys originally came from County Down, where they were historians of the MacGuinness clan. After the late eighteenth century expulsions, however, they found themselves farming the boggy land of north Leitrim. One historian, conducting field research in the area, found that many people assumed that their ancestors had arrived there during Cromwell's time when they were expelled under the dictum, 'To hell or to Connacht'.

In 1796, the local landlord Thomas Conolly became concerned about suspicious Frenchmen mapping the west coast of Ireland. An invasion by French forces was anticipated. The strategically important port of Ballyshannon was reinforced by English troops during this period.[1] The Rock barracks were constructed and a star fort and cannon were erected on Mullaghnashee hill overlooking the town. Reports of disturbances began to appear and both sides burnt houses in the area. In nearby Bundoran, the holiday home of William Cole, Viscount of Enniskillen, was attacked and burned. Tensions were mounting and the Ballyshannon garrison was taking no chances.

OLD MILITARY BARRACKS, THE ROCK, BALLYSHANNON. ERECTED ABOUT THE YEAR 1798. THE BUILDING IS NOW BEING DEMOLISHED AND A NEW STREET OF LABOURERS' COTTAGES IS TO BE BUILT ON THE SITE.

Despite the initial lack of support for the United Irishmen in Fermanagh, three centres of organisation did develop around Roslea, Enniskillen and Belleek.[2] On the same day that the Roslea Martyrs were hanged in Enniskillen Gaol (12 October 1797), John Maguire's execution went unnoticed.[3] He was the local leader of the United Irishmen in Garrison. The old fort of Belleek was rebuilt and garrisoned in 1798 by General Knox.

After General Humbert landed at Killala with more than 1,000 soldiers in 1798, a group of around twenty men from the Belleek area set out to rendezvous with the French troops. They set up camp on the Moy road (linking Kinlough with Ballyshannon) in an area known as Lug na Marbh (the hollow of the dead) where Redcoats discovered them and all but two were killed. Humbert's forces scored initial successes at Castlebar and Collooney, near Sligo. The commander of Sligo, Colonel Vereher then retreated to Ballyshannon fearing that the French would sack his town. Napper Tandy, one of the leaders of the United Irishmen, then landed at Rutland Island and intended to sweep south and link up with Humbert's forces. However, Humbert by then was forced to surrender when defeated at the Battle of Ballinamuck, County Longford. His troops were allowed to return home to France but two thousand of his Irish supporters were massacred in the aftermath of that battle. The Belleek Yeomanry Infantry apprehended three men returning home from the Battle of Ballinamuck. They tried to swim to Roscor Island but one of the men, Hugh Ward, was shot and killed. His body was interred on Dead Man's Island (also called Lonesome Island) on Lough Erne.[4]

In February 1832, six thousand Whiteboys armed with scythes and pikes marched through the streets of Ballyshannon. They were protesting against the imposition of the land tax (tithes) payable to the Church of Ireland.[5] When the leaders of the Young Irelanders, John Mitchell and Charles Gavin Duffy visited Ballyshannon during their tour of Donegal, they were dismayed by the scenes they saw that one of their entourage concluded, 'The same appearance of poverty and squalor struck us here as in the south and other parts of Ireland. No wonder like causes produce like results.'[6] The Molly Maguires, another secret agrarian organisation, were also active in the Ballyshannon area at this time. The Ribbonmen were another underground organisation that often took the law into their own hands. Landlords and tenants who took over confiscated land were attacked in the locality. In 1848, a large number of suspected Ribbonmen (and women) were arrested and tried in Ballyshannon on the word of informants. Anxious about the revolutionary zeal throughout Ireland at this time, the British government introduced various repressive measures, such as the suspension of Habeas Corpus, to counteract any impending uprising.

In May 1848, the Young Ireland leaders were arrested and transported to penal colonies at the far side of the world. Until then, the Young Ireland movement had provided an important link with the 1798 rebellion through its use of physical force. Twenty years later during the early morning hours of 7 April 1868, Thomas D'Arcy McGee, journalist, poet, historian and political activist was assassinated in Ottawa, Canada.[7] He had been a prominent member of the Young Ireland nationalist movement when they were active in Ireland from 1842 to 1848. The Young Irelanders included both Catholics and Protestants who sought to create a non-sectarian Irish national identity. Their rebellion in 1848 was a complete failure and many of their leaders were transported in prison ships, while other such as D'Arcy McGee had fled Ireland shortly afterwards.

Before the failed rebellion, D'Arcy McGee used Bundoran as his base in an attempt to build support for revolution in the area. He stayed in a lodging house in the bustling seaside town. One of the other guests was Thomas Blake, the resident magistrate who was responsible for the security of the region.[8] D'Arcy McGee had to go through Blake's room in order to enter his own. Although he was opposed to secret societies, such as the Molly Maguires and Ribbonmen, D'Arcy McGee made contact with their leaders in Sligo and Donegal and pleaded with them to take up arms. For the next ten days, he travelled throughout the area trying to persuade members of the secret societies to join the rebellion. His efforts proved fruitless. In Ballyshannon, he stayed with a Dr. O'Donnell while posing as John Kelly, a student for the priesthood at Maynooth. Blake, the magistrate, became aware what D'Arcy McGee was doing in the area but he failed to capture him. D'Arcy McGee subsequently escaped to America after the rising failed. In 1857, he moved to Montreal where he became a prominent political figure in winning support for Canadian confederation until his assassination.

The leaders of the Young Ireland rebellion who had escaped to America found a growing Irish diaspora who remained deeply resentful of Britain's indifference during Ireland's Great Famine. Within this powerful constituency, the Irish Republican Brotherhood (IRB) emerged from the Fenian movement, founded in the 1850s by John O'Mahony in New York and James Stephens in Ireland. Even though the American and Irish organisations were separate, the movement as a whole was known as Fenianism. They were opposed to constitutional tactics, believing that British rule could only be ended by armed rebellion.

In the north-west of Ireland, local Fenians are thought to have met at Quinns in the townland of Fassagh, near Belleek.[9] The Fenians in Fermanagh were apparently recruited from the Ribbonmen in many cases. The movement was more prominent in certain districts. In Derrygonnelly, the leader was Hugh Montgomery, described by the Government as 'the most dangerous man in Fermanagh'. Two of his lieutenants were Edward and Denis Greyson. Denis was arrested in March 1865, accused of drilling at Belleek.[10] In an intelligence report to Dublin Castle, the local magistrate outlined his suspicions, stating, 'Denis Greyson is suspected by me of Fenianism for the following reasons; His connection with Montgomery now in Enniskillen Gaol; his refusal to take prisoners charged with Fenianism towards Enniskillen (he has a licence for a post-car) and telling the Constabulary to go to hell; his being seen frequently with bad characters in a well-known locality in Belleek called "The Mill", the meeting place for the disaffected of the district; his connection with the movement is notorious to the whole country.'

Michael Barrett, a Fenian originally from the townland of Drumnagreshial in the Ederney-Kesh area of County Fermanagh was hanged on 26 May 1868 outside Newgate Prison (now the Old Bailey) in London. His was the last public hanging in England.[11]

Meanwhile, the post-Famine landscape of North Leitrim was a desolate, depressing place. The county had been very badly affected by disease and starvation. Empty houses, now hovels, littered the landscape. Hundreds of families who had survived huddled along the roadsides, fighting the elements, struggling to survive. A journalist from the Freeman's Journal toured the area in 1881 and recorded his discoveries: 'I found, wherever I turned yesterday, the empty homes of evicted tenants rising up before me. I found that thirty or forty families have been dispossessed of the farms and the houses where they and their ancestors struggled to gain a livelihood.'[12] To compound this calamity, apathetic landlords began to evict many of those families who could not pay their rent. In many cases, the rents were raised to punitive levels in an attempt to remove the peasantry from their lands. It was in this environment that a deep-rooted sense of anger and outrage began to foment in the local population. One of the most notorious of these was Colonel Arthur Loftus Tottenham, who owned almost 15,000 acres in North Leitrim. Not all landlords in the area behaved in such an appalling way, however. The Hamiltons of Ballintra campaigned actively for tenants' rights, opposed eviction and promoted land reform.

The Irish National Land League was founded in 1879 to promote a national campaign against landlordism. The movement quickly took hold in North Leitrim and the battle lines were drawn. Michael Davitt's Land League demanded the 'three Fs' – fair rent, fixity of tenure and freedom of sale for tenants. Interestingly, Mahatma Ghandi cited Davitt and the Land League movement as a major influence in the creation of his own peaceful civil rights movement in India. The gradual land reforms for Ireland introduced by the British Government were inadequate in the eyes of some of the more militant members of the Land League. Agrarian protests began in 1879 with well-organised mass rallies where tenants demanded a reduction in their rents. The challenge to civil authority was serious. The democratic movement was underscored by violent actions not officially sanctioned by The Land League.

The protests spread throughout North Leitrim during the autumn and winter of 1880.[13] Some local IRB men facilitated the proliferation of new Land League branches. As tensions grew, violence flared. According to one witness, it was fuelled by the 'undertones of Fenianism'. On 8 August 8 1880, a crowd of five thousand assembled in Glenade. Speakers included Judge James Croal from Ballyshannon, a veteran of the American Civil War, and Patrick Fergus, an ardent nationalist politician and organiser of the local Land League branch. During the same month, Thomas Corscadden, a landlord from near Manorhamilton, had many of his tenants evicted from his land. The Glenade people began to boycott him, the first such instance in the county. No one would herd his cattle; many of his sheep disappeared across the mountain; and his hay was scattered. At Christmas, Corscadden's stables were destroyed in an arson attack. He was jeered and ridiculed as he travelled on the roads.[14]

The tactic of ostracisation was taken up elsewhere by political and land activists. Speaking in Ennis on 19 September 1880, Irish Parliamentary Party leader Charles Stuart Parnell declared, 'When a man takes a farm from which another had been evicted, you must shun him on the roadside when you meet him; you must shun him in the streets of the town; you must shun him in the shop; you must shun him in the fair green and in the marketplace; and even in the place of worship. By leaving him alone, by putting him in a moral Coventry, by isolating him from the rest of his country as if he were the leper of old, you must show your detestation of the crime he has committed.'

Three weeks after the Glenade meeting a crowd of seven thousand assembled in Manorhamilton, where the landlord Loftus-Tottenham came in for heavy criticism. Then in October, a crowd of eight thousand gathered at Kinlough where Joseph Biggar, former member of the Supreme Council of the Fenians, addressed them. The meeting succeeded in getting some local landlords to reduce their rents. After one such meeting, a local poet penned the following lines:

> Landlords no longer can dupe or divide us
> Orange and Green to each other will stand.
> Too long my brothers we've let them o(v)erride us
> Blasting our homesteads and dear Motherland.

In 1881, however, Gladstone's Coercion Act was brought in to protect landlords and many Land League members were arrested and imprisoned. That year also saw the formal introduction of the 'Three Fs' demands and the establishment of the Ladies Land League. The latter was bitterly opposed by the Catholic Church, especially by Archbishop McCabe of Dublin. In his Lenten Pastoral of 1881, he said, 'They are asked to forget the modesty of their sex and the high dignity of their womanhood by leaders who seem utterly reckless... and who have brought misery on many families.' Despite such opposition, the Ladies Land League flourished in North Leitrim. They were particularly active in Kiltyclogher in a land war with the obdurate landlord Arthur Loftus Tottenham. He had once claimed that he 'would collect his rent in spite of man and devil'. Tottenham continued to evict tenants en masse. One member of the Ladies Land League recorded some of the events, 'The forces of civilisation were represented by five hundred military and police, the sub-sheriff and the bailiff. Eight evictions were got through the first day with the usual accompaniment of broken furniture, shivering women and children – some of them with the merest rags to cover them.'[15]

By this time, the protests had already spread to neighbouring towns and villages. After a rally in Belleek in November 1880, Parnell and his political colleague John Dillon proceeded towards Ballyshannon. Along the way, they were met by a vast torchlight procession led by a brass band. They continued their triumphal march towards town. Upon arrival at their hotel, the men addressed the vast crowd and were received with a rapturous applause.[16]

Then on 20 October 1881, more than ten thousand supporters of the Land League convened in Ballyshannon to hear the speakers denounce the government.[17] By then the gentry had been forced to discontinue their hunting activities in the district because of the Land League's action. Farmers who previously allowed hunting on their land were vociferously opposed to the presence of wealthy gentry on their farms. The Irish Times noted this turn of events, 'It has been found necessary to discontinue hunting. The most systemic opposition has been shown since the beginning of the season. On one occasion great violence was offered to two gentlemen, and the hounds were stoned.' In Dartry, a local landlord appeared on Patrick Fergus' land with a hunting party. Patrick and his brother Hugh confronted them with guns and warned 'that the first who trespassed on their farm it would be at the cost of their lives'. On another occasion, Patrick met another aristocratic trespasser who was fishing in the lake on his land. Patrick informed him that he did not have permission to fish there. The angler said, 'Do you know, sir that you are speaking to Judge May?' Fergus replied, 'I don't give a damn if you are Judge November. In you go,' and he pitched him into the lake.

Patrick Fergus was a member of the Fenian Brotherhood. Both he and his brother Charles were also members of the Loyal National Repeal Association. Charles enrolled as a member on 28 August 1845 on payment of £1. Patrick would later play a prominent role in the nationalist politics of North Leitrim. He was one of the first members of Leitrim County Council and chairperson of Kinlough Rural District Council.

Arrests under the Coercion Act were widespread throughout North Leitrim in 1881. A Police Inspector or Sub-Inspector with a 'reasonable suspicion' of a person could order their arrest. In Kinlough, witnesses for the prosecution in such cases were shunned by the locals and refused lodgings. During the Corscadden case, more than a thousand people flocked to the town to support local Land League members, some of whom were sentenced to hard labour in Sligo jail.

Boycotting was just one of the weapons that the Land League used in the land war. Quite often large groups of people gathered to thwart the efforts of the bailiffs by jamming doorways and blocking roads. In September, the unrest spread to Tullaghan after Captain Barton charged his tenants with trespassing on his bog. In response, they dug deep trenches in the roads preventing him from accessing the area. The government cracked down hard on the Land League and more and more activists were arrested. The Garrison Land League staged a meeting in Kiltyclogher in November but the assembly was forcefully disbanded. When they reconvened a few miles away, their leader, Mr Ferguson, was arrested and charged with having treasonable documents in his possession.

In 1957, a Fermanagh newspaper interviewed Hugh Maguire of Muckinagh, Garrison, after he celebrated his 83rd birthday. He recalled that a large Land League meeting scheduled to take place in Garrison in 1881 was banned and that two or three hundred British soldiers arrived in the village to enforce the ban. They included thirty mounted redcoats. When John Dillon addressed the meeting held outside the village, there were no clashes with the military, although trouble was only narrowly averted. Mr Maguire remembers the Kiltyclogher Band in the town that day, with a gentle giant in their ranks. Charlie Maguire, six feet seven inches in height, was the band's big drummer. It took a half a dozen men to persuade Charlie not to force a passage through the soldiers lined across the village streets.

The slogans and policies of the Land League were everywhere, widely proclaimed by an enthusiastic band who relished their first taste of freedom from the oppression of landlords: 'Pay no rent until the suspects are released; Turn your backs on the land courts, they are only a trap to enslave you more and more; You have been slaves too long; Down with the Landlords; No more tyranny and injustice; Be true to yourselves and to your country.'

Although the Land League campaign was founded on the principles and practices of what would become a pacifist civil rights campaign, strong undercurrent of violence permeated this period of local history. Bailiffs, 'emergency men' and land grabbers all became targets for the more militant Land League members. The police records show that landlords in the area frequently received anonymous threats.[18] Lord Leitrim was killed in Donegal while on his way to Manorhamilton. Threatening notices were often posted in the market yards of villages throughout the area. They were invariably signed by 'Rory of the Hills', an alias identity reminiscent of the 'P.O'Neill' who signed statements and warnings from the Provisional IRA almost a century later. The notices would indicate who was to be targeted and ended with the ominous caveat: 'Written and signed by Rory of the Hills, who always warns before he kills.'

Despite that undercurrent, there was a brief lull in sectarian tensions during the late nineteenth century. The Land League provided a common cause for Catholic and Protestant famers to unite in their demands for better conditions. When Parnell came to speak in Belleek, huge crowds turned out to hear him. That Belleek meeting caused quite a stir and the magistrates were alarmed by the protesters' demands.[19] Another meeting was arranged for Derrygonnelly, which at the time was a sectarian flashpoint. The meeting however was a success, causing a local journalist to comment, 'One of the signs of the times is the union of Orange men, Protestants and Catholics, in accepting the League in Derrygonnelly.'[20] Alarmed by its potential to upset the social, economic and political order, the Government proscribed the Land League in 1882 and the grassroots movement floundered in Fermanagh on the rock of loyalty and conformity. Catholics and Protestants who had united in their common struggle for more than a year now began to distance themselves once more.[21] As the Parnellites still coasted ahead on the wave of Land Reform confidence, Fermanagh elected its first Catholic MP for the Irish Parliamentary Party in 1885. The Unionist Fermanagh Times gave a terse response to the victory, stating ominously, 'The Nationalists will live to regret their victory in North Fermanagh.'

After Parnell was released from Kilmainham in May 1882, the Chief Secretary for Ireland W.E. Forster resigned in protest. His successor, Lord Frederick Cavendish, was then killed by The Invincibles, a splinter group of the IRB. After 1882, the focus of the Land League had shifted to Home Rule. In a speech that year Davitt warned, 'We will make the English people understand that no matter what concession may be made, we will never be content until we have the right to make our own laws.'

A Terrible Beauty: The War of Independence

In August 1995, Sinn Féin president Gerry Adams was addressing a demonstration in Belfast when a member of crowd called out to him to 'bring back the IRA. In an unscripted reply, Adams produced one of the most infamous soundbites of the post-Troubles era: 'They haven't gone away, you know.' From partition to the present, the IRA in its various forms has made its presence felt all along the Border.

The history of secret societies and resistance groups in Ireland stretches back over hundreds of years. From the United Irishmen of the eighteenth century to the Real IRA in the twenty-first century, these groups have sought to end British rule by military means. In the land agitation of the mid-1780s, the Defenders were formed by Catholics as local defensive organisations against Protestant Peep o' Day Boys night-time raids on Catholic homes. The Defenders were absorbed into the United Irishmen before the uprising of 1798. Then the Ribbonmen emerged from the fiasco of the rebellion with an inherited sense of violent republican radicalism influenced by the French Revolution. The hereditary connection continued in the mid-nineteenth century when the Molly Maguires became active in the parts of the country that had been the centres of Defenderism and Ribbonism.[1] The IRB and the Fenians carried on the tradition, as did the Irish Volunteers and Citizens Army of 1916, until the IRA was formed in 1919. Through various factions and splits, the ranks remained committed to violence down the decades. Many of the men and women who joined the IRA during the Troubles even saw themselves as part of an unbroken tradition that stretched back to the sixteenth century when the O'Neills, O'Donnells and Maguires united to fight against England in the Nine Years War.[2]

In the aftermath of the Boer War, there was a renewed enthusiasm for the formation of a radical nationalist party in Ireland. Therefore, in 1905, Arthur Griffith and Bulmer Hobson established Sinn Féin. The name Sinn Féin is thought to have been coined by Fr Lorcan O'Ciarain, the parish priest for Pettigo who lived at Magheramena Castle outside Belleek. Among his many friends were some of the leading figures of the Irish freedom movement, such as Douglas Hyde, Griffiths, Eamon de Valera and Michael Collins. He was present at the first meetings of the executive of the organisation that would soon become the political monolith Sinn Féin.

One of Sinn Féin's most prominent members was Sean Mac Diarmada, born near Kiltyclogher in 1883. He grew up in a small thatched cottage in the townland of Laughty Barr, also known locally as Scregg. In the early 1900s, he became active in nationalist politics. He was sworn into the Irish Republican Brotherhood (IRB) and rose to prominence in both Sinn Féin and the Gaelic League.

Shortly after the establishment of the Sinn Féin party, he became director of elections for the north Leitrim area, travelling throughout the towns, villages and countryside making speeches and rallying volunteers to the separatist cause. Mac Diarmada is widely regarded as the most determined and uncompromising of the 1916 Rising leaders and he was one of the seven signatories of the Proclamation that declared Irish independence from Britain. On 12 May 1916, he faced a British firing squad, the last of the rebel leaders to be executed.

Sinn Féin had contested the North Leitrim by-election of 1908, when Charles Joseph Dolan secured twenty-seven per cent of the vote. Sinn Féin ran its campaign, directed by Mac Diarmada, from an office on Castle Street in Manorhamilton. In the run-up to the voting, violence broke out there between the Ancient Order of Hibernians and Sinn Féin supporters. One partisan account describes the scene: 'They (AOH) were armed with knuckle dusters, life preservers, revolvers and spiked clubs and paid out of parliamentary funds. They wandered through Manorhamilton and attacked isolated Sinn Féin supporters but sought police protection when faced with trouble themselves. It was estimated that the election cost the parliamentarians between £1,500 and £2,000. Half of this money had been spent on drink and hiring roughs.'

In November 1913, Professor Eoin MacNeill published an article entitled 'The North Began' in An Claidheamh Soluis, the newspaper of Conrady na Gaeilge (the Gaelic League). He urged fellow nationalists to follow the lead given by Ulster Unionists in their formation of the UVF. A public meeting soon followed, attended by seven thousand people and the Irish Volunteer movement (Óglaigh na hÉireann) was established. They were quickly infiltrated by the IRB.[3] Companies sprang up all over County Donegal and by September 1914, the British estimated that there were 74 units consisting of 10,661 men.[4]

In 1914, Pierce Beasley, a director of publicity for the republican movement came to the Kinlough area and organised a company of the Irish Volunteers. Many of the appointed officers were also members of the Ancient Order of Hibernians (AOH). Because of their antipathy towards Sinn Féin, the local company soon floundered and the AOH issued an order that any of their members who contributed to or supported Sinn Féin in any way would be expelled.[5] That same year, Ernest Blythe arrived in Donegal to recruit local men into the IRB. In addition, after the outbreak of the First World War, the Volunteers split into John Redmond's National Volunteers and MacNeill's Irish Volunteers some of whom defied his countermanding order and turned out to fight on Easter Monday, 1916.

The aftermath of the Rising brought about major changes, which saw a rapid increase in support for Sinn Féin. The Volunteers were reorganised. After 1916, many volunteers in Donegal who were previously members of the Ancient Order of Hibernians or the National Volunteers, rallied behind Sinn Féin and the Irish Volunteers.

In 1917, the British authorities attempted to ban a Sinn Féin rally from taking place in Bundoran, where Maude Gonne McBride was due to be one of the main speakers. A decoy rally was planned in the East End of the town whilst the real meeting was taking place in the West End. The distraction worked and the military proceeded toward the East End. They raced back towards the West End with fixed bayonets after realising they had been deceived. An uneasy standoff followed until the locals quietly dispersed.

Political tensions in the area were intensified by the large-scale military presence in the area. In January 1918, a group of Sinn Féin members on their way home to Ballyshannon were attacked by soldiers of the 36th Ulster Division stationed at Finner. Thirteen Sinn Féin members were injured and one young man from Ballyshannon died because of his injuries.

Despite the best efforts of the authorities, the general election of 1918 resulted in a landslide victory for Sinn Féin in Ireland. Westminster was boycotted and the elected representatives formed their own parliament, Dáil Éireann, in Dublin's Mansion House on the 21 January 1919. On the same day, the Irish Volunteers at Soloheadbeg in County Tipperary killed two Royal Irish Constabulary (RIC) officers. The Irish War of Independence had begun.

In 1919, Ernie O'Malley helped streamline the local companies of Volunteers into the South Donegal No. 1 battalion. The Battalion included companies from Ballyshannon Bundoran, Belleek, Kinlough, and Tullaghan. Thomas Mc Shea was elected battalion commander (O/C) and Patrick 'Hun' O'Doherty became his second in command.

The military situation began to intensify in 1920 as volunteer units throughout Donegal were ordered to raid all customs offices in the area and remove all documents. On 30 May, they raided Ballyshannon customs office. The alarm was raised and soldiers from Finner quickly cordoned off the bridge, blocking the only escape route for the Bundoran men. However, Thomas McShea managed to pass through the checkpoint by 'acting like a simpleton'.

British army checkpoint on the bridge at Ballyshannon during the War of Independence

As the violence intensified, Volunteers began gathering weapons from raids on houses belonging to wealthy Protestants. The IRA raided the home of Captain Barton and Miss Tynte, Tynte Lodge in Tullaghan, and a shotgun and a Winchester rifle were taken. Then in the summer of 1920, the Bundoran IRA received information that a few houses belonging to Unionists in the townland of Clyhore near Belleek contained a store of Ulster Volunteer weapons. They mobilised a number of men, went to the district and raided the houses. The first premises they visited refused their demand for admission, however, at which point the IRA men threatened to burn the house if they were refused. They began to place straw around the house in preparation for the arson attack. Upon seeing this, the occupants of the house opened the doors and let them in. The subsequent searches did not turn up any weapons.[6]

In August 1920, simultaneous attacks were launched on the RIC barracks in Bundoran, Ballyshannon and Kinlough in order to test the reaction time of the troops from Finner. Sensing that they might well be walking into an ambush, the army was slow to react. However, the continued presence of a large military force at Finner prevented the local IRA companies from becoming involved in any large-scale engagements.

Members of Bundoran's Flying Column with Commanding Officer Patrick 'Hun' Doherty (back row, third from right)

During the Irish Railway Strike of 1920, the IRA ordered railway workers to suspend services if the British army attempted to board the trains. In August, a railway worker from Bundoran received the following instructions: 'You are hereby notified that after this date you are forbidden to drive any train, or assist in any way the transport of armed forces of the British Government, by order, Ministry of War.' By that point, the trains were often sabotaged by Volunteers to prevent the army from using them and to stop goods from Belfast entering the area. The Belfast Boycott policy had been adopted in 1920 after a series of sectarian riots in Belfast resulted in mass expulsions of Catholics from workplaces such as the Harland and Wolff shipyards.

Then in September 1920, a large group of IRA Volunteers successfully raided Belleek RIC barracks for guns using an ambulance as cover. Not all of those involved in the operation were motivated by nationalist ideals. The man who was responsible for ferrying the seized guns across Lough Melvin insisted that he be paid £25 in advance. That meant volunteer Sean 'Shaw' Carthy had to cycle to Garrison to borrow the money with the British army in hot pursuit.[7]

Members of the RIC and British army raided the family home of James Connolly at Unshinagh, Kinlough, on 14 September 1920. Connolly was a captain in the IRA's Kinlough Company. His unarmed father was shot dead during the raid. On 25 October 1920, a local IRA Flying Column ambushed an RIC patrol from Cliffoney. In the aftermath, one sergeant and four constables lay dead on the side of the road. The IRA then retreated through the Dartry Mountains to the isolated Gleniff Valley. The reprisals were swift. Ballintrillick Creamery, along with the homes of suspected sympathisers in the area, were burned in reprisal by the army and RIC.

However, other thwarted operations against the RIC made the IRA's local Intelligence Officer suspect that the police were receiving information about Volunteer activities.[8] The British went on the offensive in the intelligence war and arrests soon followed. From late 1920 to mid-1921, the Army and police conducted raids on the homes of many suspected IRA men throughout South Donegal. John Murphy was arrested in Bundoran and sentenced to two years imprisonment. Bernard Ryan, a member of the Bundoran Company, was arrested in March 1921 and detained in Ballykinlar Prison Camp in County Down. In April, Thomas McShea and Patrick Johnson were arrested in possession of 'subversive material'. They were also accused of forcing local shops to close on the day of the funeral of Cork Lord Mayor Terence MacSwiney who died after a 74-day hunger strike in Brixton Prison, England. They each received a sentence of two years hard labour.

During their imprisonment, McShea and Johnson tried to escape from Derry jail. Their failed attempt led to the death of two prison guards and both men were then charged with murder and sentenced to death. The response of the IRA was to kidnap a large number of prominent Orangemen in Border counties and hold them as hostages to stop the Derry executions. Eoin O'Duffy orchestrated the operation, which was sanctioned by Michael Collins. In February 1922, the IRA abducted more than forty Unionists including Major Myles of Ballyshannon and James Johnston, owner of Oakfield estate in Kinlough, who were detained at Classiebawn Castle in Mullaghmore. The IRA informed the British authorities that the hostages would be killed if Johnson or McShea were executed, unaware that the British government had commuted the death sentences some time earlier. The hostages were subsequently released.

In January 1921, a large contingent of Crown forces from Sligo, Manorhamilton and Finner Camp near Bundoran converged on the area in a roundup of IRA suspects. Those who were detained claimed they were badly beaten. A small party of armed Volunteers had a narrow escape. They had just evaded the army cordon when they were spotted and fired on. They retreated to the Dartry Mountains where their local knowledge of the area aided their escape.[9]

The IRA Volunteers also acted as the de facto police force in the area. A farmer from Kinlough protested that her son had removed cattle from the farm and was determined to sell them at Belleek fair. The IRA stopped him before he could sell the cattle and the herd was returned to his mother. People accused of public order offences were also fined by the republican courts and ordered to leave the area. Thieves in the district were routinely detained by the Volunteers and fined in the local Dáil-sanctioned court system.

In Fermanagh also, the Volunteer movement gained increasing support after the 1916 Rising. In 1917, there were companies in Tempo and Arney. By 1918, more companies had emerged in Enniskillen, Irvinestown, Belcoo and Lisnaskea. During the winter of 1919, the command structures were defined and Sean Carthy was placed in charge of the area that included Monea, Boho, Derrygonnelly, Toora, Garrison and Belleek. Frank Carney, later elected a TD, became commanding officer for Fermanagh, organising the Volunteers and doing rifle and open formation drills. He was arrested before his orders to burn vacated police barracks and tax offices could be carried out. John Maguire of Belcoo quickly replaced him and during Easter 1920, many of the vacant barracks and offices were burned. Raids to procure arms were also conducted on a regular basis.

During an attempt to burn Lisbellaw Courthouse, however, a local vigilante raised the alarm and a gun battle ensued. An attack on Tempo barracks also demonstrated the entirely different circumstances that IRA units in the new Northern Ireland had to deal with. The UVF vigilantes and police opened fire on the IRA during the raid on the barracks and the IRA Volunteers had to fight their way out of town. The vigilante groups drawn from the ranks of the UVF were organised by Captain Basil Brooke, later installed as Northern Ireland premier Lord Brookeborough. His strategy was adopted as the template for the 'B' Special constabulary throughout the North, but particularly in Border areas where they became the frontline defence force, whose primary role was to defend Northern Ireland against republican attacks from the South. Sixteen police officers died in Fermanagh during this violent period.[10]

As efforts by the IRA to mount a substantial guerrilla campaign in Fermanagh were increasingly confounded by this new adversary, Belleek and Mulleek IRA companies were transferred to the 1st Northern (Donegal) Division in 1921, a rearrangement that proved crucial for a subsequent episode in the Belleek-Pettigo triangle.

Finally, on 11 July 1921, a cease-fire was agreed and that same day the British soldiers began to withdraw from their outposts and retreat towards Finner Camp. Subsequent talks in London between delegations of the Irish and British sides led to the Anglo-Irish Treaty in December. After the Dáil's ratification of the Treaty, many of the IRA Volunteers throughout County Donegal retained Republican sympathies but the Collins-de-Valera pact eased internal tensions. There was an escalation of violence in the county beginning with some cross-Border raids in February 1922. In March of that year, IRA Volunteers gathered in Blacklion, County Cavan crossed the bridge into Fermanagh and attacked Belcoo RUC station. Sixteen police officers were taken prisoner and brought to Athlone where they were held hostage in the Free State army barracks in return for the release of IRA prisoners in the north.[11] A massive round up in May resulted in the majority of Fermanagh's senior IRA officers arrested and an end to its campaign.[12]

IRA marching in to take over Finner, Feb 1922

However, in May and June 1922, after the end of the War of Independence and before the Civil War had begun, the small Border villages of Pettigo and Belleek found themselves on the frontline of an all-out battle between the IRA and British forces. Even as the fledging Free State began its acrimonious decent into internecine conflict, the pro-treaty and anti-treaty Volunteers united to make a last stand against the Crown forces. Free State commander Michael Collins and Liam Lynch, commanding officer of the 'Irregular' IRA, were working behind the scenes against a common enemy.[13] Collin's rationale was defined by his concerns for the safety of the nationalist minority in Northern Ireland following the recent loyalist pogroms in Belfast. The sectarian conflict had escalated sharply and in March 1922, fifty-three people were killed in Belfast, thirty-seven of them Catholics. Collins also saw the joint strategy as a means of undermining the new Northern Ireland state.

The combined force for the operation was fewer than a hundred men and it comprised both pro-treaty Free State troops and anti-treaty IRA Volunteers. From the spring of 1922, the area between Belleek and Pettigo had witnessed a build-up in military activity and by May, Free State troops occupied both towns. A number of Anti-Treaty IRA volunteers arrived in the area to take part in the Northern Offensive. Other IRA men also arrived to avoid the roundup of republicans by the Special Constabulary elsewhere in Fermanagh.

Then on 27 May, a large detachment of Special Constabulary descended on Belleek in an attempt to recapture the town. They took over Magheramena Castle and evicted its occupant, the republican Catholic pastor Fr Lorcan O'Ciarain.[14] A group of IRA Volunteers then advanced towards Magheramena where they engaged the Specials, forcing them to withdraw to Boa Island on Lough Erne for a rendezvous with reinforcements.[15]

On 28 May, the Specials used a number of Crossley tenders accompanied by an armoured car in a renewed attempt to take control of Belleek but the IRA Volunteers in Belleek Fort intercepted them as they entered Free State territory. The driver of the Lancia armoured car was killed and the crashed vehicle created a roadblock preventing the Crossley tenders from passing through. Under fire, the British forces retreated, leaving behind the Crossleys and armoured car.[16] The captured armoured car was driven off to Ballyshannon and then on to the Free State HQ at Drumboe Castle, Stranorlar.[17]

British armoured car captured at Belleek (Courtesy of Anthony Begley)

After the Specials' attack on their base in Belleek, the IRA in Pettigo began to build defences. The British army drew up and pounded their positions with artillery from the Fermanagh side. For the next few days, the IRA repelled a series of attacks by Special Constabulary and British soldiers. Meanwhile, the unionists of Pettigo fled the village amidst rumours of an imminent full-scale attack by the combined Free State and IRA forces. The events became a diplomatic incident in which Winston Churchill repudiated the assertion by Collins that his forces had nothing to do with the campaign. Indeed, Collin had neglected to tell Churchill that he had armed the IRA men with weapons taken from Free State troops and replacing these with arms given to him by the British with which to enforce the Treaty.

A combined force of Special Constabulary and British soldiers then attempted to outflank the IRA by crossing the narrow isthmus of Donegal land known as the Waterfoot, between Letter and Lowry in Fermanagh. Waterfoot is the only part of Donegal to touch Lower Lough Erne. (During the Second World War, German diplomats would take a keen interest in visiting the area to look at what Lord Haw Haw described as the 'curious swans of Lough Erne'.) On 29 May 1922, a group of IRA Volunteers set up defences along the peninsula. Repeated attacks were launched against them but they held the line. Another section of the IRA Volunteers crept out from Pettigo to support their comrades at the Waterfoot. As the fighting escalated in Pettigo, a large number of British forces again attacked the Waterfoot. The IRA men were forced to retreat after two hours of intense fighting.[18]

As Britain's Secretary for War, Churchill deployed warships to Derry to shore up the new state and had British regular forces in Enniskillen mobilised with orders to capture Pettigo and Belleek. The British artillery soon overwhelmed the IRA in Pettigo and three volunteers, Bernard McCanny, William Kearney and Patrick Flood, died in the subsequent battle. With ammunition running out and the prospect of their positions being over-run, more than sixty IRA defenders withdrew from the town. They left the body of Patrick Flood lying on Billary Hill. When a local priest asked the British commanding officer if he could retrieve the body, he noticed a coffin with a note pinned to it saying, 'Shinners accommodated'.[19]

Members of the First Northern Division of the IRA thought that the British might even launch an attack on nearby Ballyshannon (then held by a Free State garrison), thus cutting off the 'hostile Afghanistan'. Former IRA volunteer Michael O'Donaghue speculated that if this had happened it would have resulted in a unified Irish Republican Army that would have waged renewed war on the British in Ulster and destabilised the Northern government.[20]

British forces controlled Pettigo by June 4 and then turned their attention to Belleek. A small IRA garrison occupied Belleek Fort where they flew the Irish tricolour. The British artillery opened up on the fort with 18-pound shells. The first shell missed its target and landed in a nearby field killing some livestock. The second shell landed behind the fort. In the face of overwhelming odds and under covering fire from their comrades, the IRA men retreated to defensive positions west of Belleek. The British army then moved in and occupied Belleek Fort. They made no effort to pursue or further engage the Republican column, which continued to hold defensive positions a mile away.[21] By 8 June, the British union flag was flying from the fort.

British soldiers celebrating their victory in Belleek and posing with the captured Irish tricolour

This and other battles on the Border increased tensions between London and Dublin. Prime Minister David Lloyd-George warned Churchill that 'Our Ulster case is not a good one... Let us keep on the high ground of the Treaty, the Crown, the Empire. There, we are unassailable. But if you come down from that height and fight in the swamps of Lough Erne, you will be overwhelmed.'[22] Churchill's father Randolph had coined the statement, 'Ulster will fight and Ulster will be right.' Winston was similarly disposed towards the use of military force to protect the Empire. Lloyd-George even felt that 'there was a strain of lunacy in Churchill'.[23]

In all three British soldiers and three Republicans were killed during the battles of Pettigo and Belleek. From then on, Collins's policy on the North changed to 'peaceful obstruction'. Meanwhile, British demands for Collins to act forcefully against the anti-Treaty IRA increased and hostilities between both sides broke out in late June. The British military handed over Pettigo to Free State troops in January 1923. They remained in Belleek until August 1924, when the RUC and the Specials took over the security of the village.

British Army leave Belleek Fort in 1924

As the two regimes settled into their role, splits within the Republican movement became a recurring theme. Brendan Behan once quipped, that t*he 'first item on the agenda' of any new Irish organisation 'is the split'*. The following are some examples: Fianna Fáil in 1926, the Republican Congress in 1934, Cumann Poblacta in 1936, Clann na Phoblacta in 1946, Official Sinn Féin (the Workers' Party) in 1970 and Republican Sinn Féin in 1986.

Yet even after de Valera formed Fianna Fáil in 1926 and entered the Dáil, the 'soldiers of the rearguard' continued to hold their ranks in various guises. In Donegal, IRA members campaigned against the payment of land annuities to the British government. In 1928, Peadar O'Donnell established the Anti-Tribute League. When Fianna Fáil took over the reins of power in the 1930s, festering Civil War disputes spiralled into violence. De Valera rescinded the ban on the IRA and many republican prisoners were released from jail. A reformed IRA began to disrupt meetings of the opposition party, Cumann na nGaedhael, which formed the Blueshirts for protection and thus leading to open riots.

In 1933, a disgruntled Eoin O'Duffy became the leader of the Blueshirt movement after de Valera dismissed him as Garda Commissioner. Ned Cronin, secretary of the Army Comrades Association, was arrested at the Central Hotel in Bundoran on 9 December of that year. He was taken to Bundoran Garda station and then sent to Arbor Hill prison. It had been Cronin who suggested the adoption of the blue shirt as a uniform. Next day, O'Duffy arrived in Ballyshannon to speak at a rally in the market yard. Tensions were high and a hostile crowd soon gathered. They began throwing stones and other missiles at the police. The Gardaí baton-charged the crowd. Undaunted, O'Duffy got up to speak and launched into a vitriolic diatribe about de Valera. A local reporter noted, 'The atmosphere was electric as he began to speak with a vehemence that temporarily silenced the crowd.' O'Duffy's incendiary speech led to accusations, with him quoted as saying 'that De Valera and his party had murdered Kevin O'Higgins and that the policy of the present government is to assassinate General O'Duffy'. He later denied ever saying this.

In April 1934, more than two hundred Blueshirts marched into Bundoran where a football match was taking place. Word of their arrival soon spread and some left the match to confront the marchers. A riot broke out between the two sides and Gardaí were forced to intervene. Some local men were arrested and charged with breaches of the peace.[24]

Seán Russell became IRA chief of staff in 1938 and began preparations for a bombing campaign against Britain. He travelled to Germany in 1940 to seek supplies of arms. On his return trip, he became ill and died on board a German U-boat. Stephen Hayes became the acting Chief of Staff. Helped by the German spy Hermann Goertz, Hayes prepared a plan for an invasion of Northern Ireland. It was called 'Plan Kathleen'. The proposed invasion force of some 50,000 German troops were to invade Ireland landing at Larne, Coleraine, Derry and Sligo and a 5,000-strong IRA force would move from South Donegal and North Leitrim to meet them.[25] The idea was abandoned in 1940 when Goertz, who parachuted into Ireland to assess the situation, was arrested in a raid on the home of Stephen Carroll Held, an IRA member of German descent. The invasion plans were also seized in the raid.

During the Emergency, de Valera's Irish government adopted a strong policy against the IRA. Many were interned and some members were hanged. In 1940, Minister for Justice Gerald Boland ordered the arrest of Bundoran man Sean 'Shaw' Carty, who was working as a lifeguard on Bundoran beach at the time. These repressive measures by the government severely undermined the IRA, leading Boland to conclude that 'the IRA is dead' and that he had killed it.

Germany, meanwhile, still considered using Ireland as a platform for the invasion of Britain. 'Operation Green' was a full-scale operations plan. Although the main German attack was focused on the south of the island, Donegal Bay was considered as a site for an amphibious landing of German troops. On the others side of the war, 'Plan W' was a strategic plan for British forces to occupy all of the Irish Free State. This plan was actually drafted in secret talks with the Irish government to counteract any German invasion. This event would have seen British troops cross the Border and enter Donegal to repel any German forces.

Then in August 1942, an IRA unit from Ballyshannon attacked Belleek barracks. The RUC officers were awoken by the sound of gunfire and exploding grenades. The police officers returned fire. The IRA men cut the telephone wires to prevent reinforcements arriving. Guards in Ballyshannon attempted to detain a man but where forced to release him when his companions produced two pistols. These IRA men then escaped back across the Border into Northern Ireland.[26] The Irish government dispatched hundreds of soldiers to the shore up Border security after the incident.

Then the arrival of American troops in Northern Ireland prompted the IRA to renew its campaign, resolving to sabotage war industries and military installations. In 1942, the campaign escalated with attacks on police constables in Strabane, Dungannon and Belfast. Six IRA men were captured after a ferocious gun battle in Belfast and all were sentenced to death. After a petition was endorsed by more than two hundred thousand signatures calling for mercy, the sentences were commuted except for one. On 2 September 1942, Tom Williams was hanged in Belfast's Crumlin Road jail. The execution spurred more attacks by the IRA. Cross-Border attacks occurred in Culloville, County Armagh, and on 4 September 1942, Belleek RUC barracks was attacked. However, the arrest of many IRA leaders on both sides of the Border, coupled with the executions, effectively put an end to the IRA's campaign. By the end of the war, Northern Ireland was completely free of IRA activity.[27]

From then until the Border Campaign of the late 1950s, Northern Ireland enjoyed a comparative peace. Yet in 1945, Britain's first Ambassador to Ireland Sir John Maffey predicted that partition would 'cause guns to go off in Ireland once again. The Catholics of the North will call out to the Catholics of the South, saying, "We are only doing what you did in 1916. Are you going to leave us in the lurch?"[28] The Irish Anti-Partition League attempted to highlight grievances of the Catholic minority in Northern Ireland, such as the manipulation of local government boundaries to consolidate Unionist control. However, Brookeborough's indifference marginalised constitutional nationalists and allowed more radical players to step on to the stage.

A reinvigorated IRA resurfaced in the 1950s with a determined plan to 'liberate' pockets along the Border of Northern Ireland. 'Operation Harvest' was the codename given to the IRA's new Border campaign (1956-62). By making Northern Ireland ungovernable, the IRA hoped to force a British withdrawal from the North. The IRA planned to concentrate its campaign in the south Fermanagh area and create a liberated zone there. However, the successes of its flying columns during the 1919-21 War of Independence were not repeated this time. Many of the volunteers were from southern counties and were completely unfamiliar with the County Fermanagh terrain where many of the operations took place. The lack of local support, combined with internment on both sides of the Border, ensured that this campaign could only ever achieve a very limited success.

In the 1955 Westminster elections, however, Sinn Féin put forward two candidates for Mid-Ulster and Fermanagh-South Tyrone. They were Tom Mitchell and Philip Clarke, IRA prisoners in Crumlin Road jail. Their electoral success sent shockwaves throughout the Northern Irish political establishment. Westminster invoked an old statute that prevented any convicted felon from taking a parliamentary seat. A new by-election was scheduled for August of that year, a time when many Tyrone and Fermanagh people regularly holidayed in Bundoran. IRA volunteer Sean Donnelly was given the task of going to the seaside town to convince these Tyrone and Fermanagh voters to return home and cast their ballots. He was helped by 'Shaw' Carty and Master O'Brien as they scoured every guesthouse, caravan park and hotel in Bundoran. People from both counties returned home in their droves and this resulted in an even bigger victory for Tom Mitchell.

That electoral success brought more volunteers from all over the island into the IRA. From 1954 onwards, new training camps were set up. The arrival home from America of Seán Cronin, a former Irish Army officer, brought a new level of sophistication to IRA training methods. In 1956, the Army Council reactivated its campaign against the Stormont Government.[29] During January and February of 1957, there were incidents along the Donegal-Fermanagh Border. During one altercation in Pettigo, local residents threatened to 'take matters into their own hands'.[30]

At the age of eighteen, IRA Volunteer Dónal Donnelly from Omagh had been arrested during the first year of the IRA's 'Operation Harvest' campaign. Then four years later on 26 December 1960, St Stephen's Day, the RUC and B Specials began a massive manhunt when Donnelly made a daring escape from Crumlin Road jail in Belfast. He eventually made his was to his aunt's guesthouse in Bundoran's West End. Almost ten years later, the same guesthouse, Saint Enda's, was used as a safe house for the then IRA chief of staff Daithi O'Connell during the early part of the Troubles. After Donnelly's arrival, he met Philip Donoghue, a member of the IRA active service unit that operated along the Donegal-Fermanagh Border. Donoghue was present during the infamous raid on Brookeborough Barracks when Seán South and Fergal O'Hanlon were killed. Their funerals, attended by up to 50,000 people produced a strong emotional reaction among the public.

In order to prevent IRA units from pouring across the Border, a number of bridges in County Fermanagh were destroyed. The RUC informed the Garda sergeant in Kiltyclogher that many of the roads between Leitrim and Fermanagh were to be blown up. The IRA had considerable support in the Kiltyclogher area. This occasionally led to cross-Border incursions by the RUC.

During one particular firefight between the IRA and the security forces in August 1961, the RUC crossed the Border to search for the IRA unit. They were confronted by the Gardaí and forced to turn back 'with a very bad grace'.[31] The following day, a Detective Garda found a group of men (presumed to be B Specials) setting up ambush points in a field near Kiltyclogher. The Chief Superintendent in Sligo contacted his RUC counterpart in Enniskillen and was assured that the RUC would not cross the Border again.[32]

By 1960, the IRA's Border campaign was fizzling out. In November 1961, Minister for Justice Charles Haughey established military courts, which handed down long prison sentences to convicted IRA men. The ability of the IRA to sustain its campaign was also thwarted by the use of internment on both sides of the Irish Border. In 1962, the IRA Army Council issued a statement that it was ending its 'campaign of resistance to British occupation'.[33]

Have They Gone Away?

When the Border campaign ended in 1962, Cathal Goulding became Chief of Staff and he set about moving the IRA away from the armed struggle towards socialist politics. However as Northern Ireland erupted between 1969 and 1970, the IRA split into two factions – the Official IRA and Provisional IRA.

The Provisionals, under Ruairí Ó Brádaigh, were solely focused on re-establishing the IRA's military capability to instigate a new, armed campaign. From the outset it pinned its colours to the mast: 'We declare our allegiance to the 32-County Republic proclaimed at Easter 1916, established by the first Dáil Éireann in 1919, overthrown by force of arms in 1922 and suppressed to this day by the existing British-imposed Six-County and 26-County partition states.'

To accomplish its aims, the Provisional IRA was modelled initially on the British army, with commands, brigades and company structures. It was led by a seven-member Army Council; which was chosen by the 12-member Army Executive; which, in turn, was elected by the General Army Council.[1]

The PIRA consisted of both a northern and southern command. The Northern Command included all six counties in Northern Ireland, plus the five Border counties in the Republic. The Southern Command included the rest of the counties in the Republic of Ireland. The Southern Command facilitated the storage and movement of armaments, funding and volunteer training.

The founding membership of the Provisionals included families with long ties to the IRA dating back to the 1920s, and in some cases back to the Fenians of the 1860s.[2] Recent research has shown that in many cases where a family had a history of paramilitary involvement, this could then lead directly the next generation getting involved also with paramilitary groups.[3]

As the Battle of the Bogside raged in Derry during August 1969, the Taoiseach Jack Lynch ordered the Irish Army to set up field hospitals and refugee camps along the Border in Donegal. Large numbers of refugees began streaming over the Border and Finner Camp was used as a temporary shelter. Despite the primitive conditions, one refugee is reputed to have asked if they could come again next year.

Irish Army soldiers and the refugees from Northern Ireland

Meanwhile, both Unionists and Nationalists interpreted Lynch's 'stand idly by' speech as meaning that the Irish Army would invade Northern Ireland. Lynch subsequently clarified the Government's position in late November 1969: 'We have long abandoned the idea of using force to solve partition, Force would accentuate the problem rather than remove it, and force would not be militarily successful.'[4]

However, plans were indeed drawn up for Irish troops to cross the Border in order to protect nationalist areas in the event of a complete breakdown of the civil order in Northern Ireland. Codenamed 'Exercise Armageddon' it was designed to draw Northern Ireland security forces away from Border towns, allowing Irish troops to be established there. Concerns were raised that the British might simply cut off Donegal from the rest of the Republic by moving from Belleek to seize Ballyshannon.[5] In this event, the army in Donegal would revert to a campaign of guerrilla warfare. The military planners eventually concluded that intervention would be 'militarily unsound' and that there would be grave consequences for the State and the northern nationalists it intended to assist. According to one local republican, however, some members of the IRA received training in weapons use from soldiers based at Finner Camp.[6]

It was not long before the conflict claimed its first victim on the southern side of the Border. On 20 October 1969, Thomas McDowell, a member of the UVF, was killed while attempting to place a bomb at Ballyshannon power station. McDowell was also a member of the Reverend Ian Paisley's Free Presbyterian Church and of a group calling itself the Ulster Protestant Volunteers. He worked in a quarry and had previous experience with explosives and he was already implicated in the bombings that forced the moderate Unionist Captain Terence O'Neill to resign as Prime Minister of Northern Ireland. In 1969, members of both the Ulster Volunteer Force (UVF) and the Ulster Protestant Volunteers (UPV) planted bombs at the electricity substation at Castlereagh in east Belfast. As a result, large areas of Belfast were quite literally left in the dark. At first, the IRA was blamed, but it was later established that the bombings were part of a Loyalist campaign to undermine O'Neill's government, whose moderate political reforms were seen by some Unionists as a sop to Republican violence. O'Neill said in his memoirs that those UVF bombings 'quite literally blew me out of office'.[7]

In the lead up to the Ballyshannon attack, Thomas McDowell scouted the area looking for suitable targets. He and two other men stayed in a local bed and breakfast establishment posing as anglers. They settled on the power station since McDowell had the Castlereagh experience of bombing electrical installations. However, as McDowell was placing the bomb, a car drove past and he was caught in its headlights. He ducked for cover but in doing so, he grabbed one of the power lines that were carrying thousands of volts of electricity. The injuries were horrific; he had burns to most of his body and internal organs. He clung on to life for three days in the Sheil Hospital in Ballyshannon under armed guard.[8] In a cruel twist of fate, the Gardaí who attended the scene did not know if the seriously injured bomber was a Catholic or a Protestant. They called a local priest who administered the Last Rites at the scene, something that was no doubt anathema to a Free Presbyterian.

By the end of 1970, several of the Civil Rights objectives had been conceded. However, by that time, events in Northern Ireland had developed their own momentum. From 1972 onwards, the conflict progressively took the form of violence between the Provisional IRA and the security forces, with intermittent bloody involvement by loyalist paramilitaries.

The situation in Northern Ireland had already begun to have a destabilising effect across the Border. Due to the IRA's presence in Border towns such as Bundoran, a series of raids were carried out in South Donegal in December 1971 on the direct orders of Minister for Justice Des O'Malley. The arrest of prominent republicans Joe O'Neill Peter Gilmartin and Patrick Hughes in dawn raids sparked riots in both Bundoran and Ballyshannon. O' Neill, and his co-accused were charged with possession of illegal firearms. The court was held in Bundoran Garda barracks, which was protected by around two hundred gardaí. During the hearing, a crowd of several hundred people gathered outside. The three men were greeted with cheers as they left the station.

The following excerpt from Time magazine describes the scene that ensued: 'Irish police arrested three IRA suspects on charges of illegally possessing arms and ammunition at their homes in Bundoran, a favourite frontier sanctuary of gunmen. One of them was Joseph O'Neill, a prominent IRA political leader. The response to the arrests was a series of fierce riots of IRA sympathisers in Bundoran and nearby Ballyshannon. Gangs of youths in Ballyshannon stoned the gardaí, and more than a hundred additional police had to be brought in to deal with at least five hundred protesters.'[9]

Violent scenes at 'The Siege of Ballyshannon" (Courtesy of Marc McMenamin)

In fact, Irish troops were eventually used to defend Ballyshannon Garda station against rampaging youths.[10] One of the guards present during that incident recalls that 'one man who had great nerve climbed into the lorry that had the rocks in it and drove it off the bridge. That took some of the pressure off us.' He also noted that 'there were some locals involved but there was a fair few rioters from North Donegal and Northern Ireland'.[11] Sinn Féin president Ruairí O Brádaigh stated the arrest of the three republicans in County Donegal was a blatant act of collaboration with the British regime in the six counties. Former Fianna Fáil minister and now leader of Aontacht Éireann (United Ireland) Kevin Boland even claimed that the Ballyshannon incident made it plain that talk of civil war was 'not a warning but a threat'.[12]

Prior to the riots, there had been rumours throughout Bundoran and Ballyshannon that internment was to be introduced in the south, just as it had been brought in north of the Border during the previous August. The Ballyshannon Cumann of Sinn Féin had a leak from an informer within the government. According to Joe O'Neill, 'word came down from Dublin, from a source within the Government that there was going to be internment'.[13]

However, none of the three main parties in the Dáil favoured internment and the raids were widely seen as the government's best attempt to contain the IRA problem without going down that road. Bundoran and Ballyshannon had both seen a significant amount of IRA activity due to the proximity to the Border and the relocation of IRA activists to avoid internment. Bundoran was already widely regarded by as a safe haven for IRA members who were still on active service in Northern Ireland. According to Jim White, former Ballyshannon Town Commissioner and Fine Gael TD from 1973 to 1982, 'Ballyshannon was never an IRA town or never had that name as a republican town; not like Bundoran where there were always marches and that.'[14]

Dáithí Ó Conaill, elected vice-president of Provisional Sinn Féin in 1970, was teaching woodwork at the Donegal VEC technical school in Ballyshannon at this time. He lived with his wife, a cousin of Provisional Sinn Féin president Ruairí Ó Brádaigh, in a small cottage beside Finner camp on the main road between Bundoran and Ballyshannon. A native of Cork, he was previously involved in the IRA's Border campaign when he was shot eight times during the infamous raid on Brookeborough Barracks on New Year's Day 1957 in which both Seán South and Fergal O'Hanlon were killed. Ó Conaill led a covert life as a leading member of the Provisionals.[15] Along with local Bundoran republican Joe O'Neill, he attempted to import arms from Czechoslovakia into Ireland via Amsterdam.[16]

Following the Ballyshannon riots of December 1971, the government in Dublin asked the army and police chiefs for detailed reports and assessments of the prospect of similar events breaking out in other Border towns. The attack marked a new development in the republic. With the hindsight of history, this situation did not escalate but it did prompt the state to ramp up its Border security measures. The 1972 Offences against the State (Amendment) Act meant that IRA suspects could be convicted on the word of a Garda Chief Superintendent. Convictions could also be secured if suspects were unable to account for their movements. The introduction of this legislation led to the incarceration of senior IRA figures such as Ruairí O Brádaigh. In 1973, a Bundoran-based Garda sergeant saw several men leave a well-known republican bar and get into several cars before moving off in the direction of Ballyshannon. The Gardaí pulled over one of the cars and discovered 250-pounds of gelignite and more than four thousand rounds of ammunition. One of the occupants, when questioned, gave his name as Martin Mc Guinness. He received a six-month jail sentence.[17]

Bundoran became an increasingly popular holiday destination for the Catholic community in Northern Ireland during the Troubles, due to its proximity to the Border and the obvious appeal of escaping sectarian violence during the summer months. Writer Nell McCafferty confirms this: 'Crossing the Border into the Republic always felt like an escape – a relief, a flight towards sanctuary, a release of tension – even though the people of the Republic might resent the implications of a Northern accent, bringing trouble down their way.'[18]

On the other hand, overseas visitors, particularly those from Scotland, and 'upmarket' tourists from Dublin stopped coming. Bundoran's increasing reputation as a 'republican town' also deterred many potential tourists from other parts of Britain.

In 1972, Operation Motorman was launched by the British army to quash the 'no-go areas' of Belfast, Derry and other towns. That brought a fresh influx of what were by then, relatively experienced guerrilla fighters. They brought a new level of militancy in their campaign against the North's security forces. The level of attacks on Belleek Barracks increased dramatically. Some IRA volunteers also came to Bundoran from southern counties such as Clare and Limerick. Fresh from training in explosives and weapon handling and operating from Border billets in Bundoran, Ballyshannon and Kiltyclogher, they began coordinating attacks on security targets just across the Border in Fermanagh. Safe houses were reactivated. Donnelly's in Bundoran's West End, where Dáithí O Conaill laid low for a time, and the Kiltyclogher home of Katie B. Keeny, a niece of Sean Mac Diarmada, had housed fugitive Volunteers during previous IRA campaigns. British security forces identified five active service units (ASUs) operating along the Border at this time, including one based in Bundoran.[19] The same file contained a list of names and addresses of suspected IRA members based in the Border area.

The presence of high-profile Republicans in Bundoran prompted the British security forces to keep a close eye on activities in the seaside town. During the 1970s, SAS soldiers crossed into Border towns like

117

Bundoran that were known for their republican sympathies. Some of these undercover soldiers dressed like businessmen, while others grew their hair and moustaches to blend in with the crowds and gather low-level intelligence.[20]

Meanwhile, following complaints of torture of detainees arrested by the British army in the North's internment swoops of August 1971, the Irish government brought a case against Britain for the human rights violations. Aidan Browne, the Senior Counsel on the case, interviewed alleged torture victims, including one man from Bundoran who had been arrested in Northern Ireland and beaten in custody. Browne was also Junior Counsel for the prosecution in the Arms Trial proceedings against former government ministers Charles Haughey and Neil Blaney. He was also married to the grand-niece of Patrick Fergus, the nationalist politician from north Leitrim.

Pictured are Neil Blaney, Kevin Boland, Sean McEniff (Bundoran) and Charles Haughey during the 1970 Arms Trial. Haughey and Blaney went on trial accused of importing guns for distribution in Northern Ireland. They were later acquitted.

Some of the 'five techniques' described in the Irish Government's case against Britain would later be applied in other theatres of war such as Iraq and Afghanistan. These included being forced to stand for hours in a 'stress position,' water-boarding, hooding, white noise, sleep deprivation and the denial of food and water. The European Court of Human Rights found five interrogation methods used by the United Kingdom in its counter-terrorism efforts against the IRA to be violations of Article 3, deeming it 'inhuman' and 'degrading' but not torture.[21]   Following the revelation of more evidence, an appeal of that finding is being considered at present.

The level of attacks on the Donegal-Fermanagh Border prompted the British to ask the Irish Government to clear the wood on the southern side of the Border near Belleek to prevent the IRA from launching rocket attacks. The appendix of the document making the request highlights the catalogue of events.[22]

- 3 August 1972: 20 shots fired from Éire.
- 26 August 1972: 2 Gunmen fired 4 shots at RUC station.
- 31 August 1972: 4 gunmen fired 12 shots at RUC station.
- 5 October 1972: 1 shot fired at foot patrol from the area of the fort.
- 28 November 1972: Gunman fired a rocket and about 30 shots at RUC station. One member of the RUC was killed.
- 28 February 1973: Gunmen fired a rocket at RUC station.
- 30 March 1973: 10-15 automatic rounds fired at RUC patrol.

Security alert on the Donegal-Fermanagh Border

There were many other incidents of cross-Border attacks on Belleek. On 4 November 1971, gunmen placed a bomb in the foyer of the Carlton Hotel. After they crossed the Border, British troops and the RUC opened fire on the fort, which the IRA unit was using as a staging post. A member of the RUC was hurled across the road by the blast as he was directing traffic away from the hotel.[23]

Aftermath of the explosion at the Carlton Hotel

A week later, the RUC barracks was attacked from positions on the southern side of the Border. Soldiers in the barracks returned fire. Three IRA men were believed to have fired from high ground on the southern side of the Border overlooking the station.[24] In September 1973, another bomb wrecked windows in the Carlton Hotel and a second bomb caused considerable damage to the Post Office and surrounding buildings.[25] In November 1973, Belleek's RUC station was attacked again by rockets.

The plight of the village was highlighted by Omagh-born writer Benedict Kiely, who was scathing of the IRA in his writings: 'When you consider that the IRA attack a little village like Belleek and they blew up the hotel at the bridge for about the fifth time, and then they blow up, to judge by their names, a series of shops obviously owned by Nationalists and Catholics, and then issue a statement saying that they will fight until Britain realises that she must leave Ireland. So, remember the jokes that one used to make about the British army: the British were always so clever to get people to do their fighting for them in Europe, that they would fight Hitler to the last Frenchman; but I think the IRA are going to fight Britain to the last house in Belleek. Well if that's not comic, I don't know what is.'[26]

Despite the continuing violence and suffering of the period, other incidents worth recording did occasionally occur. During the early days of the Troubles, local IRA units often attacked the Customs huts on the Border at Belleek. Some of the Customs officers did not vociferously oppose them, possibly because one of them is alleged to have secured a lucrative contract to provide the huts and each burning brought more money for the supplier.[27] On one occasion, a local IRA unit arrived to burn down the hut. After ordering the officers outside, they doused the hut with petrol. Then they realised that they had no means of setting fire to it. They had to borrow matches from one of the Customs officers to complete the task.[28] On another occasion, a well-known nationalist was stopped and searched on the street in Belleek by British soldiers. He remonstrated with them in Irish (Gaelic) and was quite surprised when one of the soldiers corrected his grammar.

In 1971, Taoiseach Jack Lynch informed the Dáil that British troops had crossed the Border into the South on forty occasions between August 1969 and October 1971. He also stated that there were seventeen known occasions where British Army aircraft had flown over Irish airspace.[29] In 1973, senior security officials in the Northern Ireland Office outlined the problem that policing the Border represented for the British security forces: 'the Border is over three hundred miles long; in many places it passes through difficult terrain and is not clearly delineated on the ground; moreover different maps give varying information on its location. Apart from authorised Border crossings, there are 187 unapproved roads crossing the Border as well as many tracks and farm trails."[30]

The early 1970s saw some of the most violent events of the Troubles. The death toll at the end of 1970 was twenty-nine. By 1972 it had risen to four hundred and ninety six.[31] This was the bloodiest year of the Troubles, encapsulated by two terrible days in particular, Bloody Sunday in Derry and Bloody Friday in Belfast.

Tensions increased along the Border and, amid a climate of fear and anxiety, the security presence was stepped up on both sides. Michael Leonard, a 23-year-old cattle dealer from Tievemore near Pettigo, was shot dead by RUC officers on 17 May 1973, during a high speed chase along a Border road near Belleek. He was not a member of the IRA, and his reluctance to stop was prompted by the fact that he had been disqualified from driving. As the car chase neared the Border, one of the RUC officers fired a single shot that fatally wounded him. The coroner said that it was a 'million to one chance he had been killed'.[32]

On 30 August 1973, two carloads of IRA men crossed the Border at Pettigo to plant bombs in the nearby Post Office and Customs station in Tullyhommon. The Post Office staff were lined up and asked for their names and addresses. When the owner, a UDR member, gave his name, the IRA men tried to shoot him but he escaped to his house a hundred yards away where he returned fire. A 13-year-old boy was wounded in the arm during the exchange. A

British army bomb disposal unit later attempted to remove the bomb. However, Staff-Sergeant Ronald Beckett (37) was killed when the 20lb bomb exploded as he dragged it from the Post Office. He was married with two children. He was the tenth bomb-disposal specialist to die in Northern Ireland.[33]

According to State papers from 1977, the IRA had around two hundred and fifty hard-core activists in the Border counties. This included a Bundoran-based active service unit.[34] By the late 1970s, the IRA had begun to imitate the SAS in the Border areas, operating at night, laying mines and preparing other booby traps for the security forces.[35] The violence occasionally spilled over the Border. On 24 August 1979, an off-duty Garda in Bundoran noticed a well-known IRA man in a car with two others. Sometime later, he noticed that the car, now empty, had stopped several miles south of Bundoran near the turn-off for Mullaghmore, County Sligo. He noted its registration and ran a check. The yellow Ford Cortina was registered at Carrick-on-Shannon, County Leitrim. Unknown to the Gardaí at the time, this car was being used in surveillance for a potential attack on Lord Mountbatten, a member of the British royal family. Three days later, on 27 August 1979, the IRA assassinated Mountbatten near his holiday home at Classiebawn Castle in Mullaghmore.

Gardaí based in Bundoran had routinely patrolled Mullaghmore harbour but Mountbatten did not want a heavy security detail following him around. That day he had gone out on his boat which had been booby-trapped with an IRA bomb which was detonated from the shore. Following the explosion, the bodies of Mountbatten, his grandson Nicholas Knatchbull and his daughter Lady Brabourne were taken to Finner camp. The Royal Navy sent helicopters to remove the bodies. Paul Maxwell, a 15-year-old boy from Enniskillen, was also killed in the blast. Later that same day, the IRA killed eighteen British soldiers when they staged two coordinated bomb attacks near Warrenpoint, County Down. Writer Benedict Kiely, who had a strong connection with Bundoran, spoke of his brother Gerard's friendship with Mountbatten: 'The murder of that aged man, who had so loved and trusted Ireland, afflicted him with a sad silence into which one did not dare to intrude.'[36] The outrage was palpable. An employee of Bundoran's Allied Irish Bank wrote a letter to Timothy Knatchbull's aunt: 'My anger and disgust is such that I feel I must write... I am absolutely ashamed to be a member of a race which can commit such an outrage. I can assure you that this feeling is shared by everyone I have met in the last few days... Please try to forgive us.'

As the bloodiest decade in the Troubles came to a close, a new campaign was emerging from within the prisons of Northern Ireland.

It would propel the Republican cause onto the political stage and have far-reaching consequences for this Border area, making the year 1981 a watershed for the Troubles. IRA hunger striker Bobby Sands was elected as MP for Fermanagh and South Tyrone a month before he starved to death on 5 May 1981. Sinn Féin candidate Owen Carron held the seat in another by-election and this electoral success helped to develop serious political ambitions, setting a path that would eventually see Martin McGuinness sharing office with Ian Paisley. During the campaign, members of the Bundoran H-Block Committee had entered Classiebawn Castle and locked themselves in the tower room to protest in support of Bobby Sands. Classiebawn was chosen as a 'symbol of British Imperialism in Ireland'. The siege ended quickly and peacefully.

Then in June 1981, Fianna Fáil Taoiseach Charles Haughey called a general election. The National H-block Committee nominated nine prisoner candidates to run for the Dáil. They included four hunger strikers: Kieran Doherty, Martin Hurson, Joe McDonnell and Kevin Lynch. Both Hurson and Doherty had strong connections with Bundoran and there were tense scenes as Haughey campaigned in the Border counties. Supporters of the republican prisoners attempted to interrupt his rallies with repeated chants of 'Gardaí RUC' and violence often broke out. Haughey arrived in Bundoran to speak from a mobile platform and there were shouts and jeering from the H-Block supporters during his speech. He was hit in the face with an egg when he spoke at Ballyshannon, and violent scuffles broke out between the Gardaí and H-block supporters.

As an outcome of the political support garnered by the H-Blocks campaign, the IRA began to reassess its strategy as the 1980s progressed. It decided on a two-fold approach to achieving its goals: electoral activity combined with military operations. It was summed up in Republican leader Danny Morrison's memorable reference to having 'a ballot paper in one hand and an Armalite in the other'. Yet the legacy of the hunger strikes continued to cause controversy in Bundoran throughout the 1980s. The presence of the New York Police Department's Emerald Society Pipe Band at the Hunger Strike Commemoration in Bundoran, held at the end of August, caused an international diplomatic incident. The Irish Government of Dr. Garret FitzGerald asked the American authorities to prevent the NYPD band marching. One of the Emerald Society pipers recalls a trip to Bundoran where the local Gardaí denounced them as traitors. It should be noted that, by that time, eleven Gardaí had been killed as a result of the Provisional IRA's campaign. In 1986, Gardaí on duty at the H-Block Hunger Strike Commemoration in Bundoran heard lightly veiled threats against them from two of the speakers.[37]

According to an article by Professor Andrew Silke, Terrorism Studies program director at the University of East London, senior figures within the IRA held an emergency summit in a public house in Bundoran in 1981 to discuss the movement's finances. The PIRA leadership discussed how irregular resourcing was causing considerable problems for the group. They concluded that, to fight a long war, a more prescribed system would have to be implemented. The result of this meeting was the inclusion of expert accountants, businessmen and solicitors to revamp the movement's finances and offer guidance on how the paramilitaries' assets should best be managed. Research by the murdered journalist Veronica Guerin revealed that the PIRA's financial interests included 'extensive property holdings, guest houses, pubs, taxi and hackney services, courier services and a number of video outlets'. By the mid-1990s these businesses provided regular cash income and were an ideal cover for laundering money. In an intricate scheme, the true ownership of these businesses was concealed in a multitude of holding companies.[38]

In 1982, Ian Paisley acknowledged Bundoran's reputation as a bastion of militant republicanism: 'Without a shadow of a doubt, well-known IRA nests and holes such as Buncrana, Bundoran, Clones and Drogheda would have long since been cleaned out and a buffer zone established right along the Border.'[39]

That same year on 30 April, Private Colin Phillip Clifford (21) of the 1st Royal Hampshire Regiment was killed when a 1000lb culvert bomb exploded when his eight-man patrol passed through the Meenatully, near Belleek. The landmine was detonated by a command wire from across the Border.

In 1983, South Donegal was once again the focus of international scrutiny when the Fleet Street newspapers carried front-page pictures of two men who were alleged to be part of an assassination squad aimed at British political leaders. Both turned up a few days later in their home towns of Tralee and Ballyshannon, claiming to have been there all along. In December, a gun battle between the IRA and the British Army on the Border near Belleek.[40] On 17 August 1984, the British army defused a 100lb anti-personnel mine found at Belleek after an exchange of shots with IRA men.[41]

British Army helicopter on the Fermanagh Border

Another incident of note involved IRA volunteer Antoine Mac Giolla Bhrighde (aka Tony Mc Bride). He had worked in Bundoran as a barman after he was court-martialed from the Irish Army after being arrested in Northern Ireland in possession of weapons. Bundoran solicitor Peter Brady represented him at his court-martial hearing. He died on 2 December 1984 near the Fermanagh Border. According to the book Lost Lives, 'he was shot in disputed circumstances in an incident... which left two members of the IRA dead together with a member of the SAS'.

Then in 1987, Bundoran councilor Joe O'Neill proposed a vote of sympathy for the nine IRA Volunteers killed by the SAS in an ambush at Loughgall, County Armagh. O' Neill said that many of those men holidayed in Bundoran and some of them had caravans there. Only one other councilor supported the motion which was not passed.[42]

Meanwhile, the war raged on in Belleek. 'Expert IRA snipers had the advantage of surprise, local knowledge and local help. Such an attack mounted from a carefully chosen spot is almost impossible to prevent. The alternative is not to patrol the streets.'[43] Lance-Corporal Hewitt was just 21 when he arrived in Belleek with the Royal Green Jackets. On one of his first patrols, he made his way towards the corner outside the Carleton Hotel. His role was to cover the patrol as it made its way from the barracks to the main street. The army were most venerable approaching the bottom of Cliff Road where they were in full view from Belleek Fort. Unknown to Hewitt, an IRA sniper lay in wait near the fort. He fired one round which struck the soldier in the head. Security forces believed that an Enfield 303 rifle with a telescopic sight was used. [44] The corner where he was hit was chillingly referred to as 'splat corner' by the security forces based in Belleek.[45] Today a sculpture marks the spot where the young soldier died.

In 1988, a man from Belleek was jailed for three years for possession of a weapon. In his defense, he said he was ordered to pick up two men at a car park in Ballyshannon and then they proceeded to Clyhore, near the Border. The two got out of the van and he was told to drive up the road and check for police patrols. He told the court that he heard a loud bang and saw the two men running towards his van. They got in and he drove them out of the area.[46]

Also in 1988, the IRA killed a former RUC officer in Ballintra, County Donegal. His death caused widespread revulsion. It was not the first atrocity attributed to the unit. The group was linked to the deaths of two Protestant civilians shortly after they drove out of Belleek barracks where they were working contractors. They also killed an innocent young girl from Leggs, near Belleek. She was shot while sitting in her father's car with her fiancé outside her home. The IRA said that their intended target was her brother, who they claimed was in the UDR. However, the family had no connection with the security forces. The victim was twenty-one years old at the time. Her employer in a local pharmacy shop said, 'She was the kind of girl who was always smiling. I don't think I ever heard her say a bad word about anyone. People are just horrified.'

The fall-out from these events was decisive. In a statement, the IRA leadership said it had 'stood down and disarmed' the west Fermanagh brigade behind the killings. The Irish Times added, 'There is considerable speculation that the disbanded unit was also responsible for the Enniskillen Remembrance Day bombing, but security forces say they have no evidence to confirm this.' The unit was disbanded in the run-up to the Sinn Féin Ard Fheis before European and local elections later that year. Sinn Féin was keen to build on its political successes and quickly moved to distance itself from operations mounted by the group.

In 1989, an anonymous document handed to journalist David McKittrick provided photographs names, addresses and dates of birth of alleged IRA suspects living in south Donegal, including twelve living in Ballyshannon and nine in Bundoran. The document was headed, 'South Donegal – Stop and Hold'.[47] Councillor Joe O'Neill claimed the photographs had come from Ballyshannon Garda Station,[48] but McKittrick thought the leak came from a loyalist source.[49]

Some key events in 1990 signaled a new phase in the conflict. Relationships between the British Tory government and Unionists had begun to unravel after the 1985 Anglo-Irish Agreement established a constitutional role for Dublin in Northern Ireland affairs. As a result, there was less conviction in the constitutional guarantee of the Unionist veto over further change. In November 1990, Northern Ireland Secretary of State Peter Brooke said Britain had 'no selfish or economic interest' in the Union. This was seen as a means for bolstering the constitutional approach of SDLP leader John Hume.

There was change on the ground along the Border as well. By 1992, the British Army had relocated many of its checkpoints to avoid attacks launched from within the Republic. One was moved five miles inside County Fermanagh. The IRA had begun to use long-range weapons, such as mortars and heavy machine guns. They also employed a new and extremely controversial tactic, the proxy bomb. Benedict Kiely's 1977 novel, Proxopera, predicted the events that took place thirteen years later when the IRA began forcing people to drive car bombs into British army Border installations. The most notorious of these incidents occurred when the IRA targeted Patsy Gillespie, a Catholic from Derry's Shantallow area who worked as a cook in Fort George British army base in the city. On 24 October 1990, Gillespie was forced into a van loaded with 1,000 pounds (450 kg) of explosives and told to drive to the permanent Border checkpoint at Coshquin on the Buncrana Road. The bomb detonated while he was still in the driver's seat and he was killed along with five soldiers.[50]

A civilian worker for the RUC in County Fermanagh was also forced by the IRA to carry a bomb in her handbag into the police station in Belleek. Family members were held hostage while the woman carried out the instructions.[51] Once there, she raised the alarm and the bomb caused only superficial damage. The incident was widely condemned in the media and by politicians.[52]

Then on the night of 6 February 1992, IRA volunteer Joseph McManus of Sligo was part of an IRA unit that took over a house in Scardens Upper between Belleek and Kesh. A bogus call was made to the local warden that there was a dog worrying sheep. The warden who responded was a part-time lance-corporal in the UDR. As his van approached the house, the IRA opened fire. He was hit in the legs but returned fire with his personal protection weapon, killing McManus. One member of the IRA group was arrested in County Donegal after the incident. His trial made legal history when the three judges of the non-jury Special Criminal Court travelled from Dublin to Enniskillen to hear evidence from two prosecution witnesses. This was the first time judges from the Dublin court heard evidence in Northern Ireland under the Criminal Law Jurisdiction Act of 1976. One of them was Justice Frederick Morris, who would later head the Morris tribunal investigating Garda corruption in the Border areas.

During the early 2000s, a memorial plaque honouring IRA volunteers Antoine Mac Giolla Bhrighde (Anthony McBride), Kieran Fleming and Joseph McManus was placed at a site near where two Protestant civilians were ambushed in 1988. It caused an outcry. After some discussion, republicans decided to relocate the memorial. In a statement one of the relatives of the victims said they welcomed the decision to move the monument, which was causing great suffering the families: My mother died of ill health as a direct consequence of my father's murder... Nothing can bring them back but we want their memories to be kept with dignity.' In 2008, the appointment of Anthony McBride's sister to the four-member Victims Commission caused controversy after she described her brother as an IRA 'Volunteer' killed while on 'active service'.

In the lead-up to the historic ceasefire announcement of 1994, local IRA units stepped up their campaign along the Donegal-Fermanagh Border. In his book Deadly Beat, author Richard Latham, a former RUC officer who was stationed at Belleek from 1991 to 1996, indicated the dangers that officers faced: 'One day in August 1994, my colleagues were in the RUC station when a mortar bomb was planted outside, it was a barrack buster... The Army Technical officer later told us it was "an Act of God" it did not actually go off.'[53]

Finally, with just one hour to the ceasefire coming into effect on 31 August 1994, an IRA unit opened fire on Belleek barracks. Some homes were damaged by gunfire but no one was injured. The IRA 'cessation' of its military campaign marked the end of one process and the beginning of another. Although the ceasefire ended with the Canary Wharf bomb on 9 February 1996, talks continued and an agreement on power-sharing was concluded on Good Friday, 10 April 1998. By then, disgruntled IRA men and women were leaving the organisation to form the 'Real IRA', while other dissident republican organisations such as the Continuity IRA (CIRA) remained active throughout this time. In 1996, a bomb had ripped apart the Killyhevlin hotel in Enniskillen. The attack was the first to occur in Northern Ireland since the Provisional IRA proclaimed its 1994 ceasefire. Suspicion quickly fell on a group known as the Irish National Republican Army, a purported military wing of Republican Sinn Féin. Bundoran councillor Joe O'Neill denied that RSF were involved in the incident.[54]

However, one of the most bizarre events concerning local republicans involved an American businessman named David

Rupert, who was linked to the FBI, MI5, An Garda Síochána and its Special Branch, Crime and Security Branch (Garda Intelligence unit), the Continuity IRA and the Real IRA. Rupert became a well-known figure in the town since he first arrived in August 1992 with Linda Vaughan, a lobbyist for Noraid, the pro-Republican Irish-American fundraising body. At 6ft 7 inches, Rupert was difficult to miss. He has been bankrupt three times and married four times. He subsequently turned out to be an informer for the FBI and the British Secret Services. He was called as a witness for the prosecution in the trial of Michael McKevitt, alleged leader of the Real IRA which had carried out the 1998 Omagh bombing that killed twenty nine people and two unborn babies. McKevitt was sentenced to twenty years imprisonment in 2003 for being a member of the IRA and directing terrorism. The file entitled 'The Department of Public Prosecution Verses Michael McKevitt' provides an interesting insight into the very unusual character of David Rupert.

Linda Vaughan was a guest speaker at the Hunger Strike Commemoration ceremony in Bundoran. That was where Rupert met a number of prominent Republicans, including Joe O'Neill. Special Branch detectives who spotted them together, then became interested in the mysterious American. They contacted the FBI, which then invited Rupert to provide information about his Irish republican contacts. Rupert agreed to do so in return for money. He is also alleged to have had Mafia connections and a background in smuggling. According to 'Black Operations: The Secret War' Against the Real IRA, by John Mooney and Michael O' Toole, Rupert was 'colourful, entertaining and bright, he was also a philanderer and con artist. His professional life had been a disaster. In his formative years in business, Rupert proved himself ruthless and capable of anything. He betrayed anyone who trusted him; there was nothing he wouldn't do.'[55]

After agreeing to spy for the FBI, Rupert came to Ireland several more times. He became involved in fundraising activities in North America and achieved a position of trust within Republican Sinn Féin. He also met senior figures in the Continuity Irish Republican Army (CIRA) in Bundoran.[56] In 1996, he leased the Drowes bar in Tullaghan, County Leitrim. The pub also had a caravan park out the back. During McKevitt's trial, Rupert referred to it as 'my IRA theme park' because of its republican patrons. The FBI gave him $8,500 to pay for the lease.[57] Then in October 1996, Rupert returned to America. Yet from 1997 onward, he supplied both the FBI and the British Secret Services with information on republican activities. Rupert went on to infiltrate the Real IRA and gained McKevitt's trust.

During the court case, McKevitt's lawyers strongly argued that Rupert had no credibility as a witness. They claimed he was being paid as a witness by both the MI5 and the FBI (a total of £750,000).[58] They also claimed he stood to gain from giving of evidence against McKevitt. The court noted Rupert 'had a very chequered business career and operated close to the edge in many matters'. However, it rejected 'all criticisms made of the court's judgment in relation to the credibility of David Rupert'. Rupert is now said to be in a witness protection programme in the United States.

On 4 March 1996, John Fennel from Belfast, a founder member of the INLA, was found beaten to death in a caravan park in Bundoran. The incident was believed to have been connected to an ongoing internal feud in the INLA, a dissident republican paramilitary group linked to the Irish Republican Socialist Party which split from Official Sinn Féin in 1974. [59] In May 1998, dissident republicans claimed responsibility for an attempted mortar bomb attack on an RUC station in Belleek. Initial suspicion fell on the Continuity IRA, which had carried out previous attacks in Fermanagh.[60] A mortar exploded as RUC officers were leading people away from the area. Two mortar tubes aimed at the station had been discovered at 11pm in the garden of the Carlton Hotel. A wedding was taking place with more than two hundred and fifty guests. They and a hundred villagers had to be evacuated by the RUC.

Some of the major players in the peace process had local connections. American President Bill Clinton's Irish ancestor came from Fermanagh. Closer still, when Tony Blair addressed Dáil Éireann in 1998 he stated, 'Ireland... is in my blood. My mother was born in the flat above her grandmother's hardware shop in the main street of Ballyshannon in Donegal. She lived there as a child, started school there and only moved when her father died, her mother remarried and they crossed the water to Glasgow. We spent virtually every childhood summer holiday, up to when the Troubles really took hold, in Ireland.'

The Continuity Army Council was created from Republican Sinn Féin's split with the Provisionals in 1986. However, the military wing did not emerge until ten years later. Although Republican Sinn Féin denies any association with the CIRA, it is widely believed the relationship is symbiotic.[61] In 2009, security services were becoming increasingly concerned about the rise in CIRA activity in the Border area. According to a Sunday Times report, Gardaí believed CIRA has recruited new members who have no criminal records or prior associations with the IRA. They also believe CIRA were co-operating with other dissident groups that oppose the Good Friday Agreement.[62] A report by the Independent Monitoring Commission stated CIRA had sought to enhance its capabilities with the acquisition of weapons. The twenty-first IMC report (2009) concluded, 'CIRA also continued efforts to recruit and train members and in other ways to enhance its capability as a terrorist organisation. Overall, we concluded that CIRA remained a very serious threat.'[63]

A 2009 Donegal Democrat article, Continuity IRA Members Living in Donegal, then claimed that security services had identified twelve senior members of the Continuity IRA, including suspects living in Ballyshannon and Bundoran. Garda were instructed to monitor the movements of dissident republicans living in the Border area and were concerned about an increase in CIRA activity during the previous six months.[64] A leaked Garda intelligence memo also contained names, addresses and details of vehicles used by CIRA suspects living in counties Tyrone, Fermanagh, Donegal and Cavan.[65]

Republican Colour Party parading in Bundoran, August 2013

In November 2009, a group of armed men believed to be dissident republicans, arrived at the Garrison flat of a young Catholic PSNI officer. The young man had joined the police service a few weeks previously. However, acting on intelligence provided by the Gardaí, he had been removed from the house. A single shot was fired by the assailants at undercover police in the village. Police fired two shots in return but nobody was hurt. Soldiers from the elite Special

Reconnaissance Regiment were also believed to have monitored the suspects' movements for a number of days. It had been reported that the regiment was brought into Northern Ireland to help counter the growing threat from dissidents, particularly in Fermanagh where the threat to police officers was greatest. Five men were arrested after the attack.

Meanwhile, dissident republicans killed PSNI constable Stephen Carroll in Craigavon and British soldiers Patrick Azimkar and Mark Quinsey in Antrim in 2009. In 2010, they killed Kieran Doherty in Derry and mounted some forty serious gun and bomb attacks. That was also the year they began to target Catholic members of the PSNI. Constable Peadar Heffron was badly injured in a bomb attack in Randalstown, County Antrim. In 2011 Constable Ronan Kerr was killed in Omagh. On 1 November 2012, Prison Officer David Black, a 52-year-old father of two, was shot and killed by dissidents as he drove to work on the M1 in County Armagh.

In 2012, three of four main dissident republican groups coalesced in an effort to de-stabilise the power-sharing executive at Stormont.[66] The new group was formed by the Real IRA (RIRA), Republican Action Against Drugs (RAAD) and a combination of independent armed republican groups (sometimes referred to as Óglaigh na hÉireann). A statement given to Guardian journalist Henry McDonald said, 'The leadership of the Irish Republican Army remains committed to the full realisation of the ideals and principles enshrined in the Proclamation of 1916... The IRA's mandate for armed struggle derives from Britain's denial of the fundamental right of the Irish people to national self-determination and sovereignty. So long as Britain persists in its denial of national and democratic rights in Ireland, the IRA will have to continue to assert those rights.'[67]

Derry 2014

We Kept Our Heads Down

Farmer and part-time UDR soldier Tommy Fletcher was killed by the IRA on 1 March 1972 at his Frevagh home near Garrison. He was on his way to work when a group of men wearing stocking-masks stopped him. They brought him back to the farmhouse where they discovered and removed his pistol and shotgun. They told his wife they were taking Tommy away but he would not be harmed. He was then marched to a nearby field and shot fourteen times. The gunmen escaped across the Border. After his death, many Protestants from the area packed up their belongings and moved. The Border area was no longer a safe place for them.

The intimidation of Protestants living in the area was nothing new. During the War of Independence and the Civil War, Protestants often bore the brunt of nationalist ire. Fueled by stories of the 'Belfast pogroms' and the mass expulsion of Catholic workers from the Harland and Wolff shipyards, the Dáil ordered a boycott of Belfast goods in August 1920. This ultimately meant a boycott of some Protestant-owned businesses in Border counties. Protestants owned many of the local businesses in towns like Bundoran and Ballyshannon and many felt that their situation had become untenable as the Border was established. A large number sold up and moved to Northern Ireland or further afield. A mass exodus of Protestants from the South was taking place, with numbers declining by more than 33% between 1911 and 1926. The Protestant community continued to fragment after partition. Its decline was driven by a combination of economics, religion and intimidation. Of the 343,000 Protestants in 1901 in the areas that would become the Free State, only 144,000 were left in 1961 and they were concentrated in the Border counties of Donegal, Cavan and Monaghan.[1] The trend continued during the Troubles.

This migration of Protestants from the Donegal-Leitrim area had two distinct phases. The first was during the violent 1919-1923 period when many relocated to Fermanagh. The next phase took place during the Troubles with a further internal migration to 'safe' towns such as Ballinamallard.[2] Since partition, Border Protestants had found themselves a vulnerable minority in a politically and geographically contested area. Violence led to road closures and the build-up of military structures along the Border. A brooding atmosphere of silence, distrust and trepidation permeated the lives of all who lived near the boundary. This led many in the minority Protestant community to feel that they should be 'sharp with the eyes and slow with the tongue'.[3] They remained silent for many years. When a southern Church of Ireland minister was asked about his community's experience of the Troubles, he responded, 'we kept our heads down.'[4] Until recently, very little was known about their views or concerns.[5] The pain felt by many Border Protestant communities during the Troubles goes far beyond the numbers of fatalities or physical injuries. In recent years, the population has stabilised and peace in Northern Ireland has improved self-confidence.[6]

The Plantation of Ulster saw new names take on the mantle of power in the area. The O'Donnells, Maguires and MacClancys were usurped by English and Scottish settlers such as the Brookes, Coles, Johnstons and Folliotts. Settler numbers in South Donegal made up just fifteen percent of the population. In parts of East Donegal, this was closer to fifty percent.[7] The first planters were encouraged to have 'ready in their houses at all times a convenient store of arms, wherewith they may furnish a competent number of men for their defense, which may be viewed and mustered (every half year), according to the manner of England'.[8] So the newly arrived Protestants settled on the best land and those Catholics who remained were marginalised to the less arable hills and bogs. The communal memory of these events bubbled for centuries.

In 1980, the Irish Times spoke to a Catholic farmer from Fermanagh: 'This is an area of disadvantaged land, bad land... Where you get good land you tend to get them (Protestants). They have maintained their advantage over the years.' It was an accepted practice that a farmer never sold land to 'the other side'. [9] There was deep suspicion and mistrust between both communities. 'All the time he's smiling at me I can feel the knife turning,' remarked one west Ulster Protestant about his Catholic neighbour during the 1950s.[10] Although land was a divisive issue, it also brought Catholic and Protestant farmers together in rural Border areas. Farmers routinely shared machinery, helped out at harvest time and looked out for their neighbour's livestock.[11]

County Fermanagh was radically transformed during the opening decades of the seventeenth century. After 1610, more than a thousand English and Scottish settlers arrived in the county. They dominated landholdings but sixty-three 'deserving Irish' also received small grants. The initial plan was to segregate both communities, but many native Irish continued to live and work on land granted to the settlers. More settlers arrived and consolidated their position by constructing fortified settlements such as Enniskillen, Newtownbutler and Lisnaskea. Dispossessed and discriminated against, the natives resented the settlers. Yet both communities appear to have co-existed in a tenuous peace.[12]

The first major fracture between both communities appeared during the 1641 Rebellion. Traditionally seen as a revolt against the Ulster plantation, it was instigated by insolvent families such as the

Maguires of Fermanagh. In Ulster, the rebellion quickly disintegrated into sectarian violence. The deaths of thousands of Protestants held a strong psychological effect on the new settlers as indicated by historian A.T.Q. Stewart: 'The fear which it inspired survives in the Protestant subconscious... Here, if anywhere, and the mentality of siege was born.'[13] One of the most notorious incidents involved a refugee convoy at Portadown, where about eighty Protestants were drowned in the River Bann. To this day, the Portadown District Orange Lodge carries a banner depicting the massacre when it marches on the Twelfth of July. Reprisals against the Irish living in planter-controlled districts followed, most notably the massacre of the residents of Islandmagee, County Antrim.[14]

Contemporary pamphlets claimed more than 100,000 settlers were murdered. Temple's Irish Rebellion (1646) said it was an attempt to exterminate the settler population and editions of Temple's book were reprinted and distributed throughout the seventeenth, eighteenth and nineteenth centuries. Recent research suggests the number of murdered settlers was around four thousand.[15] Even the erudite William Copeland Trimble's estimation of the number of casualties is high. His comprehensive History of Enniskillen, first published in 1919, states, 'It was estimated that 80,000 Protestants lost their lives in this effort to exterminate the British, but this number may be an exaggeration and 20,000 would be nearer the mark.' Trimble (1851-1941) was the owner of The Impartial Reporter newspaper in Enniskillen. Educated at Portora Royal School, he founded the Fermanagh Tenant Right Association in 1881 but he was strongly opposed to the Irish Land League. Trimble also opposed Home Rule and was a strong supporter of Sir Edward Carson's campaign, which began in Enniskillen on 18 September 1912. A troop of horse personally trained by Trimble met Carson and the Earl of Erne at Castlecoole and led them through the town. They retired to Portora Hill, where they watched 40,000 Orangemen and Unionists marched past in a defiant show of strength.

Reinforcing the conviction that Protestants were to be driven from their land, Grace Lovett's deposition on the 1641 Rebellion claimed the rebels 'tooke away the lease writeings, will and scripts that this deponent had that concerned the Estate of the said several parcels of land'.[16] Protestant churches were burned down and some victims were denied Christian burials.[17] Ann Blennerhasset's deposition claims that she heard some of Rory Maguire's men boast that they had hanged several Protestants in the churchyard of the parish where a Mr. Flack was minister. She also said Maguire had sent Flack and his wife, along with a group of other Protestants that included children, towards Ballyshannon under armed guard. Once out of Fermanagh, they were killed by the rebels.

Conor Rua Maguire was one of the leaders of the 1641 rebellion. He failed in his attempt to capture Dublin and was later captured and hanged. His brother Rory continued the fight. Enniskillen held out despite rebel efforts to starve the inhabitants. Not for the last time, Enniskillen became a haven for Protestant settlers in west Ulster. Rory Maguire attacked Monea Castle, where he 'slew and murthered eight Protestants'. The carnage continued. Sir John Hume built Tully castle in the early seventeenth century. During the rebellion, it was attacked and burned by Rory Maguire's men. According to one story, Lady Hume surrendered the castle on Christmas Eve 1641 on condition of safe conduct for the Protestant refugees within. However, Maguire's men allegedly 'stripped the inhabitants, except Lady Hume, of all their clothes, imprisoned them in the vaults and cellars'. The Maguires killed all sixteen men and sixty-nine women and children. Only the Humes were spared. However, eminent historians, such as Professor Lecky of Trinity College Dublin, have dismissed this account.[18] Castlecaldwell, (then known as Hasset's Fort) was also attacked by the rebels who drove off Francis Blennerhasset and his wife.

Tully Castle

In 1643, Ann Blennerhassett gave a deposition stating that during the rebellion, Rory Maguire sent her husband to Ballyshannon Castle, where he was shot and killed. Other local events during the 1641 Rebellion involved Colonel Nugent and 600 Irishmen who encircled Ballyshannon Castle but were beaten back by Sir Ralph Gore's forces. Colonel Manus O'Donnell also staged an unsuccessful attack on Gore's castle near Donegal.[19]

Propaganda about the rebellion based on the victims' depositions helped legitimise the appropriation of Catholic land in the Adventurers' Act. It also provided the pretext for Cromwell's bloody campaign in Ireland, which ended in 1653. The consequences of his violent crusade meant that many more Catholic landowners were forcibly removed from Ulster and banished 'to hell or to Connacht'.

Two hundred and sixty years later, the descendants of the men who had held Enniskillen mustered once more in defence of Ulster. The Ulster Volunteers were formed to resist Home Rule 'by all means which may be found necessary'. They were followed in 1914 by the establishment of the nationalist Irish Volunteers. Both groups grew rapidly and open drilling in public areas became a regular occurrence. Events had escalated a year earlier when almost half a million Ulster Protestants signed the Ulster Covenant.

The Great War postponed the impending hostilities between Nationalists and Unionists as thousands on both sides enlisted in the British Army. In September 1914, two hundred of the Fermanagh UVF enlisted at Finner camp. Both Unionists and Nationalists believed that loyalty to England would be rewarded politically when the war ended. Carson and Redmond appealed to Unionists and Nationalists respectively to enlist. By 1916, 22,000 members of Redmond's Irish Volunteers were in the British Army and 25,000 of Carson's Ulster Volunteers had also joined by this time. A further 48,000 Irishmen, mostly from the south and of no discernible political allegiance, also enlisted.[20]

Lord Kitchener, Secretary of State for War, made it clear from the outset that he wanted the Ulster Volunteers to enlist. He met Carson, who persuaded him to keep the UVF together as a unit. The UVF amalgamated with the Royal Inniskilling Fusiliers, the Royal Irish Fusiliers and the Royal Irish Rifles to become the 36th Ulster Division. After their training at Finner Camp, they left for France in 1915. At the Battle of the Somme on 1 of July 1916, the Ulstermen left their trenches and advanced on German positions. Many were mowed down by heavy machine-gun fire, yet they became the only British division to achieve some success on the day. The first day of the Battle of the Somme became the bloodiest day in the history of the British Army.[21]

Major Myles of the Donegal UVF was the grandson of Robert Myles, who had fought with the Inniskillings at Waterloo. His family was responsible for introducing electricity to Bundoran in 1910. Myles fought at the Battle of the Somme where he was company commander in the 11th Battalion of The Royal Inniskilling Fusiliers: 'On the morning of 1 July 1916 their task was to support another battalion in the attack at the Somme. It was their first big battle and they were full of fervour to prove their mettle. They had to attack one of the best-defended German positions. It was reached at a terrible sacrifice to men. Nothing was won but glory. Captain Myles was severely wounded and was awarded the Military Cross for his gallantry and leadership. Five hundred and seventy officers and men of the battalion were killed or wounded and the losses of that fateful morning brought mourning and sadness to many Donegal homes.'[22]

The family military tradition continued and Myles's nephew Robert won the Military Cross when serving with the 6th Battalion of the Royal Inniskilling Fusiliers in Italy in 1944.[23] After the war, Major Myles had returned to Ballyshannon to run the family business and during the War of Independence, he was abducted by the IRA. In 1923, he was elected to the Dáil and enjoyed a twenty-year political career. He was a well-known personality and very popular with all members of the community.

The revolutionary period (1919-23) placed a lot of pressure on Protestants living in the Irish Free State. Many of the 'big houses' belonging to the Ascendency were burned to the ground. Numerous landlords were threatened and the economic costs of the Belfast Boycott, which was largely directed against Protestant traders, resulted in a large migration from the Free State. Protestants in the Border area suffered due to the breakdown in the rule of law. Their houses were either attacked or taken over by the IRA. In County Cork, about thirty-five percent of the civilians shot by the IRA were Protestant.[24] While the Belfast pogroms caused deep resentment among many Catholics, in some cases the chaos enabled old scores to be settled. In the glossary of colloquial terms in his 1960 memoir, Song of Erne, recalling his Fermanagh childhood, Robert Harbison refers to the 1916-1923 period as 'bad times'. A report by the British government concluded, 'Undoubtedly, loyalists in County Donegal and near the Border were persecuted and forced to withdraw eastward; but the reports brought in were grossly exaggerated, and the Northern Newspapers made the most of them for political purposes.'[25]

The Hilliard family came from the townland of Drumawark on the Lough Derg side of Pettigo. During the early 1920s, there was a lot of military activity in the area. The local IRA raided the farm and removed foodstuffs.[26] According to a family member, 'the IRA was rampant in their pilfering and also the burning and damaging of property belonging to Protestants. My grandfather spent many nights outside guarding his property in fear of an IRA attack.' When the Border was established, the family moved to Ederney in Fermanagh: 'A lot of Protestant people of today are not aware just how harshly Protestants in Border areas were treated in the early 1920s.'[27]

Willie Long was born in Kinlough. At the age of eight, he and his family moved to Garrison because of the 'pressure on Protestants'. His father fought in the Second World War and Willie joined the B Specials and the Home Guard in 1944. After a brief stint abroad, he returned to Northern Ireland, married and transferred to Garrison. In 1972, while on patrol, his unit noticed seven black flags placed near the Border. There were seven UDR men living in the locality and they viewed this as a threat. Some weeks later, the IRA shot and killed Tommy Fletcher: 'Directly after that, there was a lot of fear in the community. Every time I went out to milk I had a gun with me and it was cocked and ready to use.' On advice from a UDR officer, Willie and his family relocated to Enniskillen.[28]

Bertie Kerr's father had been in the A Specials, the full-time Constabulary force active during the time of partition. Their land ran along the shores of Lough Melvin: 'Some IRA men from about Ballyshannon and Donegal came around. My father was ploughing with two horses on the hill. They were setting up to shoot him and the Catholic neighbours all got round them, and eventually took the gun off them, and said that under no circumstances did they want Willie Kerr shot.'[29] Prior to the Troubles, that great community spirit existed in Garrison, Bertie says. They formed a committee of Catholics and Protestants to address local issues. However, when the Troubles began, Bertie asserts that it had a devastating effect: 'Things deteriorated round the Border surely with the Troubles. They blew up the road to stop the IRA coming across. They blew up the road beside our house. They cut off the Leitrim community from the Garrison community. The barracks had been closed sometime in the Sixties and it was turned into a youth hostel. The IRA came in and burned one hotel and they blew the other hotel up.'[30]

In 1923, Lady Spender travelled to Cliff House near Belleek to meet Major Moore. Moore was previously the commandant of the Special Constabulary in Derry and Grand Master of the Derry Orange Order. She recorded the events in her diary: 'After a mile or more, we found ourselves at Clift, the home of Major Moore, which is over the Border unluckily for him. We know him, so we went and looked him up, and a most pathetic figure he is. His family have lived there for generations, and he has spent most of his life there and used to be on the best of terms with the people, and his mother was endlessly good to them. But when the troublous times began again, some ten years ago or more, they turned against him in the treacherous Irish way, and he has had nothing but trouble since. He took us for a walk down the river through his estate, and took us over the house, and told us of the terrible times he has been through. Last June, a year ago, that is, he was forced to keep one hundred and fifty Republicans in his house for several weeks, and they wrecked the whole place, till it looks, with its bare rooms, broken furniture, smashed mirrors and disfigured walls, like a house in the war zone in France after the Germans had occupied it. They destroyed his water supply so that now he has to fetch his water in pails from a well. They stole his war medals; they strode about his garden in his fur coat on hot summer days like the ill-conditioned children they are; and when they finally departed, the house was in an indescribable condition of filth. Still, he lived on there, putting what he could to rights, and leaving the rest until last February when one night he heard a knocking at the door, which is of glass, went down and saw a number of men outside, one of whom fired at him point blank, but the rifle missed-fire, and he tore to the stairs, thumped his feet on them as if he were running upstairs, while they hammered at the door, and then dashed into the drawing-room, snatching up a six-shooter on the way, and out into the garden, while they, having broken in, rushed upstairs on his track, as they thought. It was a dark night, and down by the river, which was in flood, he missed his footing and fell in and was carried some way down, but he got out eventually and made his way to the road; there he saw two of the men and fired at them and downed one, and made the other walk in front of him at the point of his revolver till he reached the fort. After that he stayed away for a bit, and has only just come back to live there. Crippled with rheumatism, he is there along with his faithful old butler, and one maid servant. The house is almost bare of furniture, the beautiful grounds are all overgrown with weeds and nettles, and any moment another attempt may be made to murder him, but he is too obstinate or too plucky, whichever you like to call it, to abandon the place which he adores.'[31]

Killing members of the RUC and UDR during the Troubles was seen as a direct attack on the wider Protestant community. During the 1970s and 1980s, many members of the security forces were killed by the IRA in west Fermanagh. On 28 November 1972, Reserve Constable Robert Keys, a father of six from Bannaghmore near Kesh, was killed in an IRA rocket attack on Belleek RUC station. He was about to go off duty when the rocket pierced a steel shutter and hit him in the chest. It was followed by a twenty-minute attack, with heavy fire directed at the station from the southern side of the Border. This was one of the first attacks in which the IRA used a shoulder-launched RPG-7 rocket. In 1973, part-time UDR member and father of four Matthew Lilley was shot by the IRA while on his milk round at Kellagho just outside Belcoo. Two days earlier, Catholic farmer Patrick Duffy was killed nearby when he drove over an IRA landmine intended to kill members of the security forces.

On 1 June 1975, Margaret Kilfedder, a Protestant civilian mother of five was killed when a cylinder bomb exploded at her Garrison home. The bungalow's previous occupant was a member of the UDR who had left the area, along with a number of other Protestant families, because of their fear of assassination. It is believed that the bomb may have been intended for him. Mrs. Kilfedder and her husband had left Belfast to get away from the violence there.

In 1978, part-time UDR soldier Alan Ferguson from Enniskillen was killed in an IRA ambush near Scribbagh Post Office outside Belcoo. Norman Donaldson, a UDR member was shot as he left Derrygonnelly RUC barracks in 1980. He was collecting money for a hospital charity. In a cruel twist of fate, his friend John James Dundas suffered a fatal heart attack when he arrived at the scene.[32]

On Sunday 3 August 1980, William John Clarke, aged 59 and married with four children, was shot and killed by the IRA four hundred yards inside County Donegal in the village of Pettigo. He was from Castlederg, County Tyrone and was visiting relatives at the time. More than four hundred Irish troops and Gardaí mounted a vast search operation after the incident. Private Clarke joined the UDR in 1971, becoming a full-time member in 1973. He was one of a number of congregation members from First Castlederg Presbyterian Church who were killed by the IRA.

Then on 8 November 1987, a cold, windy Sunday morning, a large group of people gathered to honour their war dead at the War Memorial in Enniskillen. Remembrance Sunday has always been a significant and sombre day in the calendar of the Protestant community in Northern Ireland, but regarded as a British occasion by Irish nationalists, despite the fact that many thousands of Irishmen from all religious backgrounds fought with the British army in both world wars. At 10.43am, a bomb exploded in the nearby Reading Rooms, a hall owned by the Catholic Church in Enniskillen. The gable wall collapsed, showering tons of rubble onto the unsuspecting crowd below. Eleven people died in the blast. They were Bertha Armstrong, Edward Armstrong, Wesley Armstrong, Samuel Gault, Nessie Johnston, Kitchener Johnston, John Megaw, Nessie Mullan, William Mullan, Alberta Quinton and Marie Wilson. A twelfth man, Ronnie Hill, remained in a coma for thirteen years before he died in 2000. Sixty-three people were injured, nineteen seriously. Thirteen children were among the injured.

Members of an IRA unit had placed the bomb in a cupboard on the first floor of the building. An electronic timer was used to detonate the device.[33] The fallout caused by the atrocity was enormous and republicans came in for global condemnation. For instance, the Irish rock music group U2 were on tour in America at the time of the bombing. That evening they took to the stage and (significantly) during their rendition of 'Sunday Bloody Sunday', lead singer Bono made the following statement: 'I've had enough of Irish Americans, who haven't been back to their country in twenty or thirty years, come up to me and talk about the resistance, the revolution back home and the glory of the revolution, and the glory of dying for the revolution. Fuck the revolution! They don't talk about the glory of killing for the revolution... Where's the glory in bombing a Remembrance Day parade of old-age pensioners, the medals taken out and polished up for the day? Where's the glory in that?'

Bono's words echoed throughout the stadium and the clip was subsequently included in the 'Rattle and Hum' film. Millions heard the sentiments. Historian Jonathan Bardon speculates that the speech 'may have done more to discourage Irish-American financial support for the Provisional IRA than all the politician's appeals put together'.[34]

A few days after the bombing, a senior IRA source admitted that Enniskillen was a 'major setback' and 'it really hurt us badly in the Republic more than anywhere else... People in the IRA just feel sick.'[35] More than 50,000 people queued in the wind and rain outside Mansion House in Dublin to sign a book of condolence. Lord Mayor of Dublin Carmencita Hederman took the book to Enniskillen and broke down in tears as she handed it over.

The Remembrance Day Bombing will also be remembered for the heart-breaking humanity of one of the bereaved. Gordon Wilson's daughter Marie was the youngest victim and he held her hand as they both lay trapped beneath the rubble: 'I shouted to Marie was she all right and she said yes and she found my hand and said, "Is that your hand Dad?" Now remember we were under six feet of rubble. I said, "Are you all right?" and she said yes, but she was shouting in between. Three or four times I asked her, and she always said yes, she was all right. When I asked her the fifth time, "Are you all right Marie?" she said, "Daddy, I love you very much."' She died later in hospital and that evening Gordon Wilson gave an interview to the BBC. In an extraordinary act of Christian forgiveness, he said, 'I bear no ill will. I bear no grudge. Dirty sort of talk is not going to bring her back to life. She was a great wee lassie.'

The West Fermanagh Brigade of the IRA was suspected of being responsible for that bomb and it had members from both sides of the Border. [36] In the late 1980s, a series of attacks on Protestant civilians led to disbandment of the unit. In March 1988, it was alleged to have been responsible for killing Gillian Johnston, a 21-year-old shop worker while she was sitting in a car with her fiancé outside her home near Belleek. The IRA claimed that the real target was a family member who was in the UDR but the RUC stated there was no connection between the family and the security forces. On 4

August 1988, building contractor William Hassard (59) and his lifelong friend Frederick Love (64) left Belleek RUC station where they had been finishing some routine maintenance work. They were heading home to Derrygonnelly when their car was riddled with bullets by an IRA unit at Slater's Cross near the Donegal-Fermanagh Border. Almost a hundred bullet casings were recovered from the scene. The West Fermanagh IRA admitted it had carried out the attack, claiming the men had ignored warnings not to carry out work for the security forces. Frederick Love's sister said the family were horrified by what happened the two men: 'They were children together; they went to school together; they worked together for forty years; and now they have died together. I just don't know what sort of people could have murdered them. Everyone here is in a state of shock.'[37]

In January 1989, the same unit struck again when it killed Harry Keys, a farm worker and former member of the RUC Reserve. He was shot twenty-three times while sitting in his car with his girlfriend outside her home in Ballintra, County Donegal. The unit claimed that Keys was gathering intelligence for the security forces but Garda and local people believed it was a sectarian 'grudge' killing because Keys's girlfriend was a Catholic.[38] The attack was widely condemned and on 23 January 1989, the IRA Army Council announced that it had 'stood down' and disarmed the unit responsible. The dismissal came as Sinn Féin was preparing for local and European elections and republicans were concerned that the attacks would damage the party's political performance.

In an interview for a short book entitled 'Stories of Border Protestants North and South', Graham Laird recalled growing up in Ballyshannon where his family roots in the town go back to the early 1800s. He spoke of 'memories of riots, broken windows, posters calling for boycotts and threats'. He has one memory in particular of his mother being forced by an accuser to take a Bible in her hand and swear an oath that her son was not a member of the B Specials after she was told that his name was on a death list. These stresses were a great burden on the older generation. Graham concluded that the Border 'has been a challenge to anyone living in its vicinity, an influence that has undoubtedly been more destructive than constructive'.[39]

Jim White is a former Fine Gael TD, first elected in 1973. He helped to broker talks between senior members of the IRA and a group of Protestant clergymen in Feakle, County Clare on 10 December 1974.[40] As a public representative, he was an outspoken critic of republican activities in the Border area. 'A lot of things happened after the riots in Ballyshannon. After Billy Fox was murdered things changed. I had 24-hour police protection for six months of my life, seeing as I was the only Protestant in the Dáil at the time. I was the only Protestant public representative along the Border at the time too.' When Republican sentiment began to take hold along the Border area as the Troubles broke out, those opposed to the IRA found themselves at risk. In a 2008 interview, White told the reporter, 'I did get death threats; I did get intimidatory letters but I just carried on as normal.'[41] He also recalled that in the aftermath of the Ballyshannon riots, he found himself ostracised by republican sympathisers in the town: 'I can well remember walking down the street in Ballyshannon and people crossed to the other side of the road rather than having to speak to me.'[42]

Cross-community co-operation has been a constant feature of the Garrison-Rossinver area despite partition and the Troubles and it remains so to this day. In the 1950s, a committee was formed in the village.[43] 'No matter what went wrong in the village there were six or eight men, Catholic and Protestant, they always got together and, no matter what the problem was, they could always find a solution to it.'[44] After the IRA killed Tommy Fletcher there was widespread cross-community support for his family: 'We buried him a few days later in Garrison... and I never seen a storm like it in me life. There was thunder and lightning, there were slates blown off the church, what never happened in a lifetime. [Yet] there was hardly a Catholic family in the countryside who wasn't at the funeral.'[45]

After Fletcher's death, five other UDR men from the same area left because of death threats issued to them by the IRA.[46] A local reporter met one of the men who was leaving his farmhouse with the furniture and bedding in a trailer. He had been born on the farm and he and his wife had lived there for forty years.[47] The impact of many of the Border killings was profound. Many other families left the area. One Border Protestant farmer left after the IRA killed his friend: 'What you have worked for all your life was scattered... the ground was taken from under you. You were leaving home.' However, many held onto the land even though there was no one to farm it.[48]

Another Border Protestant farmer from Belcoo was a victim of both the IRA and the UVF. The IRA hijacked his car outside his home and he was held at gunpoint in his house until dark. His car was later recovered in Ballinamore, County Leitrim. The UVF then hijacked the same car, placed a bomb in it and forced the farmer to drive across the Border into the Republic. The bomb was timed to go off after he had parked the car at the Garda station. On the way, the car hit a bump in the road, but the bomb did not explode. Then when he arrived at the station, he yelled 'bomb' to warn the Gardaí but the bomb failed to go off again and the Irish Army carried out a controlled explosion. Despite the violence directed at him, the

Protestant farmer told a journalist that relations with his Catholic neighbours were very good: 'The majority around us are Catholics. We get on very well with them. If I wanted help with a sick calf in the middle of the night, it would be to them that I'd go, just as they'd come to me for help.'[49]

A powerful and lingering issue for the Border Protestant community was the result of the 1981 by-election for Fermanagh and South Tyrone. IRA hunger striker Bobby Sands was elected as MP on a substantial vote of 52 per cent, against Harry West's 48 per cent. Both then and now, many Protestants and Unionists saw it as a clear and unambiguous vote of support for the 'armed struggle': [50] 'When you've suffered at the hands of the IRA... everyone was gutted that they would go out and vote for somebody who was active in the IRA.'[51]

Given Fermanagh's history on their own side, it is not surprising that many young men from the Protestant community chose to join the security forces. Samuel Lewis spoke of the proud military tradition of Fermanagh in 1837, 'The military spirit thus drawn forth has been maintained ever since... the sons of the native farmers frequently prefer a soldier's life abroad to that of an agriculturist at home.' Yet those who joined the UDR, did so for a number of reasons. One former UDR soldier commented: 'These people were there for the money, the drink and their political bigotries.'[52] Some saw it as an extra source of income.[53] Many saw it as a justifiable and appropriate way to protect their families and community. Joining the UDR also prevented many Fermanagh men from joining the illegal loyalist paramilitary groups. In a report published by the Church of Ireland Diocese of Clogher, one contributor noted, 'The Fermanagh person despises all paramilitarism – the Fermanagh person believes no-one has the right to take life.'

So the Protestant community in Border counties such as Fermanagh and Tyrone always viewed attacks on the UDR as attacks on their Protestant neighbours, friends, and local community. Almost two hundred UDR soldiers were killed on duty and more than sixty others were killed after they left the regiment: 'To the Unionist community along the Border, they (the UDR men) are husbands and fathers, often the mainstay of Protestant families. They do what their community by and large expects in joining the UDR... The loss of men folk is a blow to the heart of any community.'[54] They had often joined from a sense of duty:

'In areas like Fermanagh... families who feel strongly about their Britishness would encourage their sons, if they wanted to commit themselves to anything, into the legitimate RUC Reserve or UDR... But I believe it's getting difficult for them to do that, because immediately they are an easy target.'[55] Furthermore, in joining up, life was changed forever for Protestants along the Border: 'I served seven years in the B Specials. After the B Specials disbanded, seven of us then joined the UDR. After we joined the UDR, we couldn't cross the Border except for a very odd funeral and even then you always arrived late and you didn't travel in your own car. The Free State was a no-go area for us.'[56]

The Ethnic Cleansing of Fermanagh

Henry Patterson, professor of Irish Politics at the University of Ulster, delivered an address in 2006, at the Sixth International Conference of the Spanish Association for Irish Studies. Entitled, 'War of National Liberation or Ethnic Cleansing: IRA violence in Fermanagh during the Troubles,' it reignited the heated debate about the impact of sectarian violence within the county.

By 1980, approximately fifty Protestants, mostly members of the RUC or UDR, had been killed in County Fermanagh by the IRA.[57] Unionist leaders labelled the campaign as genocide against the Protestant people. In 1994, the Dublin-based Sunday Independent newspaper published a story about an alleged plan of the Ulster Defence Association (UDA) to carry out 'ethnic cleansing'. It involved the repartition of Northern Ireland followed by the forced removal of Catholics from the remaining area.[58] The use of the term 'ethnic cleansing' had emerged from the Balkan conflicts and first entered the Northern Ireland lexicon in 1992. That was when UUP leader James Molyneaux claimed that Protestants in Border areas 'had been the victims of ethnic cleansing for over twenty years'. Thousands have been 'intimidated from the Border regions of Fermanagh and Tyrone,' he said'[59] Another opponent of the Northern Ireland peace process, commentator Simon Jenkins also used the term in a 1996 article: 'The ethnic cleansing of Ulster west of the Bann has continued. The predominantly Catholic areas, especially the Londonderry conurbation, are virtually parts of the Republic... From Fermanagh to Londonderry lies a sickle of nationalism, a cordon sanitaire between Protestant Ulster and the Irish Republic.'[60] In an interview with writer Susan McKay, Unionist politician Ken Maginnis said, 'There would be quite a few elderly mothers still holding on to the land along the Border, even if there is no one left in the family to farm it.'[61]

Many Border Protestants perceived the IRA's concerted campaign by IRA as 'ethnic cleansing'.[62] While Fermanagh and South Tyrone had traditionally been a mainstay of moderate Unionism, the IRA's targeting of off-duty UDR men caused widespread anger among the unionist community and Ian Paisley began to make his presence felt in the area. In 1980, Paisley toured the Fermanagh Border claiming the IRA had drawn up a list of prominent Protestants to be assassinated and calling this 'genocide'. He urged Protestants to be vigilant. On 23 June 1980, more than seven thousand Protestants from all over Fermanagh assembled in Newtownbutler for a rally addressed by Paisley and UUP leader Molyneaux. When the Irish Times interviewed Church of Ireland Primate Dr. John Armstrong, he said, 'There seemed to be a disturbing pattern in the killings. Sometimes the person killed would be the natural successor to the farm, like an elder son. It is difficult to find evidence of a plan to eliminate Protestants. The only evidence is that so many people have been killed.'[63]

However, other academics such as cultural historian Graham Dawson contest the 'ethnic cleansing' description: 'Such claims rest on a questionable treatment of evidence. While migration, including Protestant migration, away from the Border is a reality, this is due to a range of factors, including rural youth unemployment... The pattern of violent death is clearly more complex than Unionist claims about "ethnic cleansing" allow. In the course of the Troubles, Border Protestants and Unionists have been subjected to a politics of intimidation and terror, but this has not taken place on a scale, nor with the consistency of pattern to warrant the description "ethnic cleansing".' [64]

In 1995, Dr. John Dunlop, former moderator of the Presbyterian Church in Ireland wrote, 'More than any other single factor, the observed decline in the Protestant population in the Republic has confirmed northern Protestants in their prejudices and fears.'[65] That observation was shared: 'The condition of the Border Protestant community... is a window through which northern Protestants view the Republic of Ireland.' [66]

Certainly, the community has been hit hard and is characterised by migration and in some cases post-traumatic stress. For many Protestants near the Border, life was difficult and dangerous. Many felt they had to be 'sharp with the eyes and slow with the tongue'.[67] Although many others reported that they never felt themselves to be in danger or experienced any form of sectarianism, for the most part they opted to keep a low profile during the Troubles. [68] They felt that raising their heads above the parapet might lead to attacks from paramilitaries: 'Our attitude was, don't get involved in case you draw attention to yourself.' This feeling was compounded among those who had members of their family in the security forces.

Many Protestants were angry that Irish security forces did not do more to seal the Border during the Troubles. They felt more could have been done to prevent the IRA from escaping after attacks in Northern Ireland. When the Foot and Mouth outbreak occurred in 2001, the Gardaí hermetically sealed the Border, prompting one observer to remark, 'For thirty years, they claimed they couldn't close the Border. They closed it twice in the last four years. Now you couldn't get a sandwich through.' Then in September 2013, Tánaiste Eamon Gilmore told journalists that 'the state could have done more to prevent IRA activities in Border areas.'[69]

The annual Twelfth parade at Rossnowlagh has long been lauded as a celebration of Orange culture and a great family day out. Writer Darach MacDonald posed the question as to whether this is the future for many such parades.[70] Certainly, the concept of an Orange festival is gathering some momentum as an alternative to contentious parades and a repeat of Drumcree. At Rossnowlagh, Orange leader Drew Nelson acknowledged the sterling work done by both former Irish President Mary McAleese and her husband Martin in bringing both communities together. From 1998, President Mary McAleese held a Twelfth of July reception for southern Orangemen, their families and others at Áras an Uachtaráin. The language has softened and whilst there are flares of anger such as the flag protests in Belfast, the dialogue continues. The shared history approach has borne fruit and Anglo-Irish relations have seen a seismic shift in recent years. The recognition of First World War service provided the impetus for a more open dialogue on a variety of subjects. Queen Elizabeth's royal visit had a massive impact on Irish society and many were moved by her carefully chosen words.

Another indication of how far both communities have come in recent years, was the historic address by Drew Nelson, Grand Secretary of the Grand Orange Lodge of Ireland, to Seanad Éireann on 3 July 2012. He told the senators that Orangemen 'want to remember 1690; we don't want to live in 1690'. He continued, 'Three things, in particular, on this side of the Border have created a very positive climate which sets a good foundation for working towards that normalisation of relationships, namely the development of the visitors centre at the Boyne battlefield site; the funding of Cadolemo, our community development and capacity-building organisation (in Cavan, Donegal, Leitrim and Monaghan), by the Irish Government; and the royal visit. I believe that these three things really were all done in the spirit of cherishing "all of the children of the nation equally".'

'Will it be a pint or Ballyshannon?'

When politician Brian Lenihan senior was asked for his name when found drinking after hours in a Dublin pub, he responded by asking the Guard, 'Will it be a pint or Ballyshannon?' The reference to a Border posting indicated the perception among Gardaí that it was the Irish equivalent of being sent to Siberia. Until relatively recently, policing the Irish Border was an extremely hazardous task. More than three hundred RUC officers were killed and almost 9,000 injured during the Troubles.[1] The RUC had the reputation of being the most dangerous police force in the world in which to be a member. Twelve Gardaí were killed by republicans or other subversive groups during the same period. Since the demilitarisation of the area, the danger has subsided but the threat remains.

Policing was introduced into Ireland during the early nineteenth century. The County Constabulary was created in 1822 and it later became the Royal Irish Constabulary (RIC). After the War of Independence, the RIC was disbanded in the Irish Free State and the Civic Guard was established and renamed An Garda Síochána in 1923. After 1920, the RIC were charged with policing the newly formed Northern Irish state, being renamed the Royal Ulster Constabulary in the process. However, they were not trusted fully by the Unionist population, which had already set up its own paramilitary forces, particularly in County Fermanagh. The Unionists prevailed on the British government to sanction the creation of a Special Constabulary from these units. That happened in 1920, when it was divided into A, B and C classifications. There were 2,000 full-time A Specials and some 19,500 B specials. The latter were part-time, unpaid and patrolled their own areas. The 7,500 C Specials were older, also unpaid and non-uniformed reservists, sometimes used for static guards on installations. Northern Ireland Premier Craig informed British Prime Minister Lloyd George that the Specials would resist any move to enforce boundary changes that Unionists did not agree with. A showdown with Crown forces never came but the Specials were used to suppress nationalist dissent. General Ricardo, one of the founders of the original UVF, commented, 'The Nationalist is shown a list with his name at the top and is told that if any "B" man is touched, the list will be attended to from the top.'[2]

In April 1920, as the War of Independence raged throughout Ireland, Sir Basil Brooke founded the Protestant militia group, Fermanagh Vigilance, in an effort to combat the local IRA. Along with many other prominent Unionist from families such as the Archdales and the Irvines, Brooke had been instrumental in the formation of the UVF in Fermanagh from December 1912. Brooke asked Dublin

Castle to recognise his new paramilitary force as an official special constabulary. When this offer was declined, he remarked, 'Dublin can go to hell... We'll look after ourselves.'

Even before the outbreak of the First World War, there was an Ulster Unionist administration in waiting, backed by a well-armed paramilitary force supplied through illegal gun-running. After the loyal sons of Ulster had sacrificed so much on the blood-stained fields of France, they were more determined than ever to hold their beloved Ulster, albeit now a truncated six-county version of the province. From 1920 onwards, the arming of Protestants had taken official shape in the Ulster Special Constabulary.

By November 1921, there was serious discontent throughout the RIC in Northern Ireland when a form was circulated asking members to state their religion and whether they were prepared to serve the new government. One RIC officer told the Irish News this was 'a step to get an exclusively Orange or purely sectarian force in the Six Counties and no one resents the plan more than the decent Protestants in the RIC of whom there are many'.

The political environment of Northern Ireland influenced the internal make-up of its police force from the start. The Royal Ulster Constabulary (RUC) was then established in 1922. Many of its members, possibly up to half, were former Specials and they imported some of the features of that force into the new one. The religious and political partisanship was reinforced by the force's close relationship with the Orange Lodge.[3] From then on, the RUC was so much under the direct control of the Stormont government that it came to be regarded as 'the armed wing of Unionism'. [4]

From its inception, the RUC was equipped with 'some of the most draconian policing powers ever passed in a liberal policing democracy'.[5] The Civil Authorities (Special Powers) Act enabled the government to intern people without trial, which it did between 1922 and 1925, 1938 and 1946 and between 1956 and 1961. Other powers, such as the Flags and Emblems Act (1954) made it illegal to display any Nationalist paraphernalia such as the Irish tricolour flag. Non-violent protest was outlawed by the Public Order Act (1951). It was in this environment that many Nationalists looked at the RUC as a biased police force supporting the Protestant parliament's control over Northern Irish society.[6]

Yet one former Bundoran-based Garda recalls that during the 1960s 'relations between the RUC and the Guards were very good. We knew each other and we co-operated when we needed to.' He also said that before the Troubles, 'there was one fella from Belleek RUC station who used to drink in Ballyshannon. No one ever said a word to him.'

Meanwhile, out of a force of approximately 6,500, the Garda Síochána had only a few hundred stationed near the Border when the Troubles broke out. In August 1969, the Irish Army's strength was just over 7,000 with a part-time reserve force of 20,000.[7] Then the influx of refugees from the North, along with an increasing number of IRA men on the run, raised the political temperature in Border towns such as Bundoran and Ballyshannon. The political violence threatened to spill over the Border and the police were initially unprepared to deal with the unfolding events. The showdown with republicans came in 1970 when Joe O'Neill and two other IRA suspects were arrested and detained at Ballyshannon Garda Station. The Gardaí found bullets in a drawer at O'Neill's bar. They were acting on information that the senior republican had been seen carrying a weapon at Clyhore.

One officer said, 'When we arrested Joe O'Neill, he refused to move and went as stiff as a board... We had to carry him down the stairs.'[8] The arrests sparked riots in Ballyshannon. The Irish government was very concerned that this could cause a ripple effect along the Border and inflame tensions. The violence prompted a build-up of Irish security forces and the Minister for Justice began sending newly recruited Gardaí directly to the Border. After the Ballyshannon riots, according to one former Guard, 'We were always ready for the next time. It would have been a change in the system of working, or a change in attitude, whatever way you would like to say, we were aware of the dangers that were around.'[9]

By the mid-1970s, the Irish security forces were making their presence felt on the Border. The Gardaí and the Irish army set up more than 10,000 checkpoints along the frontier in 1975 alone. That same year, they conducted 5,400 mobile patrols of the Border. Much of the Border police work involved house searches and weapons caches were regularly uncovered.

For some RUC officers, a Border posting came about as a result of being 'blocked', an in-house term for disciplinary action. Border posting were extremely dangerous. Conditions at the stations were often basic and frequent attacks by the IRA ensured that it was not a popular assignment. It did, however, foster a sense of comradeship among the police involved. A former RUC officer from Fermanagh commented, 'I preferred working in hard areas because the camaraderie was better, our friendships were forged under fire. In soft areas like Bangor, your superior officer had more time to focus on things like unshined shoes.' The same former officer speculated that some may have been motivated by career prospects in joining the RUC. Others saw it almost as a vocation to make Northern Ireland safer.[10] Being in the RUC made officers an immediate target for republican paramilitaries. The threat meant that Fermanagh-based members of the force resided only in 'safer areas' such as Enniskillen, Ballinamallard, Lisbellaw and Kesh.

When an Irish News journalist in the late 1980s was shown a series of documents containing the names of alleged republican activists living in Border towns, including Bundoran, he was told that the list was drafted by a covert group of officers within the RUC. The group's aim was to eradicate 'Republican terrorism' and 'bring down the Anglo-Irish Agreement'.[11] The revelation confirmed the fears and misgivings of most Catholics.

Before the Troubles, nationalist protests in Northern Ireland were heavily policed while loyalist counter-protests did not receive the same level of scrutiny.[12] Many nationalists never regarded the RUC as a legitimate police service, viewing it as part of an unacceptable political system. During the 1980s, Chief Constable Jack Hermon made concerted efforts to improve the impartiality of the RUC and by the mid-1990s, the force had ratcheted up many successes against loyalist paramilitaries. A former officer stated, 'Sectarianism wasn't tolerated by anyone... There was a bit of banter, but you'd have to expect that.'

Meanwhile, the outbreak of violence in Northern Ireland caught the Irish Defence Forces by surprise. There was a lack of preparation and training for a Border security campaign. For instance, some of the accommodation at Finner camp was built before the First World War and soldiers had to endure cold and damp in overcrowded and primitive sleeping quarters. They could be called on to patrol at short notice and often without sufficient rest. Extended periods away from home posed further problems for soldiers and their families. One former soldier spoke of the strain, 'Family life would be disrupted, especially when an operation was on, such as a big search for weapons. We'd arrive at the barracks and be told we wouldn't be going home until next week. That would happen regularly.'[13]

The 28th Battalion was activated on 1 September 1973 to strengthen Border operations by securing one hundred and twenty-six miles of the frontier with Northern Ireland. That was the longest stretch of Border protection for any Irish battalion, encompassing the territory between Blacklion in County Cavan to Castlefin, County Donegal. Its area of operations had more than eighty recognised Border crossings and a further twenty non-approved roads. The soldiers based at Finner Camp had to maintain nine static checkpoints and carry out patrol duties, as well as set up 'snap' checkpoints at other locations. Their other duties involved call-out operations. In 1989 alone, the 28th Battalion carried out almost three thousand patrols, set up more than two thousand, two hundred checkpoints and dealt with more than twenty bomb threats. Its primary role was to provide assistance and protection to the unarmed Garda Síochána and the heavy military presence acted as a deterrent against IRA activity in the Border area. Yet the continuous violence in Northern Ireland meant soldiers at Finner were in a constant state of 'blue alert'. That required them to be always ready, either at home or in the barracks.

Irish Army Checkpoint at Clyhore near the Donegal-Fermanagh Border

Border duty also posed many threats to the southern security services. In addition to the bombs and shootings, there was always the danger of mortar attacks, and command wire booby-traps aimed at British targets were often operated from the southern side of the Border. Although the Irish Army had very little direct engagement with the IRA, social tensions increased between republican sympathisers and soldiers in Border towns such as Bundoran and Ballyshannon. Incidents of intimidation of soldier's families and restrictions on social liberties also added to the stress of patrolling the Border. One soldier commented, 'We were called "Free State Brits".' Another soldier spoke of the exclusion he felt in his own community, 'I was ostracised... There were guys I went to school with and they would just ignore me if I met them on the street.'[14]

Some soldiers found it difficult to deal with the aftermath of scenes of violence, such as the gunfire surrounding the release of kidnapped businessman Don Tidey from a Leitrim hide-out in 1983: 'I witnessed a colleague being killed when we were trying to release a kidnapped victim and the IRA opened fire on us. A Garda was also shot dead at that incident. I'm still reliving the trauma since.'[15] Another soldier told of how he 'saw the body of an RUC officer which had been booby-trapped. The body was also defiled.' A study conducted by Oglaigh Náisúnta na hÉireann Teoranta (ONET), an organisation for ex-servicemen and women, revealed a high incidence of mental stress among former soldiers who had served on the Border. Many of the participants displayed various symptoms of Post-Traumatic Stress Disorder (PTSD).

Locally seized IRA weapons on display at Finner Camp

A secret, intelligence-led war was waged against the IRA by the Irish Army and Garda Special Branch. As the technology improved, remote reconnaissance methods of surveillance meant that the army was able to monitor the movements of known republicans in the Border area. Meanwhile, the Irish Army had specialist units that dealt with bomb disposal and suspect devices. On one occasion, the army had information that there was an IRA weapons cache at Rossinver graveyard near the Border. A group of soldiers from Finner set out to investigate: 'One of the lads who was new and a bit inexperienced shouted that he'd found something. He forgot to follow protocol and attempted to open the box himself. I shouted to everyone to hit the ground. These weapons stashes were often booby-trapped. This one wasn't, but that was our immediate reaction.' [16]

Clyhore Checkpoint

Co-operation between Irish and British soldiers was commonplace by the end of the 1970s. Both sides came up with pragmatic solutions to local problems posed by the Border. For instance, the Irish Army protected the British if they had to cross the Border briefly at Belleek to re-enter Northern Ireland. Conversely, Irish security forces were unofficially allowed to enter Northern Ireland at a Border crossing near Pettigo. Soldiers from both sides were also susceptible to 'map-reading errors' along the Border. These led to some incidents when the British Army was inadvertently stopping cars on the southern side of the Border. Both armies also co-operated closely on bomb disposal techniques, particularly if the command wire was traced back to the southern side of the Border. Personal relationships formed and a former soldier in the Irish Army even stated, 'If I went through a British Army checkpoint, I was saluted.'[17]

On the other side of the Border, one former British soldier from County Fermanagh has fond memories of his service. His grand-uncle had received a Victoria Cross for valour in the First World War. His uncle fought with the British Army in the Second World War (and later became a prominent member of the Civil Rights movement). His father joined the British Army in 1950 and served with the Ulster Rifles in Hong Kong, Lahore, Singapore and Malaysia during the counter-insurgency campaign there. However, a posting to Northern Ireland posed many additional dilemmas and difficulties. There was always the danger of being recognised on a patrol and targeted. Visiting relatives who had moved to the south always involved risk. The ex-soldier recalled his experience of patrolling the Border in Northern Ireland as 'ninety-seven percent boredom and three percent terror... the other big problem was sleep deprivation and getting petrol-bombed. We also used to get lots of abuse, so you were always on edge.' During one incident, he witnessed a young woman having difficulties with her pram. When the pram fell over he helped to turn it upright but was treated to a torrent of abuse from the young woman.

During the early part of the Troubles, there was little communication between the two police forces. This was due in part to some reported actions of the RUC and the widespread belief among Protestants in Northern Ireland that IRA volunteers could live with impunity in the Republic.[18] Over time, however, many discreet channels were opened. The Irish government was concerned about the rise of Protestant paramilitaries and their threat to the south. The bombs in Monaghan and Dublin were planted by members of the UVF and one of the earliest incidents of the Troubles had been an attempted attack on Ballyshannon Power Station by a close associate of Ian Paisley. By the 1990s, co-operation was commonplace. One police officer interviewed at the time, told a reporter, 'On the likes of the Fermanagh Border the RUC have a very good working relationship with the Gardaí, there'd be a fair degree of co-operation.'[19] Some local Gardaí enjoyed a collegial relationship with their counterparts in the RUC. At Christmas, they were invited into the police station at Belleek for drinks.

In 1992, Fortnight magazine examined the issue of Border policing. The journalist spoke to one RUC officer who said, 'On the Border you're more open to terrorist attack, because the terrorist has more opportunity to exploit the element of surprise. He has more escape routes, more places to hide, he knows exactly where his support lies in these areas.' Meanwhile, a Garda policing the other side of the Border highlighted the difference: 'We've one main advantage over the RUC; we're not targets... If there's a problem, for example, a road traffic accident, we have no hesitation in going straight to the scene. They have the danger of being got at.'

The isolation that RUC officers faced in Border areas made it a very unpopular posting. And though the Gardaí are not alienated from Border communities in the same way, many viewed a Border posting unfavourably: 'Most Gardaí working here wouldn't live locally. It's like being sent to Siberia. Normally they send young members. Most people would have to spend around a year up here.'[20]

Policing an area like Belleek during the Troubles was still a very different experience to a posting in the Andersonstown district of Belfast or in South Armagh. West Fermanagh has a tranquil, rural feel to it and relations between the two communities have never been marked by the same levels of sectarianism that was evident in other Border areas. However, alcohol played a large role in alleviating the stress and boredom of Border duty for security forces on both sides of the Border. One former officer told the Belfast News Letter: 'The RUC had more people with alcohol problems because of the level of stress involved... There were men reliant on drink who would bring in drink to get through the day.'[21] Another officer admitted, 'Some of my colleagues drank themselves to death.' The stress of the job made life difficult for many married members of the force. A frontier posting meant long periods away from families and contributed to the break-up of many marriages. A former member of the force confided, 'The job led to quite a few divorces.'[22]

Belleek RUC station in the 1980s

A former RUC officer told the following story: 'One night on patrol, my sergeant was blown up in a landmine attack. I had driven over

157

that spot a few times that day. After he was killed, we had to pick up what was left of him. When we got back to the station, the Super came out with a few bottles of whiskey and said 'There you go lads.' Nowadays, there's counselling for that type of thing.'[23] Many veterans suffered from Post-Traumatic Stress Syndrome after witnessing or being a part of violent confrontations along the Border. Neither government have ever adequately addressed this issue.

British Army on patrol in Belleek

Even when calm, the conditions at Belleek police station were quite basic and police officers worked in a closed environment. They shared the base with the army, whose tours of duty lasted six months. The policing section consisted of an operations room, a sergeant's office, a radio room and a kitchen. Each officer had a room upstairs, which was considered a luxury by Border station standards. In the attic was a secure room used by Special Forces, whose members would arrive in the station at night and take up residence for days or weeks. During that time, they had no contact with either the police or regular army. The police shifts would last three or four days and, at the end of the duty period, the men were brought to and from the base by helicopter. It was too dangerous to travel by road as some landmine attacks had taken place on the road from Enniskillen.

British Army Checkpoint on Boa Island

The police station had been fortified at different stages during the Troubles. Large sangars were built and a mortar-proof roof was put in place to protect those serving within its walls. During the late 1980s, the IRA had intensified its 'barrack buster' campaign, forcing the British Army to fortify its bases and increase the number of troops in Northern Ireland. The IRA came very close to destroying the Belleek base in 1994. A 200-lb bomb was mounted on the detached bucket scoop of a JCB digger on the Cliff Road. The explosives were packed into a modified gas cylinder and placed in a metal firing tube welded to the bucket base. The arming device was attached to a light switch. The operation was abandoned when a routine British Army patrol stumbled on the scene. The disarmed mortar is now reputed to be the centre-piece of a British army regimental museum in England.[24]

For those stationed at the Belleek police-army barracks, the threat persisted to the very end. With just one hour to go before the 1994 ceasefire began, the Provisional IRA launched one final attack on Belleek station. No one was injured in the incident. After the ceasefire, the RUC were served openly in the shops for the first time. Things were changing in Belleek. When dissident republicans attacked the station ten years after the ceasefire, it was unmanned at the time. Yet policing the Border remained a dangerous job when the PSNI took over the role of the RUC long after the Good Friday Agreement. In 2009, the former PSNI Chief Constable Matt Baggott described the terrorist threat in Fermanagh as 'severe' because of the increase in republican dissident activities along the Border. In a 2010 interview with the Impartial Reporter, a PSNI constable said they had to approach areas such as Belleek with caution. When the police visited the area with the journalist, their car was followed by another patrol car as back-up and all of the officers were armed with guns indicating a situation that 'has become the norm' in the PSNI's war against dissidents. His colleague told the reporter, 'We don't go down as often as we want to Belleek. There is no pattern but we are down several times a week, but it is probably no more than that at the moment and that is because of the current dissident threat.'[25] His colleague agreed, 'It was relatively quiet for a while but we seem to have swung into action again, particularly in places like Belleek. It's close to the Border; it's far away from assistance and we have to go down with some caution.'[26]

Both police forces courted controversy. The Morris Tribunal revealed a high level of corruption among some Gardaí in Donegal. RUC interrogation methods, the alleged 'shoot to kill policy' and accusations of collusion with loyalist paramilitaries brought the force into disrepute. Despite historical antipathies in the Border area, moreover, there was a high level of co-operation and a large degree of mutual respect between members of both forces.[27]

North-South police co-operation has continued to grow, especially among Gardaí and PSNI officers on the ground. While they cannot cross the Border to collect statements, higher levels of informal co-operation are apparent. Meanwhile, legal and political developments throughout Europe have allowed co-operation between police forces to develop. The Independent Monitoring Commission (IMC) stated that the 'high level of dissident activity would... have led to more deaths, injuries and destruction had it not been for the operations of the law enforcement and security agencies North and South and their ever closer cross-Border co-operation.'[28]

Members of An Garda Síochána and the Police Service of Northern Ireland on Belleek Bridge in December 2014

The Rod and the Reel

Despite the political division of the area, two cathartic activities have continued to transcend the divide. Lough Erne, Lough Melvin and the Drowes River are internationally renowned as some of the premier fishing locations in Western Europe whilst the region has produced some of the finest exponents of traditional Irish music on the entire island.

The Erne rises in Beaghy Lough in County Cavan and flows for 64 miles through Upper and Lower Lough Erne before entering the Atlantic at Ballyshannon. For centuries, the River Erne had an international reputation for its abundance of salmon. The O'Donnells, Chieftains of Donegal for almost 400 years were known as "the kings of the fishe".[1] It was a major source of revenue for them and they exported the fish in exchange for wine and other goods. When Assaroe Abbey was established in the late 12th century, the monks were awarded fishing rights on the river.[2] This provided them with a rich diet of mackerel, mullet, hake, herring and eel. Commercial eel fishing has an extensive history on the Erne, which stretches back to the monks at the Assaroe Abbey in the 12th century. In 1740, Sir John Caldwell leased a weir. His son, James discovered that he could harvest up to 3000 eels in one night during their winter migration. After the Plantation of Ulster, the Folliotts and then the Conollys developed the local fishing industry. The salmon were salted, cured, and exported to England and Europe.[3] Around 1867 R.L. Moore bought the fishery and developed angling on the river. This system continued until the construction of the power stations.

In the 1800s, Ballyshannon became very popular as a tourist destination for aristocratic anglers. Their arrival prompted ancillary employment in the catering industry and gillies very much in demand. Hugh Allingham provides an indication of the economic benefits of commercial salmon fishing for Ballyshannon in his book Ballyshannon, Its History and Antiquities: "As many as 2,000 fish have been taken in one day, and 400 in a single haul".[4] In 1825, Ballyshannon produced seventy-five tons of salmon.[5] Writing in 1851, Reverend Henry Newland stated that 'the Erne is decidedly the best fisherman's river in Ireland' and that 'the number of fish which it contains is altogether inconceivable'.[6]

Artist's impression of the falls on the River Erne

The Erne yielded an average of 100 tonnes of salmon (approximately 23,000 fish) every year. These fish were then exported to British and European markets. Until 1937, the Erne was the largest fishery in Ireland, employing 120 people directly. However, the construction of two hydroelectric dams between 1946 and 1955 led to the loss of many spawning and nursery areas with the result that there is no longer a self-sustaining wild population in the Erne system.[7]

In 1928, a legal dispute broke out between local fishermen and the landlord in control of the river. The case was known as the "Kildoney men's case" In 1933 judgement was delivered in favour of the local men and the river Erne was opened for public use.[8]

The river attracted angling tourists from all over the world. In times past, it was not unusual to see over fifty boats on the river and catches of trout weighing from 15 to 25 lbs were commonplace. The decimation of the salmon stocks led to the Erne system becoming better known for course fishing. On waters around Enniskillen, many world-angling records have been achieved. The key species are Bream, Rudd and Perch. In the past Roscor near Belleek played host to the World Coarse Angling Championships.

In angling terms, Ballyshannon is synonymous with the Rogan family's fly-tying artistry. As the angling industry in the town began to flourish in the early 19th century, the Rogan's capitalised on their unique ability to produce world-class flies. The anglers soon realised that the Rogan flies were very successful at catching salmon on the

Erne. Michael Rogan senior was born in Ballyshannon in 1833 and he learned the trade from his father James. Apparently, by the age of twelve he was so proficient at the craft that anglers were more than willing to purchase his elaborate creations. His flies were compared to 'fine pieces of jewellery'.[9] His minimalist approach employed just scissors and a comb. He also used a special wax that remained a family secret. Tradition has it that the urine of a stallion ass was used as a dyeing agent to achieve the luminous colours of his flies. The urine was supposedly kept in a barrel at the back of the shop much to the chagrin of near neighbours. When Michael senior died in 1905, his son James took the business and in 1938, his son Michael continued the tradition. He was the last of the name to carry on the tradition.

Due to the frequent flooding in centuries past, locals had an expression that "In the summer, Lough Erne is in Fermanagh and in the winter, Fermanagh is in Lough Erne". In the 1880s, a drainage scheme lowered the level of the lake and many new drowned-drumlin islands emerged. For millennia, the river was a major highway and people traversed its path from the Stone Age to modern times. The development of the road networks meant that it was no longer a significant transport route but today thousands of people continue to sail along its path for recreation.

For millennia, the Drowes has been seen as the historical boundary between Ulster and Connaught. It is one of the best salmon rivers in Ireland. Every year anglers flock to the river to catch the prestigious first salmon on New Year's Day. The Drowes begins its journey at Lough Melvin and runs its course for six miles until it reaches the Atlantic Ocean at Tullaghan.

The area where the Drowes enters Lough Melvin is known as Lareen. In the past, it was home to a number of Anglo Irish families. The story of Lareen is a microcosm of the decline of the Ascendency in Ireland. Luke White (Jnr) built Lareen House in the 1820s. He inherited Lareen, Mullinaleck and Rossfriar from his father. When Luke Junior died in 1854, Lareen was passed to his nephew John Thomas Massy, who became the 6th Baron Massy. His great grandfather, General Hugh Massy, was one of the English commanders sent to Ireland to suppress the 1641 Rebellion. Baron Massy used Lareen as a sporting estate and hosted many hunting parties there. For a time, life was good to the Massys by virtue of birth, but like many Ascendancy families, their fortune began to decline in the late 19th century. The costs of running the various estates were a significant drain on the family's dwindling wealth. He continued to live lavishly and made some poor investment decisions.

In 1912, Baron Massy sold Lareen, "the bed and soil of Lough Melvin and the waters thereof..." to Maxwell Blacker-Douglas. Blacker Douglas continued to use it as a sporting estate. The Blacker Douglas family entertained many guests including George Bernard Shaw's family and fishing legend T.C. Kingsmill Moore. According to Kingsmill Moore, the walls of the main rooms were covered in monochrome art depicting scenes from classical mythology. These life-sized nudes were too much for prudish Victorian tastes and the lurid appendages were airbrushed. When their descendants tried to restore the paintings, they found that the damage was irreversible. Blacker-Douglas's son Charles inherited Lareen and in 1926, he sold it to Maxwell Boyle. In 1933, a fire destroyed the house and the estate and fishery were sold to the owner of the Hamilton Hotel, Bundoran. A 1943 Irish Tourist Association survey indicates that it was still in a ruined condition due to the fire. Lareen Sporting Estates Ltd and Tunny Hotels bought in 1965. In 1977, the estate and fisheries were bought by Thomas and Betty Gallagher of Edenville and it has remained in the family since.

Fishing legend T.C. Kingsmill Moore fished out of Lareen for four years, twice a year. The house was in decline by the time he arrived: "Already the house was an anachronism, a manor house without an estate...the dust was settling; the Big House was dying at its roots...Then at one stride came disaster. Father and then mother were dead; the son, always delicate, became incurably ill. The Big House had fallen. Another old Irish family had come to its end."[10]

Lough Melvin is widely regarded as one of the best wet fly fisheries in Ireland. It hosts four genetically distinct types of trout namely the brown trout, sonaghan, ferox and the famous gillaroo. T.C. Kingsmill Moore described the gillaroo as 'the panther of the water' in his influential book 'A Man May Fish'. The gillaroo or *Salmo stomachicus* is a species of trout, which eats primarily snails. Its name is derived from the Irish language *Giolla Rua*, which means "Red Fellow". This is due to the fish's distinctive colouring. It has a bright buttery golden colour in its flanks with bright crimson and vermillion spots. The gillaroo feed almost exclusively on bottom-living animals (snails, sedge fly larva and freshwater shrimp) with the exception of late summer when they come to the surface to feed. The area around the lake is home to a large variety of flora and fauna included white fronted geese, otter, Atlantic char and rare plants such as the globe flower. It is a very important resource for scientists and the local community. Lough Melvin remains one of the few examples of a post-glacial salmonid Lough and remains in a relatively pristine state. Its chemical content is noticeably lower than Lough Erne or Neagh. The lake was an important tourism resource for towns like Garrison and Kinlough. In 1986 writer Colm Tóibín spoke to a woman called Mrs. Gregory from Garrison who described village life during the 1930s, "The fishing was wonderful between the wars. Everyone knew everyone else, came to the same hotel at the same time of year and in the evening they were having drinks before dinner in the bar of Casey's Hotel or McGovern's Hotel all the fish caught that day would be laid out on the table. Things were different then." [11]

The lakes and rivers continue to draw people to the area. The Erne experience offers a cautionary tale about the long-term impact of harnessing our natural resources.

The Reel

The music of the Border area is derived from a confluence of influences that produce its unique sound. The hard-driving, heavily Scottish-influenced music of north Donegal becomes distilled south of Bearnas Mór Gap and is fused with the lively, rhythmic influence of North Leitrim and West Fermanagh.

Given the antiquity of 'Ireland's oldest inhabited town', it is not surprising that Ballyshannon has a musical tradition that stretches back for hundreds of years. The blind harpist and composer Ruaidri Dáll Ó Catháin wrote "The Hawk of Ballyshannon," also known as "Port Athol," (later retouched by O'Carolan as "O'Moore's Daughter). It is thought the tune was written as a tribute to the Fermanagh chieftain Philip McGuire.

The 'gentleman piper', Patrick Haly was born in Ballyshannon in 1748 and died in 1813. He became Burgess of the Town Corporation when Ballyshannon was one of the most prosperous commercial towns in the northwest. Hugh Allingham, author of Ballyshannon Its History & Antiquities (1879) and half-brother of the poet William described the environment in which Haly performed: "In by-gone days there lived a race of musicians in Ireland which have become extinct. For such there was always an open door and a hearty welcome. They were received and treated as honoured guests, and, in return, charmed the ears of the company with their performance on the pipes and harp."[12] Haly was a much sought after musician and a frequent honoured guest of Sir James Caldwell at Castlecaldwell. The plaintive sound of his pipes echoed over Lough Erne as Caldwell and his guest sailed across the lake in his "St. Patrick" barge. Haly's visits to Castlecaldwell are remembered in a once popular song:

"With his pipes and songs
And chanter longs,
He sits in high decorum

165

And at his (e)ase he snuffs and plays,
And pushes about the jorum"

William Allingham is best known as a poet but he also played fiddle and collected tunes from the area.[13] He scoured the workhouses to record the repertoires of the locals. In 1847, he collected 'Ain Kin Dearie' and 'Paudeen O Rafferty' from Tom Read in Ballyshannon. He submitted songs to 'The Petrie Collection of the Ancient Music of Ireland', one of which was a local song named 'It was an Old Beggarman, Wet and Weary'. He also submitted a tune in 9/8 time (slip jig) named Kitty O Hea. His other contributions to the music collections were the airs of Van Diemen's Land and Mo Chailín Deas.[14]

Another famous ballad associated with the town is 'Colleen Bawn'. It is the story of a Squire Folliard's daughter who falls in love with Willy Reilly. They decide to elope only to be recaptured by Folliard and his men. Reilly is then transported for kidnapping. However, Colleen waits for him and eventually he returns to Wardtown Castle, near Ballyshannon and marries her.

From the mid-nineteenth century, traditional musicians in the area played at house dances in homes known as 'céilí houses'. The music was performed one or more musicians. The fiddle was the most popular instrument. The music was performed for solo couple or set dances. In the early 1900s, large outdoor musical gatherings (Aeridheacht) were also popular in the area.

The ownership of gramophones and wireless sets introduced Irish people to a wider selection of music. Jazz was becoming quite popular. According to Daniel Cassidy's book 'How the Irish Invented Slang', the word jazz may have come from the Irish word teas (pronounced j'ass) meaning passion or excitement. The word has sexual connotations. According to Louis Armstrong, the first use of the word Jass (from which jazz evolved) was in 1917 when a group of Irish and Sicilian musicians in New Orleans recorded a track called Dixieland Jass One Step. However, the Catholic Church saw the new music as decadent. In 1924, the Irish Catholic Directory described jazz and its influences as "importations from the vilest dens of London, Paris and New York leading to evil thoughts and evil desires." County Leitrim became the centre of the Anti-Jazz campaign and its leader was the parish priest of Cloone, Fr. Peter Conefrey. On New Year's Day 1934 over three thousand people from South Leitrim and the surrounding areas marched through Mohill shouting slogans such as 'Down with Jazz' and 'Out with Paganism'. Taoiseach Eamon de Valera sent his regrets that neither he, nor any of his ministers, could attend but sincerely hoped that the efforts of the Gaelic League to restore 'the national forms of dancing' would be successful. The Leitrim Observer published an article in support of the campaign: 'Let the pagan Saxon be told that we Irish Catholics do not want and will not have the dances and the music that he has borrowed from the savages of the islands of the Pacific'. Fr. Conefrey stated that jazz 'borrowed from the language of the savages of Africa.' The Anti-Jazz Campaign ran out of steam as 1934 progressed but due to clerical pressure, the government introduced the Dance Halls Act of 1935. That same year, the Nazi party introduced a law banning Jazz from being played over the radio.

In addition to its function as a form of entertainment, house dances were very often used as fund raising events within the local communities. The clergy were very weary of these events where men and women could dance together unsupervised. The church successfully lobbied the government to introduce the Dance Hall Act in 1935. The act prohibited private house dances and ensured that future music making took place in a controlled environment. They church began to open their own halls that became a lucrative source of funding. The 1930s saw a large increase in the building of parochial halls throughout the country. The local clergy applied successfully for dancing licenses and the money raised became an important source of revenue for parishes and for the government, who took a 25% tax on each ticket sold. The socialising of young men and women at dances would now take place under the strict supervision of the local priest. The new venues required more volume and the céilí band was born. The new line-up included drums, piano and double bass. The Assaroe Céilí Band was formed in the late 1940s and is still active today. Both Charlie Lennon and Charlie McGettigan (winner of the 1994 Eurovision Song Contest with Paul Harrington) played with the Assaroe Céilí Band in their youth.

After the Dance Hall Act of 1935, 'house céilís' declined in the area. It would take many decades for the traditional music in the region to recover. In the 1970s, Irish traditional music enjoyed a revival. This marked the period known as the 'golden age of traditional music in Ballyshannon'.[15] John Gordon and Kevin Loughlin from Belleek were regular performers at the time. Mick Hoy from Fermanagh was also a regular visitor. Ben Lennon from Kiltyclogher often performed in McIntyre's bar, a favourite haunt for traditional music players from

Donegal, Leitrim and Fermanagh. Ballyshannon Folk Festival was launched in 1978 and continues to this day.

One of the first recorded mentions of music in Bundoran was given in a legal deposition by Francis Kerrigan, a local fisherman in 1870. The people of Bundoran challenged a landlord's decision to close off access to the beach, claiming that it was a public right of way. Kerrigan, who was 75 at the time, said that he was born in Bundoran and lived there all his life. His father had lived in Bundoran all his life too and recalled that the 'pleasure ground' had always been used by the public for 'walking, dancing, music and all kinds of entertainment'.[16]

In the mid-19th century, Bundoran was two separate villages. In the West End was the Ascendancy resort of Bundoran where many of the hotels had pianos that classically trained musicians would sight-read the latest hits off the ballad sheets. Here, the music was more refined than the informal communal music making that was taking place a mile away in the East End Catholic village of Single Street.

Throughout the late 19th and early 20th centuries, during the summer months, musicians from far and wide would congregate in the town and line up on the cliffs to warm up for their concerts that night. During the 1920's Aeridheacht or out-door céilí were very popular. There were organised by local schoolteacher and local IRA intelligence officer Joseph Murray, whose aim it was to reinvigorate the Gaelic Revival in the town. The Bundoran Gala Week in the 1930s featured fiddle and dance competitions. In the 1940s, dancers would meet on Sundays to dance the 'Haymakers Jig'. From the 1960s until the present day, the tradition has been kept alive by a handful of stalwarts.

Dancing by the sea at Rougey, Bundoran in the 1940s

Paddy Kelly was born in Fintona, County Tyrone and by a young age had established himself as an accomplished fiddler. His reputation was such that he found himself being regularly booked to perform in Bundoran. He would often cycle from Fintona to Bundoran with his fiddle on his back during the summer months. Over time, he settled in the town. In 1951, he won the senior fiddle title at the first Fleadh Cheoil na hÉireann. His son Pat, also an accomplished musician toured Britain with the late great Sean McGuire.

The area that stretches from Kiltyclogher to Derrygonnelly and Belleek has a rich heritage in traditional music. The region has produced many fine singers and musicians, who were steeped in local tradition, notably Eddie Duffy, Mick Hoy, John Gordon, the Lennons and Paddy Tunney to name a few. The tradition stretches back to the mid-18th century when O'Carolan was a regular welcome visitor to many of the 'Big Houses' on the shores of Lough Erne. O'Carolan married Mary Maguire of County Fermanagh, and they had a family of six daughters and one son. They settled on a small farm near County Leitrim. Protestant settlers, who had been at most for three generations in the country, seemed to have been just as devoted to the Irish harp music as the old Gaelic families.[17] O'Carolan had a long association of friendship and hospitality with the Maguires of Tempo. He composed a song to honour Mrs Archdall of Castle Archdale and played in Castlecaldwell.

John Gordon had a very distinctive playing style. He was born in 1928 and grew up on a small farm in the townland of Drumcully, between Belleek and Belcoo. Both his parents were musical and from an early age, he showed an interest in music. His first instrument was the mouth organ and his father taught him to play the fiddle when he was about six years old. At the age of ten, his mother entered him in the Fermanagh Feis and he won first prize.

Ben Lennon was born in 1938 in Kiltyclogher. In his younger days, there were over 50 fiddlers in the area. He learned much of his repertoire from nearby Fermanagh fiddlers John Timoney and John Gordon. He was strongly influenced by Michael Coleman but equally influenced by styles from the neighbouring counties of Fermanagh and Donegal proximity. His brother Charlie is a prolific composer. He began playing piano at the age of seven. Ben taught him to play the fiddle. At fourteen, he joined Michael Shanley's 'Seán McDermott Céilí Band'. At 17, he toured professionally with the Richard Fitzgerald band and later the Assaroe Céilí Band. In 1984, he released his first composite piece 'The Emigrant Suite' the 'Island Wedding' premiered in Moscow in 1993. The 'Famine Suite' (Flight from the Hungry Land) followed in 1995. He has recorded on over 25 albums over the decades and remains one of Ireland best-known composers of traditional music.

In 1972, Ben Lennon and his wife Patsy moved to Donegal town where he worked for the Magee Company. Patsy became the postmistress in Rossinver and eventually they made the village their base. This move prompted a dramatic change in the music of the area. Over time, Ben met many of the musical stalwarts of Fermanagh's rich musical tradition. He played with Mick Hoy and Eddie Duffy in Derrygonnelly. McIntyre's bar in Ballyshannon became a favourite haunt of traditional players. Saturday night sessions took place in the Thatch cottage hosted by John Gordon and Kevin Loughlin from Belleek. Phil Rooney from Kinlough also attended the sessions. During this time Ben also met the legendary Donegal fiddler John Doherty, whose version of the 'Gravel Walks' is still a favourite at traditional sessions in Donegal. There were regular sessions in Derrygonnelly. They were attended by Gabriel McArdle and Ciaran Curran (bouzouki player with Altan). Brian Rooney (The Godfather) was also a regular performer at the sessions in Gilbrides. Desi Wilkinson the flute player would also glean tunes from Ben's extensive repertoire. Cathal Mc Connell from Boys of the Lough fame also regularly played music with Ben. The culmination of all this playing was the 1989 album Dog Big Dog Little, named after the two hills in Fermanagh. According to legend, two hounds of Cúchulainn's were chasing a dove, who was in fact a witch. She turned the two dogs into two hills Dog big and Dog little.

Paddy Tunney (1921-2002), the Man of Songs was an Irish traditional singer, poet and writer. At an early age, his family moved to Mulleek, in County Fermanagh near the Border village of Belleek. Tunney described the area around Lough Erne's shores as 'a land where men walked and talked tall and there was a rich music in their mode of speech'.[18] His father got a job on the construction of the Boa Island bridges. His mother, Bridget Gallagher from Pettigo came from a long line of traditional singers. She was the biggest influence on his music. In his book 'The Stone Fiddle', he described the first time, he heard the song 'As I Roved Out': "Meadow mane rippled with corncrakes and scythe steel sang to whetstone. The air ached with the pain and joy of loving. It was the time that turned my mother to songs of love and longing...She sang me for the first time that exquisitely beautiful song: As I Roved out or The False Bride."

He attended Derryhollow National School and later Ballyshannon Technical School. During the Second World War, he became involved with the IRA and in the summer of 1943 was sentenced to seven years penal servitude for smuggling explosives. Reminiscing on the experience, he apparently quipped 'it was quite normal in those days to be writing poetry and planting bombs'. Throughout his life, he was hugely influential in Irish traditional music circles and his songs have been recorded by artists including: The Chieftains, Planxty, Paul Brady and Andy Irvine, Altan, Dervish and Cara Dillon.

On August 13th 1770, Sir James Caldwell was entertaining guest on his 'St Patrick's' barge. Music was provided by local fiddler Denis McCabe. Both McCabe and the guest had been drinking and McCabe fell overboard. He drowned and Caldwell commissioned a stone fiddle to commemorate the musician. The fiddle can still be seen at the entrance to Castlecaldwell. The inscription reads...

Ye fiddlers beware ye fiddlers fate
Don't attempt ye deep lest ye repent too late
Ye ever were to water foes
So shun the deep till it with whiskey flows
On dry land ye can exercise your skill
There ye can play and drink your fill
D.D.D.

Locals believe that D.D.D. stands for Denis Died Drunk or Drink Drowned Denis.[19] It appears that Sir James Caldwell had a museum at the castle and among his most treasured possessions was the skull of Turlough O'Carolan. His skull was removed his grave and changed hands many times before it was sold to Caldwell. After he died, it ended up in Belfast.[20] In 1926, it was transferred to the National Museum, Dublin. [21]

Paddy Tunney was also a renowned raconteur. In 'The Stone Fiddle', he relates the humorous tale of two local men's encounter with the paranormal.

"Two local fiddlers decided to set up a poteen still near the graveyard at Castlecaldwell in preparation for Hallow Eve. As the distillation process began, one of the men took out his fiddle warmed up with the Salamanca Reel. Suddenly, two shadowy figures emerged. One was wearing a long black cloak with a hood and the other was dressed in a swallowtail and knickerbockers. The fiddlers noticed that the figure in the long black cloak had no head. They were frozen with fear until the man dressed in a swallowtail picked up the fiddle and played 'The Boys of the Lough' in a manner that would 'draw tears from a stone'. He then played the haunting melody 'Ceann Dubh Dílis'. When he finished he turned to his headless companion and said to him 'Come on Terry, your skull is no longer here. If it was I'd have found it years ago'. He returned the fiddle and urged the musicians to 'Keep McCabe's music alive'. It was only after that the two men realised that they had met ghosts of Denis McCabe and Turlough O'Carolan."

Index

Bibliography

Allingham, H., 1879. *Ballyshannon Its History & Antiquities.* Londonderry: s.n.

Anderson, J., 1995. Agrarian Revolution: Tirhugh 1715-1855. In: W. Nolan, ed. *Donegal History & Society.* s.l.:s.n.

Anderson, M. & Bort, E. eds., 1999. In: *The Irish border: history, politics, culture .* Liverpool University Press: s.n.

Andrews, J. H., 1965. The papers of the Irish boundary commission. *Irish Geography,* 5(2), pp. 477-481.

Anon., 1970. Bréifne. *Journal of Cuman Seanchais Bréifne,,* 4(13).

Anon., 1974. An Interview with Benedict Kiely. *James Joyce Quarterly,* 11(3), pp. 189-200.

Anon., 1985. Defenders and Defenderism in 1795. *Irish Historical Studies,* 24(95), pp. 373-394.

Anon., 2009. *Garrison attack and policing.* [Online]
Available at: http://www.sluggerotoole.com/

Anon., 2011. *Carson's Home Rule opposition began in Enniskillen.* [Online]
Available at: http://www.impartialreporter.com
[Accessed 15 December 2013].

Anon., 2011. *Cross Border Community Plans Rossinver-Garrison, Kiltyclogher-Cashel and Glenfarne-Blacklion-Belcoo.* s.l.:Leitrim County Council, West Cavan West Fermanagh Regeneration Project & Broadmore Research.

Anon., 2011. *Tullaghan Kinlough Integrated Community Plan,* s.l.: Leitrim County Council, West Cavan West Fermanagh Regeneration Project & Broadmore Research.

Anon., 2012. *New IRA: full statement by the dissident 'Army Council'.* [Online]
Available at: http://www.theguardian.com/
[Accessed 23 June 2013].

Anon., 2014. *Census 2011 - Preliminary results.* [Online]
Available at: http://www.cso.ie/census/Table8.htm

Aoidh, C. M., 1994. *Between the Jigs and the Reels.* Manorhamilton:
Drumlin Publications.

Bardon, J., 1992. *A History of Ulster.* Belfast : Blackstaff Press.

BBC News, 2009. *Three released over police attack http://news.bbc.co.uk/.*
[Online]
Available at: http://news.bbc.co.uk/
[Accessed 19 May 2013].

Beattie, S., 2013. *Donegal in Transition. The Impact of the Congested
District Boards.* Sallins: Merrion Press.

Begley, A., 2009. *Ballyshannon and Surrounding Areas: History, Heritage
and Folklore.* Ballyshannon: Carrickboy Publishing.

Begley, A., 2011. *Ballyshannon: Genealogy & History.* Ballyshannon:
Carrickboy Publishing.

Bell, J. B., 1972. *The Secret Army: A History of the IRA, 1916-1970.* London:
Sphere Books Limited.

Bell, R., 1994. 'Sheep Stealers from the North of England': The Riding Clans
in Ulster. *History Ireland,* 2(4), pp. 25-29.

Bishop, P. & Mallie, E., 1988. *The Provisional IRA.* Reading: Corgi Books.

Borderlines Project, 2008. *Borderlines: Personal Stories and Experiences
from the Border Counties of the Island of Ireland.* Dublin: Gallery of
Photography.

Bottomley, P. M., 1974. The North Fermanagh Elections of 1885 and 1886:
Some Documentary Illustrations. *Clogher Record ,* 8(2), pp. 167-181.

Bowcott, O., 13 April 2002. *Army urged to halt border security campaign.*
s.l.:The Guardian.

Bradley, J., 1996. *An Island Economy – Exploring Long-term Economic and
Social Consequences of Peace and Reconciliation in the Island of Ireland,*
Dublin: Forum for Peace and Reconciliation.

Busteed, M., 2006. *Castle Caldwell, Co. Fermanagh. Life on a west Ulster estate, 1750-1800.* Dublin: Four Courts Press.

Cairns, E. & Darby, J., 1998. The conflict in Northern Ireland: Causes, consequences, and controls. *American Psychologist,* 53(7), p. 754.

Conway, V., n.d. *Policing the Border during the Troubles.* [Online] Available at: http://www.humanrights.ie

Coogan, T. P., 1991. *Michael Collins: A Biography*: Arrow Books.

Coogan, T. P., 2004. *Ireland In The 20th Century By. London arrow book 2004,* London: Arrow Books.

Co-operation Ireland , 2005. *Proposals for Effective North-South Co-operation: A Policy Paper*.

Coulter, H., 1862. *The West of Ireland: its existing condition, and prospects.* Dublin: Hodges & Smith.

County Donegal Book of Honour Committee, 2002. *County Donegal Book of Honour. The Great War, 1914 - 1918.*

Crawley, M., 2002. *Protestant Communities in Border Areas Research Report*: Rural Community Network NI.

Creamer, C. et al., 2008. *Fostering Mutual Benefits in Cross-Border Areas ,* Armagh: International Centre for Local and Regional Development (ICLRD) .

Cuellar, F. d., *Captain Cuellar's Adventures in Connacht and Ulster.*

Cunningham, J. B., 2006. *The Pettigo History Trail.* Pettigo: Pettigo Mens' Group.

Cunningham, J. B., 1987. The Castle Caldwell Estate in 1780 and the Recent Arrest of the Highwayman Francis McHugh (Prionsias Dubh). *Clogher Record,* 12(3), pp. 261-264.

Cunningham, J. B., 2006. The Lost English Plantation of Fermanagh. In: B. S. Turner, ed. *Migration and Myth: Ulster's Revolving Door.* Downpatrick: Ulster Local History Trust, pp. 92-96.

Cunningham, J. B., 2010-04. *The Way We Were in Fermanagh in World War II and the 1940s: The Golden Years of Smuggling.* Belleek: Davog Press.

Cunningham, J. B., 2013. *Fermanagh in Space. The 500 person in space has Fermanagh ancestors..* [Online]
Available at: http://erneheritagetours.com/magento/wp/?page_id=16. Fermanagh in Space
[Accessed 12 February 2014].

Cunningham, J. B. & McGowan, G., 2008. *Fermanagh In Sight: The Fermanagh Highlands.*

Cunningham, J. & Herbert, V., 2004. *From Ballyjamesduff To Ballyshannon (A Guide To The River Erne).* Enniskillen: Erne Heritage Tour Guide .

Curtis, L., 1994. *All Along the Watchtowers.* s.l.:New internationalist, Issue 255.

Darwin, K., 1990. *Familia 1990: Ulster Geneological Review: Number 6.* s.l.:Ulster Historical Foundation.

De Paor, L., 1990. *Unfinished Business: Ireland Today and Tomorrow.* London: Hutchinson Radius.

Derry and Raphoe Action, *Protestants and the Border. Stories of Border Protestants North and South.* s.l.:Derry and Raphoe Action.

Dewar, M., 1996. *The British Army in Northern Ireland.* London : Arms and Armour.

Doinnléibhe, P. M., 1963. Fermanagh (1870-1900). *Clogher Record,* 5(1), pp. 7-29.

Donagher, P., 2001. *Donegal Bay angling guide: a definitive guide to game, coarse and sea angling in South Donegal.* Ballyshannon: Erne Enterprise Development Company.

Donegal County Council, n.d. *The Unemployment Landscape of County Donegal. Donegal County Council.* [Online]
Available at: http://www.donegalcoco.ie/
[Accessed 14 March 2014].

Donnan, H., 2010. Cold War along the Emerald Curtain: rural boundaries in a contested border zone. *Social Anthropology,* 18(3), pp. 253-266.

Donnelly, D., 2010. *Prisoner 1082. Escape from Crumlin Road, Europe's Alcatraz.* Cork: The Collins Press.

Duibhir, L. Ó., 2009. *The Donegal Awakening: Donegal and the War of Independence.* Cork: Mercier.

Duigneáin, P. Ó., *North Leitrim in Famine Times, 1840-50.* Manorhamilton: Drumlin Publications.

Dungan, M., 1993. *Distant Drums. Irish Soldiers in Foreign Armies.* Belfast: Appletree Press.

English, R., 2004. *Armed Struggle: The History of the I.R.A..* London: Pan Books.

Fealty, M., 2013. *Good Friday Agreement at 15: The dour fatalism of our political Calvinists.* [Online]
Available at: http://sluggerotoole.com/
[Accessed 14 April 2013].

Feeley, T., 2013. *From Glack to Bunduff.* Kinlough: s.n.

Ferriter, D., 2005. *The Transformation of Ireland: 1900-2000.* 2nd ed. London: Profile Books Ltd.

Fitzpatrick, D., 2002. The Orange Order and the Border. *Irish Historical Studies,* 33(129), pp. 52-67.

Fitzpatrick, R., 1989. *'A Peculiar People' God's Frontiersmen: The Scots-Irish.* London: Weidenfeld & Nicolson Ltd.

Fortnight, 1972, . *Fortnight Guide to Ulster Demography*: Fortnight Publications Ltd, No. 33 pp. 4-6.

Fraser, T. G., 2007. Partition. In: S. J. Connolly, ed. *The Oxford Companion to Irish history.* Oxford: Oxford University Press, p. 455.

Gallachair, P. Ó., 1975. The Parish of Carn. *Clogher Record,* VIII(3), pp. 301-380.

Gardiner, D., 2008. *Whatever you say, say nothing. A report on the views and experiences of Border Protestants for the Church of Ireland Diocese of Clogher*: Hard Gospel Project.

Geagan, M., 2011. *Dancing By the Sea: A Journey Through Time in the Bundoran Area.* Bundoran: Stracomer Press.

Glenravel Local History Project, 1971. *The Troubles.* [Online]
Available at: http://www.glenravel.com/
[Accessed 28 January 2014].

Gray, P., 2007. Thomas D'Arcy McGee. In: S. J. Connolly, ed. *Oxford Companion to Irish History.* Oxford:: Oxford University Press, p. 352.

Group, N. L. M., 2000. *North Leitrim Mens' Group.* [Online]
Available at: http://homepage.eircom.net/~nlmensgroup/
[Accessed 18 November 2013].

Hand, G., 1969. *Report of the Irish Boundary Commission (1925).* Shannon: Irish University Press .

Harris, R., 1972. *Prejudice and Tolerance in Ulster: A Study of Neighbours and "strangers" in a Border Community.* Manchester: Manchester University Press.

Hayes-McCoy, G. A., 1932. Ballyshannon: Its Strategic Importance in the Wars in Connacht, 1550-1602. *Journal of the Galway Archaeological and Historical Society,* 15(3/4), pp. 141-159.

Heslinga, M. W., 1979. *The Irish border as a cultural divide: a contribution to the study of regionalism in the British Isles.* 3rd ed. s.l.:Van Gorcum.

Independent Monitoring Commission, 2009. *Twenty First Report of the Independent Monitoring Commission.*

Independent Monitoring Commission, 2010. *Twenty Fifth Report of the Independent Monitoring Commission.*

Institute for the Study of Conflict & Beckett, J. C., 1972. *The Ulster Debate: Report of a Study Group of the Institute for the Study of Conflict,* London: Bodley Head.

Johnston, J., 1980. Settlement Patterns in County Fermanagh, 1610-1660. *Clogher Record,* 10(2), pp. 199-214.

Kenny, K., 1998. *Making Sense of the Molly Maguires.* Oxford : Oxford University Press .

Kerr, D. A., 1982. *Peel, Priests and Politics: Sir Robert Peel's administration and the Roman Catholic Church in Ireland, 1841-1846.* Oxford: Clarendon Press.

Kiely, B., 1945. *Counties of Contention,* Cork : Mercier Press.

Kiely, B., 1991. *Drink to the bird: a memoir.* London: Methuen.

Kinlough Rossinver Askill Garrison Partnership (K.R.A.G), 2008. *Melvin Drive.*

Laffan, M., 1983. *The Partition of Ireland, 1911-1925.* Dublin: Historical Association of Ireland.

Laffan, M., 2004. The Emergence of the 'Two Irelands', 1912-25. *History Ireland,* 12(4), pp. 40-44.

Latham, R., 2001. *Deadly Beat: Inside the Royal Ulster Constabulary.* Edinburgh: Mainstream Publishing Company.

Leitrim County Council, West Cavan West Fermanagh Regeneration Project & Broadmore Research, 2011. *Tullaghan Kinlough Integrated Community Plan.*

Livingstone, P., 1969. *The Fermanagh story: A documented history of the County Fermanagh from the earliest times to the present day.* Enniskillen: Cumann Seanchais Chlochair.

Logue, P , M. K. S. P., 2007. *The Border Protestant Community and the Peace Programmes.*

Logue, P., 1999. *The Border: Personal Reflections from Ireland North and South.* Dublin : Oak Tree Press.

Mac Doinnléibhe, P., 1963. Fermanagh (1870-1900). *Clogher Record,* 5(1), pp. 7-29.

Mac Donagh, J. C., 1947. Counsellor Terence Mac Donagh: A Great Catholic Lawyer of the Penal Days. *Irish Quarterly Review,* 36(143), pp. 307-318.

Mansergh, N., 1991. *The Unresolved Question: The Anglo-Irish Settlement and its Undoing 1912-1972.* London: Yale University Press.

Marron, P., (1976). Ballyshannon to Enniskillen in 1776. *Clogher Record,* 9(1), pp. 64-66.

Martin, G., 1999. Origins of Partition. In: M. Anderson & E. Bort, eds. *The Irish border: history, politics, culture.* Liverpool: Liverpool University Press.

McCoy, C. & Ó Siochrú, M., 2008. County Fermanagh and the 1641 Depositions. *Archivium Hibernicum,* Volume 61, pp. 62-136.

McCracken, E., 1947. The Woodlands of Ulster in the Early Seventeenth Century. *Ulster Journal of Archaeology,* 10(3), pp. 15-25.

McCreary, A., 1996. *Gordon Wilson: An Ordinary Hero.* London: Marshall Pickering.

McCusker, B. & Morris, F., 1999. *Fermanagh: Land of Lake and Legend.* Donaghadee: Cottage Publications.

McDaniel, D., 1997. *Enniskillen: The Remembrance Day Bombing.* Dublin: Wolfhound Press.

McDermott, J. J., McNeary, R. & O'Conor, K., 2009. *Rosclogher castle: The late medieval lordship centre of 'Dartry MacClancy' Lough Melvin, Co. Leitrim.*

McDonald, H. & Cusack, J., 1997. *UVF.* Dublin: Poolbeg.

McGarry, J. & O'Leary, B., 2000. *Policing Northern Ireland: Proposals for a New Start..* Belfast: Blackstaff.

McGearty, S. et al., 2005. *The Emerald Curtain The Social Impact of the Irish Border,* Carrickmacross: Triskele Community Training & Development.

McGreary, A., 1996. *Gordon Wilson: An Ordinary hero.* London: Marshall Pickering.

McKittrick, D., ed., 2001. In: *Lost Lives: the stories of the men, women and children who died as a result of the Northern Ireland troubles*: Random House.

McVeigh, J., 23 March 2005 . *Michael Barrett (1841-1868) - The forgotten Fenian from Fermanagh*: An Phoblacht.

Mearáin, L. Ó., 1958. The Apostasy of Miler McGrath. *Clogher Record,* 2(2), pp. 244-256.

Minogue, R., 2002 . *Landscape Assessment of County Leitrim*: Comhairle Chontae Liatroma.

Moody, T. W., 1935. XXVIII.-The revised Articles of the Ulster Plantation, 1610. *Historical Research,* 12(36), p. 178–183.

Mooney, J. & O' Toole, M., 2003. *Black Operations: The Secret War Against the Real IRA.* Ashbourne: Maverick House Publishers.

Moore Institute for Research in the Humanities and Social Studies, National University of Ireland, Galway, n.d. *Landed Estates Database.* [Online]
Available at: http://landedestates.nuigalway.ie
[Accessed 10 January 2014].

Moore, T. K., 1960. *A Man May Fish.* Buckinghamshire: Colin Smythe Limited.

Muldoon, O. T., 2008. Adolescents' explanations for paramilitary involvement. *Journal of Peace Research,* 45(5), pp. 681-695.

Murray, P., 2004. Partition and the Irish Boundary Commission: A Northern Nationalist Perspective. *Clogher Record,* 18(2), pp. 181-217.

Newland, H., 1851. *The Erne: Its Legends and its Fly Fishing.* London: Chapman and Hall.

NISRA, 2001 . *Northern Ireland Census of Population.* [Online]
Available at: http://www.nisranew.nisra.gov.uk/census/start.html
[Accessed 24 July 2013].

Northern Ireland Office, 2003. *Responding to a Changing Security Situation.*
[Online]
Available at:
https://cain.ulst.ac.uk/issues/politics/docs/nio/nio1003security.pdf
[Accessed 8 May 2014].

Ó Canann, T. G., 2013. Dynastic Conflict in Medieval Donegal, AD 800-1400. In: *An Historical, Environmental and Cultural Atlas of County Donegal.* Cork: Cork University Press, pp. 116-124.

Ó Duibhir, L., 2011. *Donegal & the Civil War: The Untold Story.* Cork: Mercier Press.

Ó Duigneáin, P., 1987. *North Leitrim in famine times, 1840-50.* Manorhamilton : Drumlin Publications.

Ó Gallachair, P., 1961. *Where the Erne and Drowes meet the sea, fragments from a Patrician parish.* Ballyshannon: Donegal Democrat Ltd.

Ó Gráda, C. & Walsh, B. M., 2006. *Did (And Does) the Irish Border Matter?*: Institute for British-Irish Studies. Working Papers in British-Irish Studies. No. 60.

O'Loughlin, J., 2009. *The Border Belleek 1910-1930.* [Online]
Available at: www.joeoloughlin.co.uk
[Accessed 24 August 2013].

O'Loughlin, J., 2011. *A History of Keenaghan Abbey & St. Michael's Church, Mulleek.*

O'Loughlin, J., *The Border at Belleek 1910-1930.* [Online]
Available at: http://www.joeoloughlin.co.uk/
[Accessed 16 March 2014].

O'Brien, B., 1999. *The Long War: The IRA and Sinn Féin.* 2nd ed. Syracuse: Syracuse University Press.

O'Hart, J., 1892. *Irish pedigrees; or, The Origin and Stem of the Irish Nation. Volume: 1.* Dublin: J. Duffy and Co.

O'Neill, J., 2009. *The Forgotten Soldiers of Peace*: Óglaigh Náisiúnta Teoranta (ONET).

Patterson, H., 2006. *Border Killings – Liberation Struggle or Ethnic Cleansing?.* [Online]
Available at: http://news.ulster.ac.uk/releases/2006/2223.html
[Accessed 11 November 2013].

Patterson, H., 2010. Sectarianism revisited: the Provisional IRA campaign in a border region of Northern Ireland. *Terrorism and Political Violence,* 22(3), pp. 337-356.

Patterson, H., 2011. *'Deeply anti-British' The Irish state and cross-border security cooperation 1970-1974.* London, 61st Political Studies Association Annual Conference. Transforming Politics: New Synergies.

Patterson, H., 2013. *Ireland's Violent Frontier: The Border and Anglo-Irish Relations during the Troubles.* Basingstoke : Palgrave Macmillan.

Peter Quinn Consultancy Services Ltd, *Garrison Integrated Village Action Plan.*

Peter Quinn Consultancy Services, 1998. *'The Way It Is' Area Profiles. A Comprehensive Review of Community Development and Community Relationships in County Fermanagh.*

Phoenix, É., 2011. *The Impact of The Great Famine of 1845-51 with special reference to Ulster*, Department of Arts, Heritage and the Gaeltacht.

Piraprez, F. V. N. J. & Gaffney, M., 2011. *Ben Lennon - the Tailor's Twist: Ben Lennon's Life in Traditional Irish Music.* Dublin.

Plummer, C., 1922. *Bethada Náem nÉrenn. Lives of Irish Saints.* Oxford: Clarendon Press.

Pollak, A., 1985. Why Northern Ireland Needs a Military Back up: A UDR Officer's Point of View.. *Fortnight*, 7-20 October, pp. 6-8.

Rankin, K. J., 2006. *The Provenance and Dissolution of the Irish Boundary Commission.* Dublin: Institute for British-Irish Studies, Working Papers in British-Irish Studies No. 79.

Reporter, I., 2011. *Carson's Home Rule Opposition began in Enniskillen.* [Online]
Available at: http://www.impartialreporter.com/
[Accessed 9 November 2012].

Robson, B., 1994. *Relative Deprivation in Northern Ireland,* Belfast: Northern Ireland Statistics and Research Agency (NISRA).

Roger Tym & Partners, 2005. *Donegal County Council Erne Maritime Link Socio-Economic Assessment Final Report ,* Glasgow.

Rúnaí, L. O., 1996. *From Rosclogher to Rooskey: The Leitrim Story.* Cumann Seanchais Ros Inbhir.

Rural Community Network, 2002. *You'd feel you had no say. Rural Protestants and Community Development.,* Rural Community Network: Cookstown.

Ryder, C., 1997. *The RUC 1922-1997: A Force Under Fire.* London: Mandarin Paperbacks.

Schlegel, D., 1997. A Clogher Chronology: October, 1641 to July, 1642.. *Clogher Record,* 16(1), pp. 79-94.

Shuttleworth, I et al., 2000. The Tail of the Tiger: Experiences and perceptions of unemployment and inactivity in Donegal. *Irish Geography,* 33(1), pp. 56-7.

Simms, J. G., 1979. The Williamite War in South Ulster. *Clogher Record,* 10(1), pp. 155-162.

Simms, K., 1977. The Medieval Kingdom of Lough Erne. *Clogher Record,* 9(2), pp. 126-141.

Simms, K., 1995. Late Medieval Donegal. In: N. W. R. L. Dunlevy, Mairead, ed. *Donegal, History & Society.* Dublin: Geography Publications, pp. 183-202.

Staunton, E., 1996. The Boundary Commission Debacle 1925: Aftermath & Implications. *History Ireland,* 4(2), pp. 42-45.

Stewart, A. T. Q., 1989. *The Narrow Ground: The Roots of Conflict in Ulster..* London : Faber and Faber Ltd.

Todd, J. et al, 2005. *Borders, States and Nations. Contested Boundaries and National Identities in the Irish Border Area*: Geary Institute. Geary Discussion Paper Series. Geary WP 2005/03.

Tóibín, C., 1987. *Bad Blood: A Walk Along the Irish Border.* Picador – Ireland.

Tonge, J., 2004. 'They Haven't Gone Away, You Know' Irish Republican 'Dissidents' and 'Armed Struggle'. *Terrorism and Political Violence,* 16(3), pp. 671-693.

Trew, J. D., 2010. Reluctant Diasporas of Northern Ireland: Migrant narratives of home, conflict, difference. *Journal of Ethnic and Migration Studies,* 36(4), pp. 541-560.

Trimble, J., 1979. Carolan and His Patrons in Fermanagh and Neighbouring Areas. *Clogher Record,* 10(1), pp. 26-50.

Tunney, P., 1979. *The Stone Fiddle: My Way to Traditional Song.* Skerries: Gilbert Dalton, .

Turner, B. S., 1975. An Observation on Settler Names in Fermanagh. *Clogher Record,* 8(3), pp. 285-289.

Walker, B., 2007. The Lost Tribes of Ireland: Diversity, Identity and Loss Among the Irish Diaspora. *Irish Studies Review,* 15(3), pp. 267-282.

Walsh, D. P. J., 2011. Police Cooperation across the Irish Border: Familiarity Breeding Contempt for Transparency and Accountability. *Journal of Law and Society,* 38(2), pp. 301-330.

Webb, A., 1878. *A Compendium of Irish Biography: comprising sketches of distinguished Irishmen, and of eminent persons connected with Ireland by office or by their writings.* Dublin: M.H. Gill & Son,.

West Virginia University Press, 2009. West Virginia History. *Journal of Regional Studies,* 3(1), pp. 124-126.

References

Chapter 1: Bordertown Blues

[1] McGearty, S. et al., 2005. *The Emerald Curtain: The Social Impact of the Irish Border,* Carrickmacross: Triskele Community Training & Development.
[2] Bradley, J., 1996. *An Island Economy – Exploring Long-term Economic and Social Consequences of Peace and Reconciliation in the Island of Ireland,* Dublin: Forum for Peace and Reconciliation.
[3] McDougall, M. D., 2010. *The Letters of Norah on Her Tour through Ireland,* Kessinger Publishing.
[4] Special Correspondent of the "Freeman's Journal". 1882. *Rack-renting in the county of Leitrim in the winter of 1881.* Ladies' Irish National Land League.
[5] Vallely, F. at al., 2011. *Ben Lennon - the Tailor's Twist: Ben Lennon's Life in Traditional Irish Music.* Dublin: Friends of Ben Lennon.
[6] Irish Times 1957. February 2.
[7] Broadmore Research., 2011. *Cross Border Community Plans Rossinver-Garrison, Kiltyclogher-Cashel and Glenfarne-Blacklion-Belcoo.* Leitrim County Council, West Cavan West Fermanagh Regeneration Project & Broadmore Research.
[8] Tóibín, C., 1987. *Bad Blood: A Walk Along the Irish Border.* Picador. Ireland.
[9] 2014. *Census 2011 - Preliminary results.* [Online] Available at: http://www.cso.ie/census/Table8.htm
[10] Plummer, C., 1922. *Bethada Náem nÉrenn. Lives of Irish Saints.* Oxford: Clarendon Press.
[11] Annals of the Four Masters (AFM) 4694.
[12] Trew, J. D. 2010, Reluctant Diasporas of Northern Ireland: Migrant narratives of home, conflict, difference, *Journal of Ethnic and Migration Studies*, 36(4), 541-560.
[13] Kinlough Rossinver Askill Garrison Partnership (K.R.A.G). 2008. *Melvin Drive.*
[14] Robson, B. (1994). *Relative Deprivation in Northern Ireland*, Belfast: Northern Ireland Statistics and Research Agency, (NISRA).
[15] Peter Quinn Consultancy Services, 1998. *'The Way It Is' Area Profiles. A Comprehensive Review of Community Development and Community Relationships in County Fermanagh.*
[16] Peter Quinn Consultancy Services Ltd, *Garrison Integrated Village Action Plan.*
[17] Northern Ireland Census of Population, 2001, http://www.nisranew.nisra.gov.uk/census/start.html
[18] Peter Quinn Consultancy Services Ltd, *Garrison Integrated Village Action Plan.*
[19] Hayes-McCoy, G. A., 1932. Ballyshannon: Its Strategic Importance in the Wars in Connacht, 1550-1602. *Journal of the Galway Archaeological and Historical Society,* 15(3/4), pp. 141-159.

[20] Marron, P., 1976. Ballyshannon to Enniskillen in 1776. *Clogher Record,* 9(1), pp. 64-66.

[21] Ibid

[22] Peter Quinn Consultancy Services, 1998. *'The Way It Is' Area Profiles. A Comprehensive Review of Community Development and Community Relationships in County Fermanagh.*

[23] Moore Institute for Research in the Humanities and Social Studies, National University of Ireland, Galway, *Landed Estates Database.* [Online] Available at: http://landedestates.nuigalway.ie [Accessed 10 January 2014].

[24] Feeley, T., 2013. *From Glack to Bunduff.* Kinlough

[25] Leitrim County Council, West Cavan West Fermanagh Regeneration Project & Broadmore Research. 2011. *Tullaghan Kinlough Integrated Community Plan.*

[26] Dublin University Magazine. 1858. *Ramblings in the North-West,* Dublin: Dublin University Magazine.

[27] *Donegal Democrat.* 2013. December 6.

[28] Begley, A., 2009. *Ballyshannon and Surrounding Areas: History, Heritage and Folklore.* Ballyshannon: Carrickboy Publishing.

[29] Roger Tym & Partners, 2005. *Donegal County Council Erne Maritime Link Socio-Economic Assessment Final Report.* Glasgow.

[30] Donegal Democrat. 2010. October 4.

[31] Gallachair, P. Ó., 1975. The Parish of Carn. *Clogher Record,* 8(3), pp. 301-380.

[32] Ibid

[33] Ibid

[34] Mearáin, L. Ó., 1958. The Apostasy of Miler McGrath. *Clogher Record,* 2(2), pp. 244-256.

[35] Webb, A., 1878. *A Compendium of Irish Biography: comprising sketches of distinguished Irishmen, and of eminent persons connected with Ireland by office or by their writings.* Dublin: M.H. Gill & Son.

[36] O'Loughlin, J., 2011. *A History of Keenaghan Abbey & St. Michael's Church. Mulleek.*

[37] Cunningham, J. B., 2006. *The Pettigo History Trail.* Pettigo: Pettigo Mens' Group

[38] Irish Times, 2001, 3 October

CHAPTER 2: 'Draw a Line'

[1] De Paor, L., 1990. Unfinished Business: Ireland Today and Tomorrow. London: Hutchinson Radius.

[2] Anderson, M. & Bort, E. eds., 1999. In: *The Irish Border: History, Politics, Culture.* Liverpool University Press.

[3] Kerr, D. A., 1982. Peel, Priests and Politics: Sir Robert Peel's administration and the Roman Catholic Church in Ireland, 1841-1846. Oxford: Clarendon Press.

[4] Bottomley, P. M., 1974. The North Fermanagh Elections of 1885 and 1886: Some Documentary Illustrations. *Clogher Record,* 8(2), pp. 167-181.

[5]Laffan, M., 1983. *The Partition of Ireland, 1911-1925.* Dublin: Historical Association of Ireland.

[6]Ibid

[7]McGearty, S. et al., 2005. *The Emerald Curtain: The Social Impact of the Irish Border,* Carrickmacross: Triskele Community Training & Development.

[8]Kiely, B., 1945. *Counties of Contention.* Cork: Mercier.

[9]Mansergh, N., 1991. The Unresolved Question: The Anglo-Irish Settlement and its Undoing 1912-1972. London: Yale University Press.

[10]Martin, G., 1999. Origins of Partition. In: M. Anderson & E. Bort, Eds. *The Irish border: history, politics, culture.* Liverpool: Liverpool University Press.

[11]Cairns, E. & Darby, J., 1998. The conflict in Northern Ireland: Causes, consequences, and controls. *American Psychologist, 53(7),* p. 754.

[12]Rankin, K. J., 2006. *The Provenance and Dissolution of the Irish Boundary Commission.* Dublin: Institute for British-Irish Studies, Working Papers in British-Irish Studies No. 79.

[13]Ibid

[14]Institute for the Study of Conflict & Beckett, J. C., 1972. The Ulster Debate: Report of a Study Group of the Institute for the Study of Conflict, London: Bodley Head.

[15] Laffan, M., 2004. The Emergence of the 'Two Irelands', 1912-25. *History Ireland,* 12(4), pp. 40-44.

[16]Connolly, S. J. ed., 2007. *The Oxford companion to Irish history.* Oxford: Oxford University Press

[17]Murray, P., 2004, Partition and the Irish Boundary Commission: A Northern Nationalist Perspective *Clogher Record,* 18(2), pp.181-217.

[18]Mac Doinnléibhe, P., 1963. Fermanagh (1870-1900). *Clogher Record,* 5(1), pp. 7-29.

[19]Laffan, M., 1983. *The Partition of Ireland, 1911-1925.* Dublin: Historical Association of Ireland.

[20]Coogan, T. P., 2004. Ireland in the 20th Century. London: Arrow Books.

[21]Hand, G., 1969. *Report of the Irish Boundary Commission (1925).* Shannon: Irish University Press.

[22]Murray, P., 2004, Partition and the Irish Boundary Commission: A Northern Nationalist Perspective *Clogher Record,* 18(2), pp.181-217.

[23]Fitzpatrick, D., 2002. The Orange Order and the Border. *Irish Historical Studies,* 33(129), pp. 52-67.

[24]Bardon, J., 1992. *A History of Ulster.* Belfast: Blackstaff Press. P.478

[25]Murray, P., 2004, Partition and the Irish Boundary Commission: A Northern Nationalist Perspective *Clogher Record,* 18(2), pp.181-217.

[26]Martin, G., 1999. Origins of Partition. In: M. Anderson & E. Bort, Eds. *The Irish border: history, politics, culture.* Liverpool: Liverpool University Press.

Chapter 3: 'Turning the Key

[1]Rankin, K. J., 2006. *The Provenance and Dissolution of the Irish Boundary Commission.* Dublin: Institute for British-Irish Studies, Working Papers in British-Irish Studies No. 79.

[2]The National Archives (hereafter 'TNA'): CAB/61/51 Submission by the County Donegal Protestant Registration Association 10 June 1925

[3]Begley, A., 2011. *Ballyshannon: Genealogy & History*. Ballyshannon: Carrickboy Publishing.

[4]Mansergh, N., 1991. The Unresolved Question: The Anglo-Irish Settlement and its Undoing 1912-1972. London: Yale University Press.

[5]Murray, P., 2004, Partition and the Irish Boundary Commission: A Northern Nationalist Perspective *Clogher Record*, 18(2), pp.181-217.

[6]Connolly, S. J. ed., 2007. *The Oxford companion to Irish history*. Oxford: Oxford University Press

[7]Martin, G., 1999. Origins of Partition. In: M. Anderson & E. Bort, Eds. *The Irish border: history, politics, culture*. Liverpool: Liverpool University Press.

[8]Bardon, J., 1992. *A History of Ulster*. Belfast: Blackstaff Press.

[9]Martin, G., 1999. Origins of Partition. In: M. Anderson & E. Bort, Eds. *The Irish border: history, politics, culture*. Liverpool: Liverpool University Press.

[10]Andrews, J. H., 1965. The papers of the Irish boundary commission. *Irish Geography*, 5(2), pp. 477-481.

[11]Staunton, E., 1996. The Boundary Commission Debacle 1925: Aftermath & Implications. *History Ireland*, 4(2), pp. 42-45.

[12]Laffan, M., 1983. *The Partition of Ireland, 1911-1925*. Dublin: Historical Association of Ireland.

[13]Bardon, J., 1992. *A History of Ulster*. Belfast: Blackstaff Press.

[14]Murray, P., 2004. Partition and the Irish Boundary Commission: A Northern Nationalist Perspective. *Clogher Record*, 18(2), pp. 181-217.

[15]Anderson, M. & Bort, E. eds., 1999. In: *The Irish border: history, politics, culture*. Liverpool University Press.

[16]Staunton, E., 1996. The Boundary Commission Debacle 1925: Aftermath & Implications. *History Ireland*, 4(2), pp. 42-45.

[17]Anderson, M. & Bort, E. eds., 1999. In: *The Irish border: history, politics, culture*. Liverpool University Press.p16

[18]Donnan, H., 2010. Cold War along the Emerald Curtain: rural boundaries in a contested border zone. *Social Anthropology*, 18(3), pp. 253-266.

[19]Bottomley, P. M., 1974. The North Fermanagh Elections of 1885 and 1886: Some Documentary Illustrations. *Clogher Record*, 8(2), pp. 167-181.

[20]Anderson, M. & Bort, E. eds., 1999. In: *The Irish border: history, politics, culture*. Liverpool University Press.

[21]Northern Ireland Office, 2003. Responding to a Changing Security Situation. [Online] Available at: https://cain.ulst.ac.uk/ [Accessed 8 May 2014].

Chapter 4: The Forgotten County

[1]Roger Tym & Partners, 2005. *Donegal County Council Erne Maritime Link Socio-Economic Assessment Final Report*, Glasgow.

[2]Donegal County Council. *The Unemployment Landscape of County Donegal*. Donegal County Council. [Online] Available at: http://www.donegalcoco.ie/ [Accessed 14 March 2014].

[3]*Donegal Democrat*. 2010. October 4.

[4]McGearty, S. et al., 2005. *The Emerald Curtain The Social Impact of the Irish Border*, Carrickmacross: Triskele Community Training & Development.
[5]Irish Independent. November 30 2012.
[6]Ó Gallachair, P., 1961. *Where the Erne and Drowes meet the sea, fragments from a Patrician parish*. Ballyshannon: Donegal Democrat Ltd.
[7]Ó Canann, T. G., 2013. Dynastic Conflict in Medieval Donegal, AD 800-1400. In: *An Historical, Environmental and Cultural Atlas of County Donegal*. Cork: Cork University Press, pp. 116-124.
[8]Simms, K., 1995. Late Medieval Donegal. In: *Donegal, History & Society*. Dublin: Geography Publications, pp. 183-202.
[9]Hayes-McCoy, G. A., 1932. Ballyshannon: Its Strategic Importance in the Wars in Connacht, 1550-1602. *Journal of the Galway Archaeological and Historical Society*, 15(3/4), pp. 141-159.
[10]Beattie, S., 2013. *Donegal in Transition. The Impact of the Congested District Boards*. Sallins: Merrion Press.
[11]Ibid
[12]Ibid
[13]Ibid
[14]Dáil Éireann - Volume 153 - 30 November, 1955
[15]Shuttleworth, I. et al., 2000. The Tail of the Tiger: Experiences and perceptions of unemployment and inactivity in Donegal. *Irish Geography*, 33(1), pp. 56-7.
[16]Ibid

Chapter 5: Inured to Toil

[1]*North Leitrim Men's Group Ltd.* [Online] Available at: http://homepage.eircom.net/~nlmensgroup/ [Accessed 22 February 2014].
[2]Ó Gallachair, P., 1961. *Where the Erne and Drowes meet the sea, fragments from a Patrician parish*. Ballyshannon: Donegal Democrat Ltd.
[3]Rúnaí, L. O., 1996. *From Rosclogher to Rooskey: The Leitrim Story*. Cumann Seanchais Ros Inbhir.
[4]Minogue, R., 2002. *Landscape Assessment of County Leitrim*, Comhairle Chontae Liatroma.
[5]Coulter, H., 1862. *The west of Ireland: its existing condition, and prospects* (1862), Dublin: Hodges & Smith.
[6]Ó Duigneáin, P., 1987. *North Leitrim in famine times, 1840-50*. Manorhamilton: Drumlin Publications.
[7]Leitrim County Council, West Cavan West Fermanagh Regeneration Project & Broadmore Research, 2011. *Tullaghan Kinlough Integrated Community Plan*.

Chapter 6: Rather Inclined to be Scholars

[1]McCusker, B. & Morris, F., 1999. *Fermanagh: Land of Lake and Legend*. Donaghadee: Cottage Publications.
[2]O'Hart, J. (1892) Irish pedigrees; or, the origin and stem of the Irish nation Volume: 1. Publisher: Dublin, J. Duffy and Co. New York

[3]McCusker, B. & Morris, F., 1999. *Fermanagh: Land of Lake and Legend.* Donaghadee: Cottage Publications.

[4]Ibid

[5]Ibid

[6]Livingstone, P., 1969. *The Fermanagh story: A documented history of the County Fermanagh from the earliest times to the present day.* Enniskillen: Cumann Seanchais Chlochair.

[7]Simms, K., 1977. The Medieval Kingdom of Lough Erne. *Clogher Record,* 9(2), pp. 126-141.

[8]O'Hart, J., 1892. *Irish pedigrees; or, The Origin and Stem of the Irish Nation. Volume: 1.* Dublin: J. Duffy and Co

[9]Johnston, J., 1980. Settlement Patterns in County Fermanagh, 1610-1660. *Clogher Record,* 10(2), pp. 199-214.

[10]Wilsdon, B., 2010. Plantation Castles on the Erne, Dublin: The History Press Ireland.

[11]Ibid

[12]Cunningham, J. B., 1987. The Castle Caldwell Estate in 1780 and the Recent Arrest of the Highwayman Francis McHugh (Prionsias Dubh). *Clogher Record,* 12(3), pp. 261-264.

[13]Wilsdon, B., 2010. Plantation Castles on the Erne, Dublin: The History Press Ireland.

[14]Busteed, M., 2006. *Castle Caldwell, Co. Fermanagh. Life on a west Ulster estate, 1750-1800.* Dublin: Four Courts Press.

[15]McCracken, E., 1947. The Woodlands of Ulster in the Early Seventeenth Century. *Ulster Journal of Archaeology,* 10(3), pp. 15-25.

[16]Turner, B. S., 1975. An Observation on Settler Names in Fermanagh. *Clogher Record,* 8(3), pp. 285-289.

[17]Bardon, J., 1992. *A History of Ulster.* Belfast: Blackstaff Press.

[18]Ibid

[19]Bell, R., 1994. 'Sheep Stealers from the North of England': The Riding Clans in Ulster. *History Ireland,* 2(4), pp. 25-29.

[20]Fitzpatrick, R., 1989. *'A Peculiar People' God's Frontiersmen: The Scots-Irish.* London: Weidenfeld & Nicolson Ltd.

[21]West Virginia University Press, 2009. West Virginia History. *Journal of Regional Studies,* 3(1), pp. 124-126.

[22]Cunningham, J. B., 2013. *Fermanagh in Space. The 500 person in space has Fermanagh ancestors.* [Online] Available at: http://erneheritagetours.com/ [Accessed 12 February 2014].

[23]Simms, J. G., 1979. The Williamite War in South Ulster. *Clogher Record,* 10(1), pp. 155-162.

[24]Mac Donagh, J. C., 1947. Counsellor Terence Mac Donagh: A Great Catholic Lawyer of the Penal Days. *Irish Quarterly Review,* 36(143), pp. 307-318.

[25]Simms, J. G., 1979. The Williamite War in South Ulster. *Clogher Record,* 10(1), pp. 155-162.

[26]Phoenix, É. 2011. *The Impact of The Great Famine of 1845-51 with special reference to Ulster.* Department of Arts, Heritage and the Gaeltacht.

[27]Impartial Reporter. 2011. *Carson's Home Rule opposition began in Enniskillen.* [Online] Available at: http://www.impartialreporter.com [Accessed 15 December 2013].
[28]BMH Gerald Doyle
[29]BMH Sean Prendergast

Chapter 7: The Road to Nowhere

[1]NA cab/66/18/1 August 15 1941. Control of the Northern Irish Border
[2]Irish Times 1957, February 2.
[3]Patterson, H., 2011. *'Deeply anti-British'? The Irish state and cross-border security cooperation 1970-1974.* London, Political Studies Association.
[4]Co-operation Ireland, 2005. *Proposals for Effective North-South Co-operation: A Policy Paper.*
[5]Patterson, H., 2011. *'Deeply anti-British'? The Irish state and cross-border security cooperation 1970-1974.* London, Political Studies Association.
[6]Rusk, D., 2007. *Irish News.*
[7]*An Phoblacht.* 18 October 2007
[8]Patterson, H., 2010. Sectarianism revisited: the Provisional IRA campaign in a border region of Northern Ireland. *Terrorism and Political Violence,* 22(3), pp. 337-356.
[9]Bowcott, O., 2002. *Army urged to halt border security campaign: The Guardian.* 13 April.
[10]Ibid
[11]Curtis, L., 1994. *All Along the Watchtowers*: New Internationalist, Issue 255.
[12]Smith, B. Dáil Éireann Debate. Vol. 445 No. 9. Adjournment Debate. Reopening of Cross Border Roads. Tuesday, 18 October 1994
[13]Reynolds, G. Seanad Éireann - Volume 139 - 10 March, 1994. Adjournment Matters. - Reopening of Border Crossings.
[14]Ó Gráda, C. & Walsh, B. M., 2006. *Did (And Does) the Irish Border Matter?* : Institute for British-Irish Studies. Working Papers in British-Irish Studies. No. 60.
[15]Creamer, C. et al., 2008. *Fostering Mutual Benefits in Cross-Border Areas,* Armagh: International Centre for Local and Regional Development (ICLRD).

Chapter 8: Orange and Green Unite (Briefly)

[1]Begley, A. 2009. *Ballyshannon and Surrounding Areas: History, Heritage and Folklore.* Ballyshannon. Carrickboy Publishing.
[2]Darwin, K., 1990. *Familia 1990: Ulster Geneological Review: Number 6.* Ulster Historical Foundation
[3]McCusker, B. & Morris, F., 1999. *Fermanagh: Land of Lake and Legend.* Donaghadee: Cottage Publications.
[4]Ibid
[5]Begley, A. 2009. *Ballyshannon and Surrounding Areas: History, Heritage and Folklore.* Ballyshannon: Carrickboy Publishing.
[6]Ibid

[7]Connolly. S.J. (Ed.). 2007. *Oxford Companion to Irish History*. Oxford: Oxford University Press.

[8]Wilson, D. A., 2008. *Thomas D'Arcy McGee. Volume 1. Passion, Reason and Politics 1825-1857*. Montreal: McGill Queen's University Press

[9]Begley, A. 2009. *Ballyshannon and Surrounding Areas: History, Heritage and Folklore*. Ballyshannon. Carrickboy Publishing. P. 116

[10]Livingstone, P., 1969. *The Fermanagh story: A documented history of the County Fermanagh from the earliest times to the present day*. Enniskillen: Cumann Seanchais Chlochair.

[11]McVeigh, J. 2005. Michael Barrett (1841-1868) - The forgotten Fenian from Fermanagh. *An Phoblacht* 23 March.

[12]Special Correspondent of the "Freeman's Journal". 1882. *Rack-renting in the county of Leitrim in the winter of 1881*. Bristol Selected Pamphlets. University of Bristol Library

[13]Ó Duigneáin, P. Ó., 1987. North Leitrim in Land League Times 1880-84. Manorhamilton. Drumlin Publications.

[14]Ibid

[15]Ó Duigneáin, P. Ó., 1987. North Leitrim in Land League Times 1880-84. Manorhamilton. Drumlin Publications.

[16]1880. The Land Agitation: Mr. Parnell at Ballyshannon. *The Irish Times*. November 12.

[17]*New York Times*. 1881, October 21.

[18]Ó Duigneáin, P. Ó., 1987. North Leitrim in Land League Times 1880-84. Manorhamilton. Drumlin Publications.

[19]Mac Doinnléibhe, P., 1963. Fermanagh (1870-1900). *Clogher Record*, 5(1), pp. 7-29

[20]Ibid

[21]Ibid

Chapter 9: A Terrible Beauty

[1]Kenny, K., 1998. *Making Sense of the Molly Maguires*. Oxford: Oxford University Press.

[2]Bishop, P. & Mallie, E., 1988. *The Provisional IRA*. Reading: Corgi Books.

[3]Ferriter, D., 2005. *The Transformation of Ireland: 1900-2000*. 2nd ed. London: Profile Books Ltd.

[4]Duibhir, L. Ó., 2009. *The Donegal Awakening: Donegal and the War of Independence*. Cork: Mercier.

[5]BMH. Martin McGowan

[6]BMH. Thomas McShea

[7]Interview with Historian Joe O'Loughlin

[8]BMH. Joseph Murray

[9]BMH. Martin McGowan

[10]Livingstone, P., 1969. *The Fermanagh story: A documented history of the County Fermanagh from the earliest times to the present day*. Enniskillen: Cumann Seanchais Chlochair.

[11]Dwyer, R., 2012. Sectarian violence and murder spreads across the North. *Irish Examiner*. 2 July.

[12] James J. Smyth. BMH

[13] Ó Duibhir, L., 2011. Donegal & the Civil War: The Untold Story, Cork: Mercier Press.

[14] O'Loughlin, J., 2009. *The Border at Belleek 1910-1930.* [Online] Available at: www.joeoloughlin.co.uk [Accessed 24 August 2013].

[15] Ó Duibhir, L., 2011. *Donegal & the Civil War: The Untold Story*, Cork: Mercier Press.

[16] BMH John Travers

[17] Anthony Begley Ballyshannon Genealogy & History p. 385

[18] BMH. John Travers

[19] Ó Duibhir, L., 2011. *Donegal & the Civil War: The Untold Story*, Cork: Mercier Press.

[20] BMH. Michael V. O'Donaghue

[21] Ibid

[22] Hopkinson, M., 2004. Green against Green: The Irish Civil War. Gill and Macmillan.

[23] Coogan, T.P., 1991. Michael Collins: A Biography. Arrow Books

[24] *The Irish Times.* October 23, 1934.

[25] Emerson, N., 2003. Reich to the heart of the Irish question. *The Irish Times.* 20 November.

[26] Cunningham. J. B. 2010-04. The Way We Were in Fermanagh in World War II and the 1940s: The Golden Years of Smuggling. Belleek: Davog Press.

[27] Bardon, J., 1992. *A History of Ulster.* Belfast: Blackstaff Press.

[28] Bowman, J., 1982. De Valera and the Ulster question 1917-1973, Oxford

[29] Donnelly, D. 2010. *Prisoner 1082. Escape from Crumlin Road, Europe's Alcatraz.* Cork: The Collins Press

[30] Patterson, H., 2013. *Ireland's Violent Frontier: The Border and Anglo-Irish Relations during the Troubles.* Basingstoke: Palgrave Macmillan

[31] Ibid

[32] Ibid

[33] The United Irishman, March 1962.

Chapter 10: Have They Gone Away?

[1] English, R., 2004. *Armed Struggle: The History of the I.R.A.* London: Pan Books

[2] Anderson, S. 1994. *Making a Killing: The High Cost of Peace in Northern Ireland,* Harpers Magazine.

[3] Muldoon, Orla T., et al. 2008, "Adolescents' explanations for paramilitary involvement." *Journal of Peace Research* 45. (5) pp 681-695.

[4] Paper on Constitutional Position of Northern Ireland, T.K Whitaker, Jack Lynch, 24 November 1969, Lynch Papers, NAI, 2001/8/13.

[5] Downey, J. "Army on Armageddon alert", *Irish Independent*, 2 January 2001.

[6] Interview with Joe O'Neill

[7]McKittrick, David, ed. Lost lives: the stories of the men, women and children who died as a result of the Northern Ireland troubles. Random House, 2001.

[8]McDonald, H. & Cusack, J. 1997. *UVF*. Dublin: Poolbeg, P.28-30

[9](1972) Ireland: War of Attrition. *Time Magazine*. 3 January.

[10]The Times, Friday December 24 1971

[11]Interview with a former member of An Garda Suiochana

[12]The Times, Friday December 24 1971

[13]Mc Menamin, M. *The Siege of Ballyshannon 22nd December 1971. An Assessment of militant Republicanism in South Donegal*. M.A. Thesis in History. National University of Ireland, Galway.

[14]Ibid

[15]Ibid

[16]Ibid

[17]Irish times, Jan 30, 1973.

[18]Logue, P. 1999. *The Border: Personal Reflections from Ireland North and South*. Dublin: Oak Tree Press

[19]1973 State papers: British contacts with IRA revealed, Sunday Business Post Sunday, January 04, 2004.

[20]Murray, R. 1991. *The SAS in Ireland*. Cork: Mercier Press

[21]Ireland v. United Kingdom 5310/71 Judgment (Merits and Just Satisfaction) Court (Plenary) 18/01/1978

[22]Letter from A.W. Stephens Head of DS10 to W.K.K. White Republic of Ireland Department, Foreign and Commonwealth Office. D/DS10/44/38/1. 4 April 1973.

[23]The Troubles, Issue 8, November-December 1971.

[24]Ibid

[25]Fortnight, No. 68 (Sep. 21, 1973), pp. 14-15

[26]1974. An Interview with Benedict Kiely. James Joyce Quarterly, Vol. 11, No. 3, pp.189-200

[27]Interview with a retired business man from Belleek, County Fermanagh.

[28]Ibid

[29]The Troubles, Issue 8, November-December 1971.

[30]"Background to Border Security Problem," 16 May 1974, National Archives.

[31]McKittrick, D., ed., 2001. In: *Lost Lives: the stories of the men, women and children who died as a result of the Northern Ireland troubles*: Random House.

[32]Ibid

[33]Ibid

[34]de Breadun, D. 2008. Provos had 250 hardcore activists in counties near Border region. *Irish Times* 2 Jan 2008

[35]Bardon, J., 1992. *A History of Ulster*. Belfast : Blackstaff Press.

[36]Kiely, B. 1991. *Drink to the bird: a memoir*. London: Methuen

[37]Irish times articles sept 1 1986

[38]Sunday Independent 23 June 1996

[39]Cusack, J. 1982. Paisley wants military push 'as far south as Cork'. *The Irish Times.* July 13, 1982

[40]Fortnight, No. 190 (Jan., 1983), pp. 14-15

[41]Fortnight, No. 207 (Sep., 1984), pp. 16-17

[42]Saorise, July 1987

[43]Dewar, M. 1996. The British Army in Northern Ireland. London: Arms and Armour

[44]Cowley, M. How sniper went unseen in Belleek. *The Irish Times.* July 21, 1987;

[45]Latham, R., 2001. *Deadly Beat: Inside the Royal Ulster Constabulary.* Edinburgh: Mainstream Publishing Company.

[46]3 years' jail for man on gun charge, Irish Times, February 10, 1988.

[47]Pyle, F. 1989 '25 people listed in leaked document'. *Irish Times* September 23 1989

[48]de Breadun, D. The Irish Times. Sep 25, 1989

[49]Pyle, F. 1989 '25 people listed in leaked document'. *Irish Times* September 23 1989.

[50]O'Brien, B. 1999. *The Long War: The IRA and Sinn Féin.* Syracuse: Syracuse University Press

[51]McCrory, M.L. 2003. Bomb reminiscent of 'proxy' style attacks. *Irish News.* March 14, 2003

[52]Fortnight, No. 295 (May, 1991), pp. 22-23

[53]McKee, R. 2001 Ex-RUC Man Warns of 'Worst Violence' Ever. *Belfast Newsletter,* February 24, 2001

[54]Moriarty, G. 1996. Finger points to dissident republicans. *Irish Times.* July 15, 1996

[55]Mooney, J. & O' Toole, M. 2003. *Black Operations, The secret war against the Real IRA,* Ashbourne: Maverick House Publishers.

[56]Ibid

[57]Walsh, L. 2003. Irish Independent, Sunday June 29, 2003.

[58]The Guardian, Thursday, 7 August 2003

[59]McKittrick, D., ed., 2001. In: *Lost Lives: the stories of the men, women and children who died as a result of the Northern Ireland troubles*: Random House.

[60]The Irish Times May 11, 1998

[61]Jonathan Tonge, J. 2004. 'They Haven't Gone Away, You Know' Irish Republican 'Dissidents' and 'Armed Struggle' Terrorism and Political Violence Vol. 16 (3), pp. 671-693

[62]Donegal Democrat. May 25 2009

[63]Independent Monitoring Commission. 2009. Twenty First Report of the Independent Monitoring Commission.

[64]Donegal Democrat. May 25 2009

[65]Mooney, J. 2009. Gardaí 'know identity' of dissident terrorists. The Sunday Times. May 24, 2009

[66]McDonald, H., The Guardian, Thursday 26 July 2012

[67]New IRA: full statement by the dissident 'Army Council'
The Guardian. Thursday 26 July 2012

Chapter 11: 'We Kept our Heads Down'

[1]Fortnight, 1972. *Fortnight Guide to Ulster Demography*: Fortnight Publications Ltd, No. 33 pp. 4-6.

[2]Peter Quinn Consultancy Services, 1998. *'The Way It Is' Area Profiles. A Comprehensive Review of Community Development and Community Relationships in County Fermanagh.*

[3]Gardiner, D., 2008. *Whatever you say, say nothing. A report on the views and experiences of Border Protestants for the Church of Ireland Diocese of Clogher,* Hard Gospel Project.

[4]Interview with Reverend Noel Regan.

[5]Rural Community Network, 2002. *You'd feel you had no say. Rural Protestants and Community Development.* Rural Community Network: Cookstown.

[6]Ibid

[7]Anderson, J. (1995) 'Agrarian Revolution: Tirhugh 1715-1855'. In: Nolan, W. et al. eds. *Donegal, History & Society.* p.453.

[8]Moody, T. W., 1935. XXVIII.-The revised Articles of the Ulster Plantation, 1610. *Historical Research,* 12(36), p. 178–183.

[9]McKittrick, D., 1980. Protestants in NI town want the Border sealed, *Irish Times* June 23.

[10]Harris, R., 1972. *Prejudice and Tolerance in Ulster: A Study of Neighbours and "strangers" in a Border Community.* Manchester: Manchester University Press.

[11]Gardiner, D., 2008. *Whatever you say, say nothing. A report on the views and experiences of Border Protestants for the Church of Ireland Diocese of Clogher,* Hard Gospel Project.

[12]McCoy, C. & Ó Siochrú, M., 2008. County Fermanagh and the 1641 Depositions. *Archivium Hibernicum,* Volume 61, pp. 62-136.

[13]Stewart, A. T. Q., 1989. *The Narrow Ground: The Roots of Conflict in Ulster.* London: Faber and Faber Ltd. Page 49.

[14]Connolly, S. J. ed., 2007. *The Oxford companion to Irish history.* Oxford: Oxford University Press

[15]Ibid

[16]Deposition of Grace Lovett, 5 January 1641(2), TCD, Ms 835, ff 133-134

[17]McCoy, C. & Ó Siochrú, M., 2008. County Fermanagh and the 1641 Depositions. *Archivium Hibernicum,* Volume 61, pp. 62-136.

[18]Cunningham, J. & Herbert, V., 2004. *From Ballyjamesduff to Ballyshannon (A Guide to the River Erne).* Enniskillen: Erne Heritage Tour Guide.

[19]Schlegel, D., 1997. A Clogher Chronology: October, 1641 to July, 1642. *Clogher Record,* 16(1), pp. 79-94.

[20]Dungan, M., 1993 *Distant Drums. Irish Soldiers in Foreign Armies.* Belfast: Appletree Press.

[21]Impartial Reporter. 2011. *Carson's Home Rule Opposition began in Enniskillen.* [Online] Available at: http://www.impartialreporter.com/ [Accessed 9 November 2012].

[22]County Donegal Book of Honour Committee, 2002. *County Donegal Book of Honour. The Great War, 1914 - 1918.*

[23]Begley, A., 2011. *Ballyshannon: Genealogy and History*. Ballyshannon, Carrickboy Publishing.

[24]Ferriter, D., 2005. *The Transformation of Ireland: 1900-2000*. 2nd ed. London: Profile Books Ltd.

[25]CAB/24/137 Report by the General Officer Commanding in charge of the situation in Ireland for the week ending June 3rd 1922.

[26]Derry and Raphoe Action., *Protestants and the Border. Stories of Border Protestants North and South*. Derry and Raphoe Action.

[27]Ibid

[28]Borderlines Project, 2008. *Borderlines: Personal Stories and Experiences from the Border Counties of the Island of Ireland*. Dublin: Gallery of Photography.

[29]Ibid

[30]Ibid

[31]Lady Spender's Papers (D1633) Public Records Office Northern Ireland PRONI

[32]McKittrick, D., ed., 2001. In: *Lost Lives: the stories of the men, women and children who died as a result of the Northern Ireland troubles*. Random House.

[33]McDaniel, D., 1997. *Enniskillen: The Remembrance Day Bombing*. Dublin: Wolfhound Press.

[34]Bardon, J., 1992. *A History of Ulster*. Belfast: Blackstaff Press.

[35]McKittrick, D., ed., 2001. In: *Lost Lives: the stories of the men, women and children who died as a result of the Northern Ireland troubles*. Random House.p.1096

[36]Ibid

[37]Ibid

[38]Godson, R., 1989. "Keys killing was 'grudge,'" *Sunday Tribune*, 29 January.

[39]Laird, G., Derry and Raphoe Action., *Protestants and the Border. Stories of Border Protestants North and South*. Derry and Raphoe Action.

[40]Interview with Joe O'Neill.

[41]Britton, M. 2008. "Jim White - the man behind the public persona". *Donegal Democrat*. January 15

[42]Interview with Jim White.

[43]Borderlines Project. 2008. *Borderlines, Personal Stories and Experiences from the Border Counties of the Island of Ireland*. Dublin: Gallery of Photography.

[44]Ibid

[45]Ibid

[46]Patterson, H., 2010. Sectarianism Revisited: The Provisional IRA Campaign in a Border Region of Northern Ireland. *Terrorism and Political Violence,* 22(3), pp. 337-356.

[47]Impartial Reporter 16 March 1972.

[48]McKay, S., 2000 *'Northern Protestants – An Unsettled People'* Belfast: Belfast: Blackstaff Press.

[49]McCrystal, C., 1994. "Living with it" *The Independent* 22 May

[50]Crawley, M., 2002. *Protestant Communities in Border Areas Research Report,* Rural Community Network NI.

[51]Ibid

[52]Borderlines Project, 2008. *Borderlines: Personal Stories and Experiences from the Border Counties of the Island of Ireland.* Dublin: Gallery of Photography.

[53]Gardiner, D., 2008. *Whatever you say, say nothing. A report on the views and experiences of Border Protestants for the Church of Ireland Diocese of Clogher,* Hard Gospel Project.

[54]*Irish Times* "Down what road?" 25 June 1980.

[55]Pollak, A., 1985. Why Northern Ireland Needs a Military Back up: A UDR Officer's Point of View. *Fortnight,* 7-20 October, pp. 6-8.

[56]Finlay, L., *Protestants and the Border. Stories of Border Protestants North and South.* Derry and Raphoe Action.

[57]Patterson, H., 2006. *Border Killings – Liberation Struggle or Ethnic Cleansing?* [Online] Available at: http://news.ulster.ac.uk/releases/2006/2223.html [Accessed 11 November 2013].

[58]*Sunday Independent.* 16 January 1994

[59]Patterson, H., 2010. Sectarianism Revisited: The Provisional IRA Campaign in a Border Region of Northern Ireland. *Terrorism and Political Violence,* 22(3), pp. 337-356.

[60]Jenkins, S., 1996. 'Ulster's real peacemakers' in *'The Times'* 3 February.

[61]McKay, S., 2000. *'Northern Protestants – An Unsettled People'* Belfast: Blackstaff Press. p.217

[62]Gardiner, D., 2008. *Whatever you say, say nothing. A report on the views and experiences of Border Protestants for the Church of Ireland Diocese of Clogher,* Hard Gospel Project.

[63]*Irish Times,* 19 June 1980.

[64]Boyle, K. & Hadden, T., 1994. *Northern Ireland: The Choice,* London: Penguin Books

[65]Walker, B., 2012. Watching the fate of the Southern Protestant. *Irish Times.* March 12.

[66]Logue, P, M. K. S. P., 2007. *The Border Protestant Community and the Peace Programmes.*

[67]Gardiner, D., 2008. *Whatever you say, say nothing. A report on the views and experiences of Border Protestants for the Church of Ireland Diocese of Clogher,* Hard Gospel Project.

[68]Gardiner, D., 2008. *Whatever you say, say nothing. A report on the views and experiences of Border Protestants for the Church of Ireland Diocese of Clogher,* Hard Gospel Project.

[69]Tánaiste Eamon Gilmore. 2013. *Belfast Telegraph* September 12

[70]MacDonald, D., 2010. *Blood & Thunder. Inside an Ulster Protestant Band.* Cork. Mercier Press.

Chapter 12: 'Will it be a pint or Ballyshannon?"
[1]Gardiner, D., 2008. *Whatever you say, say nothing. A report on the views and experiences of Border Protestants for the Church of Ireland Diocese of Clogher*, Hard Gospel Project.
[2]Coogan, T. P., 2004. *Ireland In The 20th Century.* London: Arrow Books.
[3]McGarry, J. & O'Leary, B., 2000. *Policing Northern Ireland: Proposals for a New Start.* Belfast: Blackstaff.
[4]McKittrick, D., 1999. Reforming the RUC: Ulster's Police: a century as Unionism's armed wing. *The Independent.* 09 September
[5]McGarry, J. & O'Leary, B., 2000. *Policing Northern Ireland: Proposals for a New Start.* Belfast: Blackstaff.
[6]Ibid
[7]Longwill, E., 2009. *The Irish Army and State Security Policy, 1956-74*, PhD, University Of Ulster.
[8]Interview with a former member of An Garda Síochána
[9]Ibid
[10]Interview with a former RUC officer from Fermanagh
[11]Ryder, C., 1997. *The RUC 1922-1997: A Force Under Fire.* London: Mandarin Paperbacks.
[12]McGarry, J. & O'Leary, B., 2000. *Policing Northern Ireland: Proposals for a New Start.* Belfast: Blackstaff.
[13]O'Neill, J., 2009, Óglaigh Náisiúnta Na hÉireann Teoranta, The Forgotten Soldiers of Peace.
[14]Interview with a former soldier in the Irish Army
[15]Ibid
[16]Interview with a former soldier in the Irish Army
[17]Ibid
[18]Walsh D.P.J. (2011) *Police Co-operation across the Irish Border: Familiarity Breeding Contempt for Transparency and Accountability.* Journal of Law and Society. Volume 38, Number 2. pp 301-330
[19]Magee, K (1992) Border Blues: Fortnight, No. 305 p. 25
[20]Ibid
[21]McKee, R. Ex-RUC Man Warns of 'Worst Violence' Ever. *Belfast News Letter.* 24 February 2001 p.4
[22]Interview with a former RUC officer from Fermanagh
[23]Ibid
[24]Latham, R., 2001. *Deadly Beat: Inside the Royal Ulster Constabulary.* Edinburgh: Mainstream Publishing Company.
[25]2010. 'Scandalous' anti-social issues in Belleek. *Impartial Reporter.* 18 March.
[26]2010. Police need back-up to go to Belleek. *Impartial Reporter* 06 May.
[27]Interview with a former member of An Garda Síochána
[28]Independent Monitoring Commission. 2010.

Chapter 13: The Rod and the Reel
[1] Begley, A., 2009. *Ballyshannon and Surrounding Areas: History, Heritage and Folklore.* Ballyshannon: Carrickboy Publishing.

[2] Donagher, P., 2001. Donegal Bay angling guide: a definitive guide to game, coarse and sea angling in South Donegal. Ballyshannon: Erne Enterprise Development Company.

[3] Beattie, S., 2013. *Donegal in Transition. The Impact of the Congested District Boards.* Sallins: Merrion Press.

[4] Allingham, H. 1879. Ballyshannon Its History & Antiquities

[5] Beattie, S., 2013. Donegal in Transition. The Impact of the Congested District Boards. Sallins: Merrion Press.

[6] Newland, H., 1851. *The Erne: Its Legends and its Fly Fishing.* London: Chapman and Hall.

[7] Roger Tym & Partners, 2005. *Donegal County Council Erne Maritime Link Socio-Economic Assessment Final Report*, Glasgow.

[8] Donagher, P., 2001. *Donegal Bay angling guide: a definitive guide to game, coarse and sea angling in South Donegal.* Ballyshannon: Erne Enterprise Development Company.

[9] Begley, A., 2009. *Ballyshannon and Surrounding Areas: History, Heritage and Folklore.* Ballyshannon: Carrickboy Publishing.

[10] Moore, T. K., 1960. *A Man May Fish.* Buckinghamshire: Colin Smythe Limited.

[11] Tóibín, C., 1987. *Bad Blood: A Walk Along the Irish Border.* Picador – Ireland.

[12] Allingham, H. 1879. Ballyshannon Its History & Antiquities

[13] Mac Aoidh, C. 1994. *Between the Jigs and the Reels.* Manorhamilton. Drumlin Publications

[14] Ibid

[15] Begley, A., 2009. *Ballyshannon and Surrounding Areas: History, Heritage and Folklore.* Ballyshannon: Carrickboy Publishing.

[16] 1870. Bundoran Public Right of Way. Dublin: McGlaghan and Magill,

[17] Trimble, J. 1979. Carolan and His Patrons in Fermanagh and Neighbouring Areas. *Clogher Record.*10 (1), pp. 26-50

[18] Tunney, P., (1979) *The Stone Fiddle: My Way to Traditional Song.* Appletree.

[19] Ibid

[20] Ibid

[21] Masterson, M. J., *Turlough O'Carolan (1670-1738) "The last of the Bards"*